Flight from Greatness

Studies in Austrian Literature, Culture and Thought

Translation Series

Hans Weigel

FLIGHT FROM GREATNESS

Six Variations
on Perfection in Imperfection

Translated and with an Afterword by

Lowell A. Bangerter

ARIADNE PRESS
Riverside, California

Ariadne Press would like to express its appreciation to the Austrian Cultural Institute, New York and the Bundeskanzleramt – Kunstangelegenheiten, Vienna for assistance in publishing this book.

Translated from the German *Flucht vor der Größe*
©Styria, Steirische Verlagsanstalt

The publishers Ariadne Press in Riverside and Verlag Styria in Graz wish to thank Mrs. Christine Fronius, the curator of Hans Fronius's estate, for her kind permission, granted as an exception, to publish the graphics in this book without charge.

Library of Congress Cataloging-in-Publication Data

Weigel, Hans.
 [Flucht vor der Grösse. English]
 Flight from greatness : six variations on perfection in imperfection / Hans Weigel ; translated and with an afterword by Lowell A. Bangerter.
  p.   cm. -- (Studies in Austrian literature, culture, and thought. Translation series)
 ISBN 1-57241-051-5
 1. Authors, Austrian--19th century--Biography. 2. Composers, Austrian--Biography. I. Bangerter, Lowell A., 1941-
 II. Title. III. Series.
 PT3814.W413   1998
 838'.91409--dc21
                                        97-6766

Cover design:
Art Director & Designer: George McGinnis
Illustrations courtesy Mrs. Christine Fronius

Copyright ©1998
by Ariadne Press
270 Goins Court
Riverside, CA 92507

All rights reserved.
No part of this publication may be reproduced or transmitted in any form or by any means without formal permission.
Printed in the United States of America.
ISBN 1-57241-051-5
(Paperback original)

In memoriam Adalbert Stifter

"What have future generations done for me? Nothing! Fine, I'll do the same for them!"
　　　　　(Nestroy)

"And greatness is dangerous."
　　　　　(Grillparzer)

"We are, you know, happy but unfortunate, just as many people are unhappy but fortunate."
　　　　　(Raimund)

"Usually greatness does not know that it is great."
　　　　　(Stifter)

"I am governed by a kind of gravitation toward misfortune."
　　　　　(Lenau)

CONTENTS

Attempt at an Introduction	3
Franz Schubert	13
Ferdinand Raimund	39
Johann Nestroy	75
Franz Grillparzer	107
Adalbert Stifter	151
Johann Strauss	231
Author's Afterword	323
Translator's Afterword	337

ATTEMPT AT AN INTRODUCTION

Recently, from the other end of a long coffee-house table, I overheard the sentence: "They were talking about Austria, and each one meant something different when he said 'Austria.'"

A person who publishes a book about Austria certainly risks increasing the number of diverging and differing opinions about what is meant by Austria, while intending to coordinate them at last.

Or should Austria be defined by the very fact that the definitions of the term necessarily contradict each other, and thus that the definition of Austria consists of the admission that it cannot be defined?

The question of Austria's essence is a Lohengrinian question: Its name and nature communicate themselves very reluctantly, and only in parting do we perceive what has been.

Actually, before the end of the First World War no somewhat constant entity called Austria existed, even though we celebrated "950 Years of Austria" shortly after the Second World War. But in a typical manner, the first recorded mention of the name occurred in the year 996, when a land, a region was mentioned, the "*vulgari vocabulo Ostarrichi dicta,*" which was called Austria in the vernacular. And even from then on the name was more a compromise, an abbreviation, a paraphrase than the designation of a geographical or political constant.

Two Habsburg crownlands and present-day federal provinces were and are called "Austria below the Enns" and "Austria above the Enns," or Lower Austria and Upper Austria; but there did not and does not exist for the two of them in common usage a higher concept called *Austria*. And if each of several participants in a conversation "meant something different," they are all proven to be right by the official Habsburg-Lorraine title, which contradicts itself when it identifies the "emperor of Austria" not only as the king of Hungary, Bohemia, Dalmatia, Croatia, Slavonia, Galicia, Lodomeria, and Illyria, the king of Jerusalem, the grand duke of Tuscany, the margrave of Moravia, the duke of Salzburg, Styria, Carinthia, Carniola, and many other places, but also as the archduke of Austria. How can one simultaneously be the archduke of a country of which one is the emperor?

As the first margraves of Austria, the Babenbergers did not control a region that one could call Austria in the narrower sense, because at first it consisted only of small pieces of present-day Lower and Upper Austria. Soon Bavaria also came under Babenberger sovereignty, and when the margraves became dukes who resided in Vienna, Styria was sometimes included, and sometimes it was not. Linz was added, but also part of Carniola. Even at that time, Austria was simultaneously more and less than Austria; and Salzburg did not become Austrian until after Mozart's death.

The state whose head was the emperor of Austria —as the king of Hungary, Bohemia, Jerusalem, etc. and the grand duke of Tuscany—did include Hungary and Bohemia, but it did not include Jerusalem and Tuscany. It was not called *Austria*, but it united two halves. The Hungarian half, in addition to the kingdom of Hungary, also consisted of other regions, Croatian regions, for example, but was at least unambiguously called Hungary; while the Austrian half of the Austro-Hungarian union did not officially bear the name *Austria*, but called itself "the kingdoms and countries represented in the imperial council" and officially received the name *Austrian Empire* only as the result of an imperial letter of October 10, 1915—three years before the end. (What a Lohengrinian designation!)

Where does all that leave Austria?

In 1806, Emperor Franz II. had dissolved the "Holy Roman Empire," which was not really Roman but had been involved in altercations with Rome for centuries. While doing so, he had still called himself a "constant augmenter of the empire." He had adopted the title of "Emperor of Austria" in 1804 and reduced himself to Franz I. The "House of Austria" had actually only been the family name of the Habsburg dynasty (which came from Switzerland). No emperor of Austria had had himself crowned emperor in Vienna, but some had been crowned king in Hungary.

Where does all that leave Austria? Everywhere and nowhere. Proceeding from these indications, the difficulties of giving a precise definition already become very apparent and seem almost unique.

There are countries where there can be no doubt about their identity with themselves, no matter what their current political situation may be: Italy, Spain, Greece, Sweden, Iran, China, Japan. Others derive their customary names from a nucleus, a center: We say *Russia* and mean a construct that consists of Russia, among other things; we say *England* and mean England, Scotland, and Wales, possibly Ireland as well, and perhaps even the entire Commonwealth. We name a part and mean the whole. On the other hand, we say *America*, name the whole, and mean only a part of North America.

But whatever we say, we know exactly what is meant. If we say *Austria*, however, we ourselves do not know exactly whether we mean the nine provinces of today or the system of kingdoms and countries that fell apart in 1918. And even when we use the apparently unambiguous adjective *German*, it is burdened with misconceptions. Specifically, in the Habsburg empire the "Germans in Austria" were not, as one might expect, the Prussians, Saxons, Swabians, or Bavarians, i.e., German subjects who were in Austria, but the German-speaking subjects of Franz Joseph in Tyrol, Vorarlberg, Styria, Carinthia, Salzburg, Upper and Lower Austria, as well as Bohemia, Moravia, Silesia, Carniola, Bucovina and other crownlands. It was possible for a citizen of Prague, Brünn, Innsbruck, or Graz to curse "the Germans" (in Bavaria, Swabia, Saxony, or Prussia) while he himself was cursed as "a German" in the Czech language by his Bohemian, Moravian, or Silesian "fellow-Austrians."

In 1918, when Czechoslovakia, Hungary, Yugoslavia, and Poland had become independent, and Rumania and Italy had also acquired portions of the Habsburg empire, when what had been called *Austria* had thereby been dismembered, a portion remained that was again called *Austria*. But it called itself *German Austria*—we now understand somewhat better, why it did so—and had to be compelled by the victors to get rid of the misleading first word and accept the misleading new-old name.

Then Austria existed *de facto* and *de jure* as a republic, but even one of its faultlessly patriotic ministers described what was produced by the loss of the First World War as a "nation against its will."

Since then the reluctance has visibly decreased, and a decisive contributing factor has been the situation that during what has now been the forty-two years of its existence, from the twentieth to the twenty-seventh year of its life this nation did not exist, that before and afterward it was threatened and endangered for several years, that during the periods of threat, danger, and nonexistence it experienced its own reality and learned of its own existence, and that as it said farewell, its name and nature were clearly revealed.

That Austria exists is now established, but what Austria is remains controversial. The inquiries begin to grow more and more lively, but for now the multitude of questions must take the place of the answer, and only the productive confusion of concepts can gradually pave the way to real knowledge and self-awareness.

I, myself, thought I knew what Austria is, until I received the assignment from a German publisher to write a small book about Austria for the series *Unsere Nachbarn und wir* [We and Our Neighbors]. I began with an exclamation and fell deeper and deeper into question marks. When my manuscript was finished, I knew more about Austria than before, but only because I knew how much I did not know about Austria.

Far more urgently than before I began working on my book about Austria; I felt the need to write a book about Austria.

Soon after that, the great posing of questions was intensified when I had to intellectually nurture and provide detailed information about everything pertaining to Vienna to an intelligent woman from England who came to the city for the first time, wanted to write articles about Austria, and was particularly interested in literature and art. Then I realized—in addition to the knowledge of what I did not know—what an educated contemporary woman with profound knowledge of Anglo-Saxon, Romance, and Slavic cultures did not know about Austria. But as a result of my improvised presentations about Nestroy, Raimund, Grillparzer, Hofmannsthal, Karl Kraus, and some living figures, to my very great astonishment I also discovered something that was common to all of them—was this what it meant to be Austrian?—and this common element was likewise essentially defined in not knowing: the "Austrian fate," consisting of not being recognized, of being misunderstood, and of self-misunderstanding, greatness fleeing from itself.

In what follows, only six examples of this flight from greatness are brought together, all of them from the previous century, of which we are not able to say whether it was Austria's ninth or first century, or the century before the beginning of the Austrian era.

But these examples do not even exhaust the contribution of that one century to the topic of this book, anymore than fleeing from greatness is peculiar only to the music and literature of Austria. The poet Nikolaus Lenau and the painter Anton Romako would similarly have their places of honor in the procession of misunderstanding, misjudgment and self-destruction, along with numerous scientists and politicians.

Nor can we detect a fading of the Austrian constant with either the end of the century or the beginning of the new era.

Around the turn of the century three great Austrian dramatists were born, who would now be about sixty years old and would determine the character of our theater, if fate had not continued to be hostile toward the production of dramas in Austria, so that Hans Kaltneker had to die at the age of twenty-three, Hans Chlumberg at thirty-three, and Ödön von Horváth at thirty-seven. Around the turn of the century Karl Kraus, "the faithful hater of his homeland," began his journalistic work, which banished him, like Ibsen's Brand, into the icy desert of "all or nothing." Arthur Schnitzler and Franz Molnár anticipated what we call "modern literature," and incidentally, later consequences of it as well, but did not follow up on it, and, although generally acknowledged, were not appropriately appreciated. Gustav Mahler, the Grillparzer of the symphony, was frustrated by his tragic inner conflict and his intermediate position between classical and modern music. After a radiant beginning, Hugo von Hofmannsthal had been silent for a decade; the poet became a man of letters and wasted his time in musical-literary-theatrical activity. Georg Trakl mysteriously died in the First World War as a very young soldier, Josef Weinheber died mysteriously and far too prematurely at the end of the Second World War, as did the genial Otto Weininger, who had created a great anticipatory work and then killed himself at the age of twenty-three. Franz Kafka fled into the literary fragment and ordered the destruction of his life's work. Robert Musil worked on a novel whose completion was practically unthinkable. Anton Kuh wasted his efforts, as Peter Altenberg had done before him, in witty remarks and fragments and lived the life of a writer without leaving ascertainable literary traces behind. Egon Friedell, eccentric and Bohemian like the others, only began publishing larger works as a mature man and died a self-inflicted philosopher's death in 1938. Karl Schönherr, a legitimate dramatist, fled into dialect like Nestroy. Alban Berg died too young like Schubert. The great era of the Vienna Secession, which brought together a corona of promising geniuses, hardly lasted longer than the era of the Vienna operetta. Adolf Loos, the father of modern architecture, remained in the shadows during his entire life and was able to see very few of his great plans become reality. Josef Matthias Hauer, the real creator of dodecaphonic music, never left his seclusion and died in complete isolation a short time ago in Vienna. Oskar Jellinek, the last master of the classical novella, was hardly noticed and died in 1949, longing for his home in exile in California.

The list could be expanded indefinitely, extended beyond the field of art, and continued into the immediate present. Only a short time ago, the important Viennese novelist Leo Perutz died. Nobody knew him, a missing person during his own lifetime. Shortly before his death he told the editor of a Vienna publishing house about a manuscript with the notation: "...so that you find something in the drawer of my desk," and maybe they found the manuscript, but it did not result in the appropriate, far-reaching literary consequences. A short time ago the self-willed Viennese poet Theodor Kramer died as well, a man whose life's work was virtually unknown and still has not been posthumously cared for.

Flight from greatness in all its variations: self-surrender and lack of appreciation, a permanent disruption of the relationship between possibility and reality, a powerful predominance of possibilities over realizations, completion only in the form of "premature completion." In the circle of my friends I have experienced and continue to experience the tragic or tragicomical fulfillment of the Austrian basic law, the wasting of talents, self-destruction, the failure to perceive and the ignoring of great promise, cruelly premature death:

Jura Soyfer, a highly gifted poet, died at Buchenwald of typhoid fever in 1939 at the age of twenty-seven, when his release and emigration papers had already been prepared. He left behind only a few fragmentary cabaret scenes. The great manuscript of a novel of the times disappeared. Raimund Berger, a natural dramatic talent—from his fifteenth year on he was confined to a wheel chair, hardly ever went to theater performances, and wrote some beautiful early pieces—died in 1954 at the age of thirty-seven. Hertha Kräftner, a very promising lyric poet, killed herself in 1951 at the age of twenty-three. Kurt Absolon, a genial graphic artist and painter who had to earn his living as a laborer and messenger for most of his life, perished in 1958 at the age of thirty-three in a traffic accident.

All of these hints, no matter how much they give pause for thought and suggest a special affinity of the Austrian nature for failure, for the absence of self-realization, are not intended in any way to announce a prerogative. I do not claim, in the manner of certain nationalists, that all of my countrymen are misunderstood geniuses, or that all misunderstood geniuses are my countrymen. I am very much aware that Heinrich von Kleist, Georg Büchner, and Vincent van Gogh, had they come from Austria, would fit very nicely into the pattern of "flight from greatness." I know just as precisely that not every inhabitant of Marchfeld, Pinzgau, or the Puster Valley is an important contemporary who fails because he lacks activation of his possibilities. Expressionist painting features not only the premature mastery of the Austrian Egon Schiele but also the premature mastery of the German Franz Marc; *The Art of the Fugue* is incompletely complete in just as magically meaningful a way as Schubert's *Symphony in B minor*; even outside of Austria the careers of the great minds and figures only seldom move upward in a straight line toward a rounded-out life's work and would earn fame during their lifetime; and finally the present day offers a grand exception in happy contrast to the Austrian rule, in that the important novelist Heimito von Doderer not only completes his novels, but at the age of sixty, as a great figure of literary Europe, has also received the highest recognition in his homeland.

And nevertheless, it appears that "leaving incomplete instead of finishing" (Friedrich Torberg) is especially common as a national preference in this Austria—of which we do not precisely know what we mean when we call it by name, and whose definition we must therefore also leave open—and that resignation vis-à-vis the outside world is especially intensive and supplemented by a shifting of the struggles and tensions into one's own inner world, in accordance with the immortal formulation of Nestroy's Holofernes: "I would like to set myself against myself, just to see who is stronger, I or I."

Nevertheless, it seems to me that this Austria, in its exciting indefinableness—both ancient and hardly existing yet—is distinguished from the other countries as a land of unlimited possibilities and precarious realizations, and in contrast to what has previously been called the land of unlimited possibilities, it has still not been properly discovered at all.

Hopefully the following six presentations of Austrian phenomena will point out some common facts between the lines of Austrian cultural history and in so doing accelerate the discovery of Austria inside and outside its borders.

FRANZ SCHUBERT

or

FLIGHT FROM BIOGRAPHY

"Every extraordinary person has a certain mission that he is called to perform. When he has carried it out, he is no longer needed in that form on the earth ... Mozart died in his thirty-sixth year, Raffael at almost the same age—Byron only a little bit older. But all of them had fulfilled their missions most perfectly, and it was probably time for them to go, so that something still remained for other people to do in a world that was intended to last for a long time."
(Goethe to Eckermann in the year of Schubert's death)

"...in that music is something quite innate, internal, that needs no important nourishment from outside and no experience drawn from life."
(Goethe to Eckermann three years later)

"And he lets it all go on just as it will, Turns and turns it, and his lyre is never still."
(*The Winter Journey*)

FRANZ SCHUBERT

Of course he is protected from the infamy of the novel, operetta, and film purveyors, but usually only obligatorily and moderately, in the normal way that one justifiably defends Chopin or Weber, and not with the holy zeal of a protest against the desecration of Johann Sebastian Bach or Beethoven. Of course he is close to us and dear to us, but we take our love for him too much for granted; there is far too little awe and reverence in it, and no appreciation for the actual dimensions of his work. When we protect him from distortion, we do not know with the requisite clarity whom and what it is that we want to preserve. We reject the adulterating image, but we have no authentic one.

His time will yet come, just as Johann Sebastian Bach's works were late in coming into the world from the archives and libraries, just as even Mozart, while never half-forgotten, after being obviously present for so long, was not fully perceived until our century.

Beethoven has always been there, unbounded, dominant, powerful, and startling; and for admirers and detractors alike, from his own time on into any later period, unambiguously great. When Beethoven died, Grillparzer said, "Whoever comes after him will not continue where he left off; he will have to begin over again, because his predecessor only stopped where art ceases."

Thirty-six torch bearers clothed in black had been in the funeral procession accompanying Beethoven's coffin to the Währing cemetery, musicians and poets: Raimund, Kreutzer, Lenau, Bauernfeld, Grillparzer, and even he who had long since begun again, who had taken music beyond Beethoven, and had kept it from ending with Beethoven, one whom Grillparzer knew very well and regarded very highly, but did not recognize.

In Beethoven's funeral procession, Grillparzer did not know who Schubert was. The next year, when they had accompanied Schubert's coffin along the same route to Währing, he gave him the epitaph: "Music buried here a precious possession, but even far greater promise." He did not notice that Franz Schubert was Franz Schubert and had fulfilled his life. Even enthusiastically admiring friends did not know it; only decades later did Schwind immortalize him in drawings. He loved the living Schubert, but after Schubert's death he wrote: "The more I now understand what he was...," and insight into what Schubert was still continues to grow.

Beethoven bears witness to his era and speaks of it and of himself to every new generation; upon encountering him in its own time, each generation thinks that nobody has completely grasped him before. While listening, we take complete possession of him. Schubert does not speak of himself or of his age, and to date he continues to speak past every generation. His era is the one yet to come. And the more we believe we already know about and of him, the more difficult it is and remains to understand completely who he was.

He himself, and that is a decisive component of his greatness, also lacked the understanding, the consciousness of his special nature, lacked knowledge of himself. Contemporaries call him "somnambulant" and speak of "clairvoyance." Carl Spitteler calls him "God's dreamer." He did not sketch; only very seldom did he revise. He actually never took regular, in-depth lessons in composition theory, and from the very beginning was able to do what he had to be able to do. Bewildered by the boy's brilliance, the conductor of the court orchestra, Salieri, a musical grand master of his era, directed the worthy piano teacher, violist, and organist Wenzel Ruzicka to take the fourteen-year-old boy under his care, but Ruzicka soon declared himself to be incompetent: "He has learned it from the dear Lord."

Franz Schubert did not work on his compositions, he wrote them down, wrote them out. On one occasion the complete edition of Schubert's works was submitted to an expert music copyist with the question as to how long it would take, under normal working conditions, for him to copy it. The answer given, for the purely mechanical copying, was a period that exceeded the one and a half decades of Schubert's musical productivity.

"I deliver what is within me, and that's all there is to it," he said. A fellow student from the boarding school reports: "Very calmly and hardly disturbed by the unavoidable surrounding chatter and din of his comrades in the boarding school, he sat at his little desk, bent over a sheet of music and a textbook—he was very nearsighted—bit his pen, drummed his short fingers occasionally in contemplation, and continued to write easily and fluidly without many corrections, as if it had to be just so and not otherwise." Robert Schumann notes, but only about part of the second movement of the *Symphony in C major*: "...it seems to me as if it came down from another sphere. Here everyone else listens, as if a heavenly guest were sneaking around in the orchestra." Schumann also divines that the symphony leads into an area "where we can not remember having been before." But we must also list Schumann among the underraters of Schubert, tragically cruel underraters of a special kind, who were (and still are) friends and admirers and from their deceptive proximity did not perceive the dimension of his greatness, just as you cannot estimate the height of a mountain that you approach.

Subsequent generations wronged and still wrong him as hardly any other genius. That his contemporaries and friends did not recognize him, however, that he himself did not know who he was must be acknowledged with painful gratitude as a blessing and as the prerequisite for such creativity. The Lord God, from whom he learned how to compose, also gave him his divine lightheartedness, for only he could write Schubert songs, Schubert chamber music, Schubert symphonies in such abundance, who did not know that they would go note for note into eternity as the complete works of Schubert, who was even secure against the all-too-prompt and distinct response of his own time. Only a Schubert who did not consciously compose great deeds of music history at his desk, who did not knowingly anticipate biographies, monuments, and all the attributes of immortality, was capable of composing seven, eight, and ten songs in one day, and two hundred and fifty in two years, was able to purloin the book with the texts of the *Beautiful Miller's Wife* and the following day show the owner, who came to reclaim it, the first songs of the cycle, which he had written overnight, in justification—only thus could a string quartet be put on paper in four and a half hours, a mass in six days.

And one must also add the fact that after composing seven symphonies, in a hopeless and despondent letter he confessed he had just experimented with several "instrumental pieces," for: "Actually, in this way I intend to make my way to the great symphony"—that he believed that he possessed nothing for the orchestra that he "could send out into the world with a clear conscience"—that when his brother told him they were playing Franz's quartets at home, he answered: "It will be better if you stick to quartets other than mine, for there is nothing to them." In that year, 1824, he had already written his first eleven string quartets and the quartet composition in C minor.

To that we must add that he left behind twelve hundred and fifty works and did not value some manuscripts, so that many significant ones are still missing.

Where he wrote for public response and sought to have an impact, he failed: in his experiments with musical drama.

How little he knew, how utterly ignorant Franz Schubert was about Franz Schubert, can be seen in the fact that he did not recognize one of his own songs when he heard it, and said: "That song isn't bad. Who wrote it?" He had written it only a short time earlier.

"Genius," Hermann Hesse observed, citing Goethe as an example, "wherever it appears, is either strangled to death by its environment or tyrannizes it; it is unquestionably the flower of humanity and yet causes distress and chaos everywhere. It is always an isolated occurrence, condemned to loneliness, is not hereditary, and always has a tendency toward self-surrender."

The genius Schubert, lonely, surrendering himself, strangled by the environment, and only fulfilling himself as a genius because of these prerequisites, has no real biography. His contemporary and friend Bauernfeld finds in Schubert's life "so few tangible biographical features." The entire wretched insignificance of this life becomes clear when one relates it more or less geometrically to the lives of Goethe and Beethoven, next to which it was so small and inconspicuously anonymous.

Schubert's life: A short line of thirty-one units in the second half of Goethe's eighty-three units.

Schubert is born. The forty-eight-year-old Goethe has finished *Hermann and Dorothea*, is preparing for an important journey, and prepares his will, with Christiane and his son as beneficiaries. For years he has directed the theater; he now calls for its remodeling and for the building of the castle of Weimar. His friendship with Schiller has been established; his interests are temporarily directed more toward the sciences and administration than toward purely literary activities.

The seventeen-year-old Schubert attains the status of master with the song *Gretchen at the Spinning Wheel*. The sixty-five-year-old Goethe has finished his *Elective Affinities* and completed his linguistically most perfect, most sublime poetic creation, the *Pandora* fragment. He has met Beethoven in Teplitz; he is reviewing the past in the memoirs *From My Life*; he turns to oriental poetry and will soon sublimely crystalize the fullness of his experienced serenity in the *West-Eastern Divan*.

When a work by Schubert first appears in print and Schubert has only seven more years to live, the seventy-two-year-old Goethe becomes acquainted with the seventeen-year-old Ulrike von Levetzow in Marienbad.

Schubert dies at thirty-one. The seventy-nine-year-old Goethe still has four years ahead of him. He writes his *Novella*; his wife has been dead for twelve years, Charlotte von Stein for a year. Grand Duke Karl August dies that year. Goethe's son will die two years before his father. Goethe has already been in Weimar for fifty years; a new complete edition of his works has been in print for two years. He is interested in the construction of canals, harbors, and tunnels; he continues to work "vigorously" on *Wilhelm Meister's Journeyman Years* and completes the work the following year. At eighty-one he has a hemorrhage from which he recovers.

Goethe worked on Faust for more than six decades. On July 22, 1831, at the age of eighty-two, he wrote in his journal: "The main business is finished." A month later, three years after Schubert's death, in a wooden hut near Ilmenau he saw the lines that he had written there on the wall forty-eight years earlier, fourteen years before Schubert's birth: "Over all the hilltops lies peace..."

When Goethe was born, Maria Theresa had been ruling for nine years; when Goethe died, Bismarck was seventeen years old.

The period of Schubert's musical existence from *Gretchen at the Spinning Wheel* until his death: four evening hours in the day called "Goethe's life."

If he had attained Goethe's age, Schubert would have died twenty years after Gustav Mahler's birth, eighteen years after the birth of Claude Debussy, six years after Schönberg was born, one year before Bartok's birth, and two years before Stravinsky was born. He would have outlived Chopin by thirty-one years, Berlioz by eleven. Reger, Busoni, and Puccini could have been his students.

Goethe saw Mozart as a seven-year-old boy and Mendelssohn as a twelve-year-old. Above all, he saw himself; he knew that he was Goethe. He consciously experienced his own biography, wrote his complete works, and more than in what he created his accomplishment consisted in the fact that he was able to create it in spite of the burden of that awareness.

But Franz Schubert, in his shabby, short decade and a half of productivity, which was outwardly so insignificant next to the grand period named Goethe, realized an accomplishment, a life's work, a complete edition of thirty-nine folio volumes that are not only quantitatively of equal rank with Goethe's works. He could only do it by renouncing any form of biography; he denied not only his era and himself, but also posterity a valid Schubert image. That he of all people could repeatedly (and not just since *The House of Three Girls* and the film *My Songs Plead Softly*) be distorted, abused, and degraded with impunity, is tied to this absence of an authentic image. Schubert is both taken for granted and unknown, familiar and remote. We hear him and do not know him; we think we know him and do not hear him. He is there; he is our property but far from being our possession.

The total absence of a biography also means that Franz Schubert can in no way be reclaimed as a "misunderstood genius." He was not discovered, either while alive or posthumously; he was always there, entirely present. When he gave his only public concert in the year he died, the hall was full, his success significant, the revenue considerable. Even in his early years Schubert was an honorary member of musical societies in Graz, Linz, and Innsbruck. The Viennese Society of Music Lovers authorized a remuneration for him and commissioned his biography. He was published, albeit far too late and inadequately; he was paid, albeit far too meagerly. When, on the occasion of its reorganization, the Diabelli publishing house called upon the well-known masters of the time to write variations on a waltz theme by the head of the firm, the twenty-four-year-old Schubert was also invited. A mass by the seventeen-year-old had already been repeated because of its success. Concerning the twenty-four-year-old, the *Dresdener Abendzeitung* reported: "The outstanding song writer Schubert is said to be currently occupied with the composition of a great romantic opera." He wrote two musical dramas that were commissioned by a Vienna theater, and in 1827, during his stay in Vienna, the German poet Hoffmann von Fallersleben repeatedly expressed his desire to become acquainted with Franz Schubert.

What happened, however, was peculiar. After many vain attempts, the meeting finally took place. Schubert was brought to Hoffmann. "Pleasantly surprised, I greet him," the latter reports, "mention briefly how hard we tried to find him, how very happy I am to meet him in person, etc. Schubert stands before me confused, doesn't quite know what to say, and after a few words, he says good-bye and—I never see him again. No, I say, that really is a bit much. Now I would prefer that I had never seen him. Then I would never have been able to associate a common, indifferent, or even impolite person with the creator of such soulful melodies. This way, however, aside from his behavior today, the man is in no way different from any other Viennese." Schubert did not wear the halo of the Olympian, nor the stigma of the titan during his walks through the gardens of Vienna's environs, on his sleepwalker's path through the darkness of his existence; he was in no way different from any other Viennese, and differed from almost all other Viennese composers in this one characteristic: that he was Viennese by birth.

He radiates nothing spectacular like Beethoven, against whose biography it is just as enlightening to measure Schubert's career, as it is to compare him with Goethe.

Schubert is born—Beethoven, long since in Vienna, internationally famous as a pianist, is writing the early symphonies, the early piano concertos and piano sonatas. Schubert attains the status of a composer—Beethoven has written all of his piano concertos, the violin concerto, *Fidelio*, the symphonies up to the eighth, and the middle quartets. Only the last sonatas, the last quartets, the

Missa solemnis, the ninth symphony, and the Diabelli variations follow. Into this time of the late, the "final" Beethoven, Schubert, who outlives him by a year, writes his life's work.

Beethoven's path led music from paradise to the knowledge of good and evil; Beethoven fetched fire from Olympus and brought it to mankind.

Schubert reclaimed for music its lost paradise—not permanently, of course, but his invaluable example stands for the eternal possibility of leading music back into paradise again and again.

We know composers, who, to a certain extent, wrote each of their more significant works only once; Beethoven is the paradigm of that species, in more recent times Stravinsky. A problem is presented or presents itself; it is treated, solved, or at least portrayed. The result does not become a model for new works; it is sufficient unto itself and stands on the side of the path to the next new problems. Other composers, such as Mozart and Schubert, know nothing of problems. They write their symphony, their sonata, their string quartet again and again, always new. Their music stands beyond the knowledge of good and evil.

Beethoven wrestles, Beethoven suffers under the influence of the public. Like Mozart, Schubert does not let the things of the world, including his own private affairs, touch his work. A god gave them the ability not to tell how they suffer. Beethoven changes the world at his desk; in so doing, he reaches the people of all eras. Mozart and Schubert create the world and thereby reach beyond mankind.

Grillparzer knew that music ended with Beethoven. But he did not hear that someone next to him had already gone on before Beethoven's death.

For a century after Beethoven, nobody could write another ninth symphony or a tenth symphony. But even before Beethoven's death, in nine years Schubert wrote seven symphonies, up to the symphony in B minor; he began again from the beginning, where Beethoven had begun, and made his own way, at the end of which is no "ninth," no "symphony to end all symphonies," but in the year one after Beethoven, the last, great eighth in C major, the rebirth of the symphony after its self-surrender in Beethoven's ninth, the salvation of the symphony after its declaration of bankruptcy in the recitatives of Beethoven's contrabasses, the defense of absolute music against the invasion of the literary element.

Schubert does not have to acquire his musical language, knowledge of his craft, he is endowed with them. Since he creates the world while composing, it is unavoidable that this world also contains the small next to the great, the ordinary next to the powerful. Since, however, he goes beyond the human, he touches the outer limits of mortality. In the string quintet, in string quartets and piano sonatas, in the songs of *The Winter Journey* we hear music of inexplicable uniqueness in a dimension never attained before or afterward: recorded harmony of the spheres. It was fortunate for him and is fortunate for us that Franz Schubert did not know who he was; woe to us, that we do not know who he was! When Beethoven died, the world held its breath. When Goethe died, he had hardly been there anymore and was already finished, dead before his death and alive beyond it, long since, according to Hermann Hesse, "on the point of becoming more and more depersonalized and disappearing completely into anonymity."

In Vienna, ten years after Schubert's death, Robert Schumann asked Schubert's brother Ferdinand if he was preserving other manuscripts. And they found, among other things, the symphony in C major, which Mendelssohn soon presented in Leipzig. Characteristic of Schubert concerning this symphony is not only its musical uniqueness, but also its fate. For it was not simply found among works he left behind, as the classical version of the story of the misunderstood genius would have it; it had been submitted to the Society of Music Lovers and been deemed too long and too difficult. It had been played once after Schubert's death and had not been appreciated, and had only then disappeared. Four years after the Leipzig performance, during a practice, Parisian orchestra musicians refused to play the second movement after having played the first. Another two years later orchestra musicians in London considered the work to be too long and too difficult.

Thirty-seven years after Schubert's death, they sought and found among other manuscripts in Graz the score to the symphony in B minor, which was played for the first time forty-three years after it was written.

This symphony places before us the question of the finished and the unfinished in Schubert's work and beyond.

Schubert probably intended that the symphony be performed in that form, in spite of its unconventional two-movement form, for he had sent it to the Styrian Music Society to thank them for having made him an honorary member, and it had not just been written at the time, but nine months earlier. On the other hand, sketches exist, even a page of the score, for a third movement—thus the intention to continue it had existed at one time.

In this glance at Schubert's life and works, it was not accidental that Goethe's so-called *Pandora* fragment was also mentioned, and that in the process it was consciously described as completed.

The question of the completion, the completeness of a work of art is independent of the mechanical, superficial ending, finishing of it. Goethe left *Pandora* behind, without letting the title figure herself appear. That he did not write more may have been accidental or the result of a conscious decision. Either way, in the form handed down to us, it is meaningful and fulfills its own laws; either way, *Pandora* is great and sublime. The question about what may be missing is just as trivial as the one concerning the author's original intentions. (Eckermann: "I asked him if one could perhaps view the work as a complete whole, or if something more of it existed. He said that there was no more of it, he had not continued it, specifically because the stature of the first part had become so great that he was later unable to complete a second part. And what he had written could very well be viewed as a whole, and that had reassured him concerning it.")

Schubert may have sent the score of the two symphony movements to Graz because he had no other symphony on hand—at the time it was also entirely conceivable to perform only parts of a work in concerts. Schubert may have seized the score without thinking of the fact that it consisted of only two movements. He may have mentally conceived a third movement and a fourth and thought that he had written them down. Perhaps the obligation to provide the people in Graz with a quid pro quo called forth the decision to view the symphony as a completed whole—a welcome solution that freed him from the necessity of creating a scherzo and, above all, a finale. The B minor symphony unjustly bears the name *Unfinished*; it is not unfinished, and to the extent that it might be, the lack of completion would be a characteristic of its completeness.

Every life as well, no matter how long it has lasted, is complete at the moment of death, in that it is finished —and enters eternity as it was, and can no longer be different. Viewed from the end, it acquires meaning, even in apparently arbitrary and accidental senselessness.

Viewing it from the end, we follow a career like a drama, a story whose conclusion we know and in which we are nonetheless passionately interested:

The year 1828 begins. With his *Winter Journey* Schubert seems to have already said farewell to life. He has left his apparent security and gone out into the winter as a stranger. He is some hours distant from the place where the linden tree's shade accorded him many a sweet dream. The mail brings no letter for him. Lonely and unrecognized, he has only the crow as a companion on the road along which nobody has yet returned. He has gone over to the organ grinder who stands barefoot on the ice and grinds his organ with stiff fingers—he is over there, beyond the village, in a fantasy world, with the question he directs to the strange old man whose plate always remains empty, whom nobody wants to hear, whom nobody looks at, around whom the dogs growl: "Should I go with you? Do you want to grind your organ to my songs?" What can yet come after this extreme, wintery dissolution, after the last open question? Can spring come once more?

Not even eleven months remain. Schubert has not yet written the symphony in C major, the string quartet, the last three piano sonatas, the Heine songs—and he has so little time left!

Goethe did not have to finish *Pandora* and had to finish *Faust*. Schubert did not go on after writing one movement of a string quartet and two movements of a symphony. Regardless of any subjective intentions, in the form in which they were left, both *Pandora* and *Faust*, as well as all one-movement and multiple-movement works of Schubert are at once complete and unfinished. Without regard to the dictates of the calendar and socio-political averages, the works of the last years of life are the late works of the genius, whether he has written them at the age of thirty, fifty, or eighty years. The value, validity, and enduring impact of the works of art are not decided by the answer to the question of what they say, nor the question of how they say it, but only by the answer to the question of who wrote them. With respect to Franz Schubert the answer to that question has not been given yet. And it will expose in their entire lack of understanding all the silly objections to Schubert's lack of "technique." According to Nietzsche, he was "less of an artist than the other great masters." Gustav Mahler expressed the criticism that his "ability far from matched his sensitivity and his creativity." Carl Spitteler writes of "offenses against form." And all this and many similar things come not from opponents, from people who disapprove, but from Schubert lovers who do justice to a law that is justifiably absolute, by using paragraphs and standards of other worlds, who want to impose their petty, mortal house rules on a paradise.

What later generations culpably misunderstand, Schubert himself approached in sweet ignorance. Two weeks before his death, he visited Simon Sechter and registered with him as a student of fugue composition. On that November 4, 1828 he had already contracted the fatal illness, for on November 11, he wrote in his last letter that he had "already eaten and drunk nothing for eleven days." Such a visit and decision while in such condition might be viewed as tempting fate: If what I have previously done has not sufficed, then may all of that have been just a beginning, a prelude, a prologue, then let the period of maturity, of ability now begin.

It was no beginning, it was the end. Maturity had long since been realized without higher contrapuntal book learning. The dear Lord had sufficed as a teacher. Master Sechter could save his instruction for other students; for if Schubert had gone on, "he would have gotten a hundred years ahead of his own time. That could not be, and so he died." (T. W. Werner)

He entered the throes of death unaware of his own greatness. He had paid for his works with the absence of special characteristics in his life. He had not been a virtuoso, and not a conductor, and had not taught like almost all of his colleagues who came before or were contemporary with him, for "in the mornings he felt the urge to compose, and in the evenings he wanted to rest."—His "speed in composing was extraordinary... Instead of becoming poorer through the dreadful squandering of the most magnificent melodies, the squandering seemed only to unveil even greater riches."—"His eyes glowed as he did it, standing out like glass."—"He often felt moved by his own creations, and the eyewitnesses testify that they could tell by his glowing eyes and by the changes in his speech, how powerfully things were working within him."

If his plans for the day were fulfilled, he spent the rest of it in a very normal way, usually happy, as gregariously as possible. He was hungry for association with friends, for good conversations, for relaxing cheerfulness without obligation. He was erratic, tardy in his appointments, reserved toward strangers and social superiors. Since he himself did not dance, he often had to play for dances. And if one of his improvisations in three-quarter time seemed somewhat successful to him, he repeated the piece until he could remember it, and then wrote it down. Thus the Vienna waltz came into being in a paradisiacal personal union of artistic and popular music. Lander and the older Strauss, a few years younger than Schubert, were familiar with these dances, which had been published from 1821 on, and in the ballrooms and gardens of the city, they turned what for Schubert had been only a passing fancy into the content of their lives.

Under obligation to nobody but the dictates of his mornings, Schubert was a free creative artist, unmindful of all of the pressing phenomena that accompany freedom. He wanted things precisely as he had them "in this miserable world. And just what would we do with happiness, when unhappiness is now the only attraction that remains for us." He was not egoistic, but with regard to his art completely self-confident, extremely surly toward unskillful composers, and completely hostile toward the common people. Once he wrote in his diary: "Enviable Nero! You were strong enough to destroy loathsome people while playing the strings and singing."

He was not a saint in any respect, nor did he accept without protest, without occasional outbursts the burden of sorrow that was placed upon him, but he nonetheless accepted it without serious attempts to escape. On the eve of his death, he asked his brother Ferdinand: "Hey, just what is happening to me?" A bit later he was still able to perceive: "This, this is the end for me." But as he began to fantasize, he wanted to go away "from this corner under the ground..." because "Beethoven does not lie here." For that reason they buried him in the

Währing cemetery, three graves away from Beethoven. Thus he himself probably answered the question of what was happening to him; thus, while saying farewell, he was permitted to see himself. And the next day, "at three o'clock in the afternoon he died, and his cheerful, unchanged countenance showed that he had passed away peacefully and without a struggle."

And just what has happened to Schubert since he died? The consciousness of the musical world does not pray to Schubert, does not rejoice in him; it has entered a marriage of convenience with him, one that functions well. We know, we appreciate him, love him to a degree, pat him on the back indulgently and somewhat sated. But the crows have seized hold of him to a greater extent than any other prey.

They played the well-meant but insufferable transcriptions of Liszt and others. In 1864 Franz von Suppé's musical play *Franz Schubert* appeared on a stage in Vienna. In the scene, "a practicable linden tree" stands in front of a mill. Schubert's entry is announced by an ensemble:

> See—he draws near,
> He walks—along,
> It is—his song!
> He comes at rapid pace
> Down to our space.
> His step, a rhythmic glide,
> His walk, his stride,
> As if on each path the music sweet
> Had come its master here to greet.

Schubert—according to the stage directions he comes "down from the mountains"—enters and sings:

In winter, in storm on the water I sail
In clothing soaked through by the rain and the hail,
I strike at the waves with a powerful blow,
While hoping and dreaming of days all aglow.

All: With joy and with zest
       That fill his breast,
       Exquisitely sings he his song,
       Ah, now let us sing along.

After the distortion of *The Wanderer* and *Gretchen at the Spinning Wheel*, Schubert composes on stage "I would like to carve it in every tree," and while doing so interrupts himself: "I cannot find the end / It's hard the words and notes to blend / It is annoying, to be sure!" But during the third attempt he is able "to find the end."

Felix Mottl used Franz Schubert's music with the style of a display-window designer for the background music to Ferdinand Raimund's *Chained Fantasy* (1898). Ignoring the key changes and the dissimilarity of the stanzas, leaving out the intermezzos and the middle of the minor-key section, and changing the accompaniment, Friedrich Silcher made *The Linden Tree* into a banal men's chorus. A publisher issued the last three impromptu pieces under the collective title *Easter Promenade* and with the individual titles "Soldiers and Bourgeois Girls," "Free of Ice," and "Peasants beneath the Linden Tree."

After that came the Schubert novel *Mushroom* by Rudolf Hans Bartsch in 1912.

    "Oh, Franzy, why didn't you pay any attention at all to the girl. I would have been happy to see you have her!"

"Me?" Schubert asked in alarm, and his heart convulsed with regret and desire.

His father placed his head in his hands and said nothing.

"Hey, Tschöll" said Schubert with a quivering voice, "you should have suggested that to me sooner."

"Well, it doesn't matter now. Why didn't you notice anything?"

"Because you advised me against Theresa, of course, because I was a poor boy."

"Back then you were twenty, and we didn't know yet what would become of you. Now you're somebody, and I know your heart."

"Tschöll, Tschöll," said Schubert sorrowfully. "Now you've made me as unhappy as you are."

"Do you still want her?" Tschöll asked softly.

Schubert looked down at the floor. "No," he said then, with his voice strained, "not anymore." He turned and left, even though his despairing friend called after him to stay, to listen, to let him help.

It was the last time that Schubert spent time in *The House of Three Girls*, which now stood empty, completely empty.

After that came 896 Schubert films. But even worlds below them, anticipating everything that has happened since then with respect to *lèse majesté*, misunderstanding, and desecration of Franz Schubert, there appeared in 1916, as an absolute nadir, the musical play *The House of Three Girls* by Dr. A. M. Willner and Heinz

Franz Schubert did not know that he was Franz Schubert. The deceptive consciousness of mortality guaranteed him immortality. Ferdinand Raimund wanted to be Schiller and Shakespeare; thus he could not quite become Ferdinand Raimund.

During his entire life he kept missing the right connection, and he left us the picture of his life as his only completed tragedy.

With Raimund's biography begins the gallery of eternal fiancées that Grillparzer and Nestroy and Lenau will continue: seen from the end, from the perspective of the whole, an almost fanatical, demonic inclination to maneuver one's own life into a hopeless situation from the beginning, to obstruct the happy, normal, desired relationship with a woman, to obtain grounds for regret, for unfulfilled wish dreams...the self-destructive element as an Austrian cardinal failing.

As a young man, Raimund had several unhappy love affairs, as we might expect, but then he found the woman of his life; and when her parents refused to give their consent, he let himself be caught and forced into marriage by another woman. He soon obtained a divorce, but could not marry again. We almost get the impression that he consciously planned it that way, as if he wanted, needed it to be that way and not otherwise. The chronicle of his youthful love catastrophes is tragic and pitiful; and once he wanted to die, threw himself angrily into an ice-cold mill stream, then regained his senses, cried out for help, and was saved. Later, when friends on one occasion alluded to the incident and jokingly reproached him for remaining alive after all,

Raimund answered: "You cannot continuously commit suicide."

And yet he undertook to do that very thing: he continuously committed suicide, tormented himself, punished himself, destroyed himself. His life was forty-six years of dying, a battle conducted on many fronts by Ferdinand Raimund against Ferdinand Raimund. While examining the figure of Franz Schubert, we already encountered the great misinterpreter Bauernfeld, the superficial, hardly reliable contemporary of his century. We meet him as well on the periphery of Raimund's tragedy; we have our doubts about many of the reports that the ancient, inflexible man published in 1872. But we must probably accept one of Raimund's comments as authentic, even if it was passed on by Bauernfeld: "I was born to be a tragedian; the only things I lack for it are the stature and the voice."

That would be an excellent joke, if he had been inspired by a realization of his own talent, but the genial comedian Raimund meant it in deadly earnest. Thus the antithesis—expressed, according to Bauernfeld, "in a noble outburst"—reflects his entire tragicomical, discordant disposition. If he had been as successful as a tragedian, as he was in the area of comedy, he would have been consumed by an unfulfilled longing for comic roles. He always wanted the very thing he could not have. He loved Toni Wagner and let himself marry Luise Gleich. He got rid of Luise Gleich and united himself for life with Toni—whom he could not marry because he was divorced—in a stirring oath of fidelity in front of the Saint Mary's Pillar at Neustift am Wald. He wrote her infinitely tender letters full of longing and desire and poetic rapture:

> ...I see an angel float down in the deepest distress. He holds a lily stem in his hand as a sign of his innocence, his pure love, and with the palm of peace he touches the deeply wounded heart... And behold, the passions cuddle tenderly at the feet of the cherub, who gives them a gentle king, whom he calls trust. And the miracle of this fantasy does not fade from my sight before I have recognized that the angel is you and pledged to you and me for my sake, that I will only walk through life hand in hand with you, my beloved guardian angel, and that I will eternally remain
>
>   your Ferdinand.

What a noble, pure love, after an acquaintance of five years, almost suspect in its poetically sublime loftiness! And actually: following the signature there is a postscript that asks very mundanely: "Dear Toni, I hear that you are angry. Are you being unjust again so soon?"

In the year following this and similar letters to the angel and cherub, the latter kept a diary that has been preserved; and in its faulty orthography, its terse keyword style, it presents a shocking contrast to the divine poesy of the rapturous poet: "we are bikering" [*sic*]—"bikered on the bastion"—"bikered on the pastion"—"we really bikered"—"was at his place, where we bikered again"—"evening rode around town with him where we really bikered"—

At his desk Raimund's poetic ecstasy grew, ecstasy that could not withstand reality. All his life he longed for the realization of a shared family life with Toni, knowing that it was unattainable. He was more attached to the longing than to its fulfillment. Where she provided existence, but not without his contribution, he created for himself occasions for pain. He destroyed everything that was whole and could have become whole. He could only exist coming out of conflict, going into conflict.

We encounter here for the first time another, later commentator and great misinterpreter: Hugo von Hofmannsthal, the Bauernfeld of a new century. Thirty-six years after Raimund's death, Bauernfeld observed: "One cannot perform Raimund without Raimund." Hofmannsthal reached the epitome of misunderstanding, when, in what is regarded as his classical Raimund essay of 1920, he wrote the refrainlike words: "The unity of all these things is complete." No, here is neither unity nor completeness; here disintegration becomes creative, and the flight from unity dictates the action.

Ferdinand Raimund wanted to become a tragic actor and entered the realm of comedy only against his will. In the drama *Jolanthe, Queen of Jerusalem* he played the marshall of a religious order as his fourth role in Vienna—the second role had been Franz Moor—and made a mistake in his lines. With "extreme pathos" he recited: "For a prisoner we can only give a belt and a leather dagger." There was "no end to the laughter," and Raimund "did not dare appear in a serious drama for a long time afterward, unless he wanted to be received with howls of laughter." But as a comedian he was quickly accepted. Within two years he was famous, immediately celebrated and venerated, but seven years later he still maintained that "the world considered him to be a comedian, when by nature he was really meant to be a tragedian."

Four years after the "leather dagger," reviews called him a "perfect comedian" and "unparalleled," and even that triumph was not achieved along a straight path. In 1832, after Raimund appeared on stage in Berlin, Willibald von Alexis noted that Raimund had no "natural comedic power," he fulfilled none of the other prerequisites for a comedian, "he sputters letters—and yet Raimund is the greatest comedian we see."

He always strived for the impossible; he only achieved greatness where he did not want it. His decisive breakthrough with the Viennese audience came when he played the role of the musician Adam Kratzerl in the farce *The Musicians at the High Market* that was given several continuations for Raimund's sake. The decisive factor in its success was Raimund's comical violin playing—but nothing concerning musical training is contained in the documents of his life. Had he also, like Schubert, learned it "from the dear Lord"? The learning surely happened on the side, but the accounts make it clear that he was a master at playing the violin. And he certainly never took regular lessons in composition, but he roughed out for the composers the music for the most important songs in almost all of his plays. (In the case of *The Girl from the Fairy World*, some theater programs note that the music "with the exception of the songs" was written by Joseph Drechsler.) He was an actor and a dramatic author, and he entered the highest level of immortality, where he became creative as a rank amateur, without awareness of or claim to greatness: in the melodies of the "Ash Song," the "Plane Song," the ensemble "So now farewell, you quiet house," the duet "Fine Little Brother," in all those moments of unconscious, unplanned greatness, where he, by his own admission, "while writing many songs wrote down the music along with them." Nor did he want to write any plays. "That's not for me," he said at the age of twenty-nine, when they asked him to do it. Not until six years later, then only for the last decade of his life, was he a dramatist; and only because he needed a viable play, like Nestroy, did he decide to write: an unplayable, half-finished manuscript was adapted and finished... Where outside of Austria can one imagine the meeting of a dramatist with the dramatic muse under such conditions?!

Was the conflict that already existed not enough: the heavenly and the earthly Toni, the comical figure that thirsted for tragic pathos? He projected them both into the production and achieved new, painful antitheses: between the actor and the dramatist and within his dramas.

What important dramatist only became a dramatist as a result of external stimulus, and then not until the fourth decade of his life? When Raimund was writing *The Barometermaker on the Magic Island*, a friend noted: "I made the comment that he is beginning to age a great deal."

And yet, how somnambulistically, Schubertlike he masters his unwanted new calling! "I will sing the musical pieces to Müller right out of my own head," he writes to Toni. And how infinitely right, competent, and "accomplished" is this music; how the outsider expertly and routinely masters the necessary forms of the dialogues and songs!

His success was unequivocal, the late career of the dramatist clearly marked out.

Here in this first stage play, which was produced against his will, without a great deal of reflection, under the pressure of external circumstances—here, where he is still not a dramatist, for once and only once Raimund achieves unity. *The Barometermaker on the Magic Island* is not world literature, is hardly literature at all. Out of context, taken on its own merits, it is a tradition-bound utility play of that era. The comparison with *The Magic Flute* is obvious; it came from the same sources and was the same age as Raimund. But Raimund's plays are *Magic Flutes* without Mozart, and Raimund's first play is a *Magic Flute* without Sarastro and the Queen of the Night, without Pamina and Tamino. The place of Sarastro is taken here by Tutu, the ruler of the magic island; he is introduced with the lines: "I succumb beneath the burden of my duties! Be quiet, so that I can busy myself while sleeping!" The spirit world is not taken seriously; the fairy tale is simultaneously presented and parodied. The plot with its stage props is conventional. The story of the lovers is hardly greater than that of Papageno and Papagena. "I like the girl. I'll stay with her," he says. "Oh, you golden man! I'll never let him go," she says; there is no development, no entanglement, no conflict, only cheerful mischievousness with figs that make the noses grow longer when they are eaten, and a water that reduces the long noses again—on the stage there are no people with whom we can sympathize, no ideas that we can follow—but: unity, uniformity; for the contrast expressed in the title, the folksy decent Viennese in the world of oriental mysteries, is made fruitful; the conflict does not shatter the work, it is legitimately expressed within it. But from now on, when Raimund works consciously as a dramatic author, everything becomes complicated, multifarious, intricate, more involved, more confused.

The conflict between parody and seriousness is never completely surmounted again; for even where supernatural beings have deeply serious meaning (the king of the Alps, Cheristane), a remnant of brightly colored fairytale routines still clings to them, which debases them as cheap conventions vis-à-vis the very real human figures. The conflict between tragedy and gaiety does not become fruitful in depth as it does in the works of Shakespeare. We can see breaks in it. The conflict between great and popular literature is never, can never be completely overcome. Raimund's second play, *The Diamond of the Spirit King*, is still based on a model. (The third will be his first "original magic fairy tale.") The plot is unclear, much is only suggested, not thought out. (Hofmannsthal felt quite correctly that a treasure was buried in the material of this magical play, but his fragmentary attempt at an adaptation failed.) Again the spirits are parodied and made into caricatures. They are confronted by the mortals, who are somewhat more defined, Eduard-Tamino, Amine-Pamina, but their story is dull and uninteresting. The Viennese figures Florian and Mariandel have vividness and charm, but they experience no adventures; like Papageno-Papagena they only go along on the periphery. The title motif of the diamond is unclear. The employed cast is too large. For the first time, Raimund's tendency to personify is fully cultivated. Fairies, genies, spirits, magicians, and pixies are joined by Hope and the quartet of the four seasons.

But it is also the case that for the first time, right in the initial confusion of styles and motifs, genius becomes noticeable.

A series of scenes is located in the "land of truth and strict morality." (*"Plaza, surrounded by beautiful high buildings, but without any windows, built in the Egyptian style and painted with Chinese and Egyptian figures and decorations; but all garish colors are avoided. This must also be the case with the colors of the articles of clothing, which approximate the Moroccan style."*) This country is not, as we expect from a fairy tale, an idyllic, ideal paradise. No, it is hell. The principle of the true and the moral is carried to the absurd in its total application: the land of truth and strict morality is ruled by a cruel regime; lies triumph, and the only pure, honest person is a stranger who is about to be burned as a witch.

Pattern and tradition are overcome here; this could be the beginning of something new. Here the noble, good, unambiguous elements of the fairy tale are transposed into dubious reality and thereby debased. And in two lines of verse Raimund's second stroke of genius in this *Diamond* shatters the framework of the baroque sphere, explosively destroys everything that has been valid until now:

After his death, Zephises, a magician, is accepted into the world of spirits. In distress, his son, the Taminolike hero, conjures up the spirit of his father:

> Eduard: Hear me, Father. If you still recognize the voice of your son, rise up here to me and save me from my despair. Father, Father, hear me! (*Thunder*) O joy, Amine, he heard me, he is coming!

Zephises comes from the middle stage trap in his previous spirit robe.

> Eduard: Spirit of my father, advise your unhappy son—what should I do?

The apparatus still functions. The communication of mortals with the spirits is still intact. But what kind of message does the spirit, who is conjured up and appears with so much pomp, have to proclaim?

> Zephises *with a serious expression:* I am your father Zephises and have nothing to say to you but this. *Disappears again.*

After having gone that far, how can he continue to write fairy-tale plays? But Raimund did not get away from the form, nor from the personifications. But he came closer to human beings.

He writes no further Papageno roles for himself; in *The Girl from the Fairy World* he is Fortunatus Wurzel, the "peasant as millionaire." There are not just a buffo servant and a rapturous pair of lovers present here, but more of the authentic mundane world; there is a peasant with servants and freeloading drinking buddies, there are workmen, journeymen, common people. But the piece is called *The Girl from the Fairy World.* The world theater is presented and played out around the daughter of the fairy Lacrimosa, who is in the peasant's custody. Her fate, stiltedly conventional, leaves us cold and is nevertheless the main thing. Wurzel wins our sympathy but remains on the periphery of the action that is decisive for the play. He is only a tool, not a hero. All this is already reflected in the double title, *The Girl from the Fairy World; or, The Peasant as Millionaire*, a form in harmony with the taste of the period, but for Raimund more than form, expression of his tragic disintegration. He will yet think up other titles of that kind: *The Fateful Crown, or, King without a Kingdom, Hero without*

Courage, Beauty without Youth—and in draft form *Moisasur's Magic Spell* had the subtitle: *A serious comical fairy-tale play.* He had success in comedy as a dramatist as he did as an actor, but here, as there, he defends himself against his real domain: "...I became more daring and invented material for myself, and thus *The Peasant as Millionaire* came into being, in which there are many silly trifles that I only used because I was afraid the audience would consider it to be too serious." What seems silly to him? Certainly not the thing that hinders our enjoyment, the conflicting coexistence of human nature and cheap fairy play, of authentic beings and personifications (Hymen, Contentment, Envy, Hate, Morning, Evening, Night, Nonsense, Youth, Old Age). Morning, Evening, and Nonsense are only supernumeraries in the play; Night has only two lines to say:

> From pomp you must flee!
> Night's vengeance you'll see.

None of these personifications is assimilated. The final act literally drowns in its ponderousness. Our sympathy for the girl Lottchen and her honest Karl cannot be mobilized. The drama moves infinitely laboriously and even burdened with more labels ("*Lacrimosa floats down in a carriage of clouds, above which a cherub floats with the label 'Salvation'—She waves; a waterfall arises, above which are the words: 'Spring of Obliviousness to Evil'*") toward its conclusion. In the midst of this amorphous diversity, however, decisive for his immortality and establishing Raimund's entry into world literature is the world around Fortunatus Wurzel. No longer is an ingenuous local servant the source of jokes; here the people, the contemporary figure, just now discovered for Raimund's drama, are also already inscrutable and malicious: "What do you think this is? No more money and rude besides? Ah, now I'll have to become more severe...," says the servant to the impoverished lord who was displaced from the palace into a dismal valley in front of his dilapidated cottage, and: "If you have the impudence to let me see you around here again, I'll tear off a willow and give you a hiding with it to remember me by, you spoiled, millionaire muttonhead, you!" And hypocritically whining: "I'm only a poor domestic servant, and he's cheating me out of what is mine. What kind of master is that? I've been swindling him now for three years, and now I don't even get anything out of it."

Raimund felt hurt about the success of *The Vagabond* by Nestroy and is supposed to have said: "Next to Nestroy I'm nothing anymore; well, let's move over." But in *The Diamond of the Spirit King* he himself had already carried out the devaluation of the fairy-tale sweetness, and in *The Girl from the Fairy World*, seven years before *The Vagabond*, he had anticipated Nestroy's view of man.

After a performance of Grillparzer's *Life is a Dream* Raimund said, "You see, that's what I always intended, and my *Peasant as Millionaire* is really the same idea... I just don't have the pretty words; and they wouldn't (he fell into dialect) understand them out there* either. It's a great pity about me." Why "a great pity"? He had all it took to compete with Nestroy. And as far as Grillparzer is concerned, Nikolaus Lenau thought that Raimund was "one of the mightiest dramatic talents of our time, far more original and direct than even Grillparzer was."

---

*A reference to the Leopoldstädter Theater in the suburbs.

And Egon Friedell is completely justified in observing: "Next to Grillparzer lived a stronger man who looked up to him all his life as an unattainable ideal." It is a great pity about him because he fled into the resigned attitude of the "great pity," because he had everything and did not do the right thing with it, because he wanted too much and too little and always at least two different things at once.

The peasant Wurzel, millionaire and palace owner, is visited by Youth, who sings farewell, who says "good-bye" to her "little brother," her "baby brother." Then he is afflicted by Old Age, who brings a billeting order along. The scene, at the center of the middle act, is one of the most splendid inspirations of poetic-musical fantasy. As an insert, as an intermezzo, again and again it will outshine all the previous and subsequent clumsy ponderousness and shifting of levels. Up to now it has secured the vitality of the fairy-tale play on the stage. But it is still only an episode and not the essential thing.

In the great scene of Youth and Old Age, suburban art leaves its small domain and approaches Parnassus.

In the original fairy-tale play *Chained Fantasy*, the duality of Parnassus and folk art is presented, but not mastered again. A tragic parable of Raimund's striving and failure: The suburban singer Nightingale appears before Apollo, but Raimund sees in the charming Viennese, whom he himself played, a "grotesque image" —self-destruction, self-abasement—and in the singing contest he allows a conventional, meaningless prize song to triumph:

> In wonderland, that near my father's kingdom lies,
> Where multi-colored nature glows beneath the skies,
> The queen of my deep love sits on her throne,

Adds soft appeal to meaning of her own.
The muses, who are filled with charm and grace,
Within her lovely breast have found their place...

Here are the "many beautiful words" that he did not have and yet could not leave alone; here the ground that was gained in *The Girl from the Fairy World* is even partially given up. Ever more commanding, the "high," the mythological, the exotic penetrates Raimund's plays. This time it is Apollo with his court, later it will be Hades and Thanatos, the spirit of virtue and the demon of evil, Eumenides and Furies—India, Arabia, Sicily, the realm of transitoriness become dramatic locales; Simplizius Zitternadel, a poor village tailor, will be in the theater program with Kreon, the king of Agrigent, the alpine market official with Hoanghu, the king of the diamond kingdom. The beautiful words will become more and more beautiful, and the verses more and more serious and unbearable; and they give Speidel reason to make the observation that Raimund "saw literary language floating above him as a longed-for but never quite attainable goddess." Early on, the nasty M. G. Saphir gave the following formulation with almost Raimundlike pointedness and unfortunate appropriateness: "Mr. Raimund bridles his Pegasus in the ether and then leads him to water in Lerchenfeld."*

More and more often, the name of Shakespeare appears in the writings of contemporary Raimund observers, but Raimund's impotent striving to reach Shakespeare's level, and Schiller's as well, without resolutely turning away from the magical and fairy-tale theater, simultaneously becomes clearer and clearer.

*Suburb of Vienna

And then he writes clumsily amateurish and awkward verses like:

Phalarius: Stay back, you Furies pale, the crown shields me from ill!
Alecto: It is no shield; of Kreon think, for hell is still!
Phalarius: I hate both him and you!
Tisiphone: Think of Aspasia!
Megära: And burning Agrigent!
Alecto: Know, you must pass away!

Then he writes prose like:

People of my ever victorious kingdom! I have had you assemble yourselves to join in with the great choir that begins to sing of the feeling of gratitude, because the gods have illuminated us, that we appeased the anger of the sun through Moisasur's fall; that from this moment on it victoriously turns the arrows of our army toward the breasts of our enemies.

Raimund wanted to be a Shakespeare and yet knew very well that he could not be a Shakespeare—and he was Shakespearian only where he did not want to be a Shakespeare:

In the middle of the conflicting abundance of unsuccessful dramas about magic spells and crowns and fantasy, his greatest, purest, most authentic work, *The King of the Alps and the Misanthrope*, was successful. Just once, the great conflict was captured brilliantly and effectively in the dramatic parable, became content instead of destroying the form. Raimund "began by writing his comedies on his body; he ended by writing them from his soul." (Heinz Politzer)

The drama about the misanthrope is a self-accusation and a self-aware settling of accounts, a diagnosis and an attempt at therapy. As always, when people who are ill and suffering, embittered and torn overcome darkness in their works, when they find the solution and fight their way through to the positive side, in Beethoven's excessively fanatical coda ecstasies as in Goethe's taming of the barbarian Thoas, and also in Raimund's healing of the misanthropic Herr von Rappelkopf, the wish is the father of the conclusion. The work is intended to create an order in which its creator wants to be able to believe. All great art says *no*; that *no* can even very often serve as the criterion for the presence of great art. Where it fights its way through to the crowning *yes*, its intent is to "call itself to order." If it directs itself to its own address, it overcomes the chaos in the work as a desperate contribution to overcoming the chaos inside and in the world of its creator. With the ending of his own life, Raimund contradicted the ending of *The King of the Alps and the Misanthrope*. But he overcame his physical end, in that his drama made the misanthrope immortal. And thus in another respect the continued life of the suicidal title figure at the end of the drama is legitimate again after all: After he had portrayed how Herr von Rappelkopf remains alive and makes his peace with the world, Ferdinand Raimund could die his own death, which became invalid in light of the immortal figure of Herr von Rappelkopf.

The life of the dramatist Ferdinand Raimund lasted for ten years, and in the middle of it stands the "romantic-comic original fairy-tale play" about the misanthrope, the greatest evidence of dramatic art in Austria.

Suddenly, unlike before and afterward, all the oriental elements from books, all the fairy-tale clutter, almost all the stilted pseudopoetic elements are made to disappear as if through higher intervention. We are among characters whose development progresses in clear lines, without circuitousness and mixing of the spheres. Magic occurs only where it is essential for the plot, when visions are required with good reason and transformations are desired. That the Alpine King Astragalus transforms himself into Herr von Rappelkopf and the latter into his brother-in-law Silberkern—all of that is completely necessary and desirable, for it makes the most splendid of all situations possible: Rappelkopf—externally Silberkern, internally still Rappelkopf—watches himself when Astragalus represents Rappelkopf. In Rappelkopf's absence he hears the others talk about Rappelkopf. He recognizes himself and sees how in his delusion he has become guilty in dealing with himself and those close to him. Thus he is healed by a method that "has gone far more than halfway from Mesmer to Freud." (Heinz Politzer)

So we have psychology, psychotherapy, but brilliantly captured in the form of a cheerful series of scenes, the message of Shakespeare's *Timon* (which is mentioned twice in the text) expressed with the devices of *A Midsummer Night's Dream*. Raimund, who is connected to Rappelkopf not only by the alliteration, has the hero he plays be surrounded by nothing but good-natured, helpful people, and his self-accusation goes even further, in that Rappelkopf, completely without cause or excuse, from the depths of his own heart, hates people; for his delusion cannot have been caused by the fact alone that "he ceaselessly reads philosophical books that turn his head," and even less by the fact that he "was cheated out of large sums of money that he loaned to false friends." For Rappelkopf is still wealthy when the play begins, and it remains incomprehensible to reason alone, "how one can be a misanthrope with such a great fortune, a good-natured wife, a well-behaved daughter..." The demonic is made absolute; the trappings of the spirit world are not offered here to save the person from threats from outside, but to save him from himself.

Rappelkopf's salvation works, but in order for it to succeed, Raimund must probably have been and remained as he was. A friend once reproached him that "a great deal of what you imagine is worse than reality. If only I could turn your vital organs upside down for once and clean out all the pathological things that make your life black!" To that Raimund responded: "It might well be that you would cure me of my hypochondria; but perhaps you would also clean everything out of me that I use to write my comedies!" How true, how insightful, but why, just why didn't he write all his comedies as he did this one?

It also contains the great intermezzo in the charcoal burner's cottage, often praised, but still not sufficiently appreciated in all its radicality. In these scenes the folk play is born and then cancels itself out again. The poor, starving charcoal burner family, evicted by the wealthy Rappelkopf, archetypes of heartrending victims, ancestors of the legions of "poor, but honest" pitiful people —this family is introduced when the children first cry out, "Mother, give us bread!" then demand, "Blast it, a piece of bread!" To which the drunken father responds:

> If you don't shut your mouths,
> I will kill you yet!

The children mock their drunken father, a micro-pandemonium is portrayed, and these are the kind of people who begin to sing the moving song: "So now farewell, you quiet house..." As he does with the servant of Fortunatus Wurzel and this degenerate family, in the last act of his drama Raimund will give us one more sample of his view of the upright common people; he came terribly close not only to Freud, but also to Strindberg and Horváth. In the Indian romantic legend about sun worshipers, *Moisasur's Magic Spell*, he also portrayed an Alpine couple with the extreme cruelty that only seems imaginable in the ancient Punch-and-Judy theater or in the "modern" drama of recent date. When the man learns that his wife has died, he says: "That is an outrage without equal; she dies, and nobody is home. Now they will carry away all my money."

This actor, who accidentally began to write plays, realized what all the romantics demanded and did not accomplish outside of Austria; he produced magical, fairy-tale, near natural, ironic plays that still live in the theater today. At the same time, he saw people in all the dubiousness of their inscrutability. Somehow he simultaneously drew near to both Shakespeare and a future century, but always only momentarily, closest and most completely in the misanthrope drama. His contemporaries surely did not recognize its uniqueness. But they never misjudged Raimund, and then least of all. When one critic speaks of the "*non plus ultra*," he means, of course, the "comic presentation," not its cause, but does full justice even to the latter. Another critic praises the "unquestionable proof of Raimund's extraordinary, admirable talent," a third sees in the second part of the drama "a real masterpiece." Three years after the premiere, *The King of the Alps and the Misanthrope* was performed on English as well as Polish stages (there as *Carpathian King*)—now things were as splendid in every respect as one could wish, but Raimund could not wish for it to be so; he "could now honorably get all the well-earned laurels of Shakespeare and Tasso, yet he could never be fully satisfied. The worm of eternal dissatisfaction and worry dwells insurmountable in his guts."

For, what is called the Austrian fate—lack of self-realization, failure to fulfill one's potential, living and working in the state of *nevertheless*, confusing and exchanging the importance of principal and secondary matters—can be caused, if not by the environment, by the Austria within, the Austria in one's own soul.

Herr von Rappelkopf's death sentence had been lifted by Ferdinand Raimund, but Raimund's death sentence against himself was not rendered ineffective as a result; it was only postponed. When Herr von Rappelkopf billets himself in the "temple of knowledge" as a "retired misanthrope," Raimund has only a few years to live. He will write two more plays; right after reaching his zenith, he will descend to *The Fateful Crown*, then climb halfway back up again to *The Spendthrift*. He will free himself from all firm engagements and give guest performances in Germany; he will no longer have to keep his relationship with Toni a secret and will be able to take the eternal bride along on his trips; he will acquire a country house in his beloved Alpine countryside south of Vienna; but every step toward external validity will be a step toward his suicide.

In *The Spendthrift* the great multiple conflict has been reduced completely to form again; now a *Diamond of the Spirit King* reveals once more on a higher plane all the weaknesses and all the greatness disastrously knit together. The spendthrift Flottwell is the hero, but we are not as much interested in him as in the carpenter Valentin. The latter, however, participates only peripherally in the dramatic action. The intrusion of the fairy world into human life has extremely moral, but not dramatically compelling functions. Again there is, as so often before, a variation of the motif of the double. The spirit Azur confronts young Flottwell personifying the fiftieth year of his life, but unlike the situation in *The King of the Alps*, the play derives primarily romantic-opera effects from the brilliant idea. The language is occasionally extravagant, involuntarily comical:

> A look at this fair valley take!
> Where glows the earth with charm more grand?
> The expert has no choice to make,
> The view outclasses Switzerland.

In two sentences of dialogue, the great double track of the grand and the authentic is matchlessly expressed with self-awareness:

> Flottwell: O servant's loyalty, you're like the moon; we do not see you until our sun goes down. *Exit*
> Valentin: That's a pretty speech, but I didn't understand it.

Thus division into "poetic" and real spheres, division into a hero and a Raimund main role, division as well, remarkably and interestingly enough, between heavenly and earthly love. Cheristane, the romantic lover, is projected outward into the world of the supernatural; the play begins under the sign of her requited love for Flottwell; however, in the second act he loves and abducts a quite colorless Amalie von Klugheim. This entire second act has little to do with the first and the third and is somewhat laboriously kept alive by means of inserted scenes. All the real greatness is concentrated in the final act. Its last scene takes place on the top of a castle mountain with a view of the mountains across from it, behind which the sun goes down, conjures up Raimund's beloved nature one last time, but in a strange, mysterious way does not mark a real end point, but uncertainly grows dark, leaving everything open.

In this third act, Valentin sings his carpenter's song, known as the "Plane Song," three times eight lines set to music from his "own head." It is a testament, it is something final, it is possibly also an end, to the extent that it gives life a goal—a goal before the attainment of which there could be no end—and reaches that goal.

Raimund's father had been a wood turner, had cursed the boy because he wanted to join the theater, and had died with, had died of that curse. Psychologists will know how to interpret the meaning of that macabre scene for Raimund's living and fatal illness. And it may be that the apotheosis of the old workman with his plane was an extreme task that Raimund's illness set for him before it granted itself release in death: settlement of the conflict with his father, justification of his choice of profession, transfiguration of both professions by the son, song of praise to the carpenter, presented in the theater, reconciliation.

> About the worth of happiness
> The people oft have fought,
> One scolds another's foolishness,
> None in the end knows aught.

The "worth of joy" is put in question, not happiness itself, the worth of happiness and all the philosophical evasions of the troubles of existence; "at the end"—and Raimund stands at the end—at the end one knows nothing. Secretly this song is placed under the sign of death from the very beginning.

> Thus is the very poorest man
> Too rich for other men.
> Fate sets its plane, as it but can,
> And planes them equal then.

Here, too, death is anticipated. In the second and third stanzas the plane will belong to Valentin, the hand of fate leads him there; Valentin-Raimund will form his own fate, will finally be like the others, when he applies "the" plane (later it reads "my plane" twice), when the people's conflict ends, when one no longer knows anything about the value and worthlessness of happiness, and when wealth no longer counts, when he, in reality "the very poorest man," finally no longer seems much too rich to the others, just because he is wealthy, successful, and blessed with earthly goods.*

---

* There are two equally valid text versions of the fourth and fifth lines; the dispute, which is authentic, cannot be clearly decided. Usually the following is sung and printed:
> Thus is the very poorest man,
> The other man, too rich—

One may assume—and Raimund himself may have been open to the argument—that it would be too extreme if the very poorest man in particular appeared far too rich to his fellow man. But it was probably the case that Raimund did not—or not only—interpret the "poorest" in a material sense; thus the expression receives its proper and biographical meaning: that the wealthy man, although "too rich," can nevertheless be a "poor devil," even the very poorest man.

> Youth seeks for happiness untold
> In everything by force.
> Yet if one grows a little old,
> One learns to cope, of course.

Just "a little old," Raimund is forty-three when he writes that. He still has two years ahead of him. He means himself, the man growing old before his time. In so doing, he writes—a decade after his first work—his late works. He is not more specific about what one must put up with; he puts up "with it," in general, without an object. He immediately adds the "woman," the heavenly-earthly Toni, whose favorite word from the diary entries—bicker—spelled correctly, one-sidedly allotted to her, returns here. He has resigned himself to the lack of fulfillment in love.

> My wife scolds me quite often, Oh!
> It brings no rage from me.
> I tap my plane out, thinking so:
> Well, bicker on, feel free.

Even if a marriage to Toni had occurred, like Valentin-Papageno's marriage to Rosl-Papagena, there would only have been quarreling, dread, and grumbling —and Cheristane, the supernally loving and beloved woman, unattainable in the clouds "that move around Persia and Arabia on magical heavenly paths."

The entire environment is in the first, time and love are in the second stanza, a classical paradigm of the Viennese strophic song, by the way, which poses a thesis, applies it to love in the second stanza and to death and heaven in the third; then, in the third stanza, death is invoked quite directly:

> If death comes sometime, by your leave,
> Tugs: Brother, come with me!
> At first then I will make believe
> I'm deaf, won't turn to see.

Death as little brother, as friend, crony, confidant, just as the young people called the peasant Wurzel their brother when they came to him to say farewell, to say "Adieu."

He pretends to be deaf, he does not look around, or he would have long since succumbed to the lure of death.

> But if, "Dear Valentin!" he says,
> "I want no fuss from you!"

The urgency is stressed with two exclamation points; the "little brother" death has good intentions, otherwise he would not say: "Dear Valentin!" You've made enough fuss, your father has been placated, now go! And in Viennese, "go" also means about the same as "be so good," it introduces the friendly, kind request. Viewed from that perspective, the call becomes quite friendly: "Go, dear Valentin. Don't make a fuss. Come, little brother." One cannot be summoned more cordially, more personally. And he goes:

> I put my plane there in its place
> And bid the world adieu. *Exit.*

He puts his plane down "there," "there," not "then." Deliverance is already anticipated in his mind, transferred to the present; the stage direction "exit" becomes transparent. He has done his work, he says farewell.

Under the circumstances he does not say "I will lay down my plane and go." Death "comes," he "tugs," he "says," he is completely "there." So he lays down the plane and says "Adieu," that half elevated, half common word. With the name of God, in the name of God, he quits. When Raimund was on his painful sickbed, half paralyzed, with the fatal bullet in his head, he wrote down two words with his left hand: "Worship God," a legacy that simultaneously includes both regret and gratitude. As Valentin he departed with "Adieu," as Ferdinand Raimund, with God.

The seventeen-year-old son of the attending physician, who was able to see him a day and a half after the shot, reports "that he looked at me attentively, with an indescribable expression, when I, already leaving, had stepped up to his sickbed once more."

But there are still two years between *The Spendthrift* and Raimund's death, and between Valentin's exit following the carpenter's song and the ending of *The Spendthrift* lies Rosa's great scene with Flottwell.

All discussions of Raimund simply skim over this scene and see in it a key to the understanding of neither Ferdinand Raimund nor his world. The fact that in the past it has not been recognized and appreciated for its greatness is puzzling and incomprehensible. Raimund exits as Valentin after literally laying down his plane in the present and saying farewell to the world. He is now redeemed; death has occurred symbolically, and the real occurrence is now only a formality. Now he can create freely, to his heart's content. Flottwell, old and decrepit, invited to the house by Valentin, enters and chats with Valentin's children. Then Rosa comes into the room. We have not yet seen her in this act, which takes place twenty years after the previous one. She left us as

Papagena, as a soubrette, sweet, vivacious, roguish, somewhat charmingly domineering. In the first act she sang that the carpenter was "her only happiness." During the second act she virtuously warded off the advances of the villainous manservant and the gallant nobleman. Flottwell, the gentleman, wrongs her in the second act, because the hypocritically malicious manservant has his confidence. As a result, Valentin and Rosa pack their things and leave his employ. He no longer remains a servant, but goes "back to his carpenter's shop." Their departure takes the form of a comically folksy ensemble of the chorus with Rosa and the "befuddled" Valentin.

Now the former loyal servant has taken the gentleman into his modest home, and he wins over the children as confederates in his goodness: "Be very good and polite with the gentleman in there. He will remain in our house. I will never let him go. And encourage your mother, too. She is a good woman, but sometimes a little impetuous."

Valentin is gone. Rosa comes, "dressed in simple, unpretentious clothing, older." Papagena's first words: "What, stay here, keep him, a stranger, when we have so many children to feed?" Evil presents itself in a straightforward, direct, merciless, brutal manner. Papagena has become a Strindberg figure: "...I am the housewife, it's my decision..." Between the second and third acts of *The Spendthrift* lie not twenty, but a hundred years. "It would make us happy, if you would do us the honor today at noon. We will not let anyone make fun of us. But forever? Pardon me! I can't permit that. Today in my house and never again!"

Flottwell, deeply humiliated, leaves the cottage. "Oh, woman! If I could only conjure back a tenth of my lost happiness and smash ten times the misery down on your old head, which would bring you to my feet, then my magnanimity would teach you how unjust you were in offending me so bitterly in my misery." He goes off. Rosa reasons: "... And he did say something about an old head. Do *I* have an old head?"

Now the first conflict in this drama that truly commands our interest breaks out, the battle of the sexes, in which Valentin is victorious. He threatens to leave Rosa and finally brings her to her senses...

> Rosa *after a brief struggle:* Well, as far as I'm concerned, it can be that way.

...and the play to its end.

In his Raimund essay, Felix Braun comments on this scene: "The 'golden Viennese heart' also has the hardness of that metal." No, here the gold is dissolved in the nitric acid of a new world view; here the noble is no longer noble and the villain villainous, the friendly man friendly and evil evil. The great thing about Rosa's self-exposure is the knowledge that nice people are evil and the cheerful are demonic. A century of soubrettes is preemptively refuted. The unknown "other" Austria enters the dimensionality of the stage in such an appallingly naked and glaring manner that generations will evade perceiving it. In all Raimund's previous dramas, love had never been the real focus of events. It was present in *The Barometermaker* as an outlined engagement, in *The Diamond* as a romantic ornament, in *The Peasant as Millionaire* and in *The King of the Alps* as a dutiful, hardly interesting subplot; in *Chained Fantasy* it was purely representative. In *Moisasur's Magic Spell* the sacredness of marriage and love between man and wife à la *Fidelio* was presupposed and represented in the noble couple Hoanghu-Alzinde as well as in the commoner couple Hans-Mirzel, with the evil peasant who tortures his wife to death as an extremely schematic contrast. In *The Fateful Crown* a slapstick scene occurs:

Simplizius: Tell me, girl, would you have the courage to abduct me?
Arete: You?
Simplizius: Or vice-versa?

And the poet Ewald, who has been carried into the oriental world, marries in a quite fabulous manner for the sake of the plot's conclusion.

In *The Spendthrift*, love now moves into the central focus more strongly than ever before. Flottwell, the hero, was united with a lovable girl, who reveals herself to be a fairy and leaves him. He fights for his new bride, who, hardly won, disappears from view. Valentin, however, as a factotum destined by the law of tradition to marry the chambermaid, endures with her, o horrors, the hell of marriage. Three possibilities, two romantic literary ones, one real thought-out one: the woman squabbles, he taps out his plane, saves himself in resignation. He learns to cope with it, thinks: "Well, bicker on, feel free." It will not be long and he will have laid the plane down and bid the world adieu.

Now Raimund no longer writes. He travels through Germany as an interpreter of his own plays, makes guest appearances in Vienna as well. Again and again he sings his carpenter's song, completing his death. He "continuously commit[s] suicide."

He loves his death as he loves the dogs. In his fairy-tale plays they appear again and again. In *The Barome-*

termaker the hero says: "Many thousand years ago there lived a man who had a poodle..." In *The Diamond of the Spirit King*, Florian-Raimund is transformed into a poodle; in *Moisasur's Magic Spell* the idyllically well-married couple jest:

Hans: I just don't know. I really like to have the dog with me. Should the two of us or the three of us go out together now?

Mirzel: Well, recently there were even four of us, when you had two little spitzes* with you. One you carried home with you from the tavern, the other just ran along with us.

Hans: Yes, and when he got lost recently, you were the only one who could find him.

Mirzel: *moodily* Yes, that's because I am very subtle.**

Hans: But we should stop now. We're arguing about the spitz like little boys; it's utter roguishness.**

In the charcoal burner's cottage scene of *The King of the Alps*, the dog has the final word when the family moves out:

The Dog: *in muffled tones to Rappelkopf as he is led away* Arf! Arf! He *follows, led on a rope by Salchen.*

*A play on words: the Viennese word *Spitz* also means tipsiness.
**In the original these lines contain untranslatable wordplays.

At that time, Raimund had already broken off one trip because he had eaten a piece of bread that a dog had licked. He was afraid that the dog could be rabid. "From that moment on he was never at peace and it was almost intolerable to be around him..." Nevertheless, in his country house he kept a dog. He took his "little brother," death, into his house, and when the dog had given his hand a meaningless scratch and had been killed on the suspicion of rabies, Raimund put a bullet in his own head. In so doing, he only completed what had already been determined long before. In a last conflict, in the realm between life and death that had been his own realm from the beginning, he remained conscious for six days after the shot.

The concern in Vienna was enormous. During his lifetime Raimund did not have any of his works published. In 1837, the year following his death, the first edition of his complete works began to appear, edited by the popular lyric poet Johann Nepomuk Vogl. Finally, posthumously, Grillparzer acknowledged the greater man, especially the drama about the misanthrope, which he praised: "Even Molière could not have devised a more superb conception... No comedy writer has ever chosen a psychologically more genuine, more richly developed topic."

But recognition and underrating, cultivation and indifference remained consistent for the poet, his image, and his characters. More than forty years passed before the appearance of a scholarly halfway conscientious edition that "Raimund's memory was worthy of." And the biography that was announced as the final volume of that edition has never appeared. And only a small portion of the letters and documents could be placed in safekeeping. Around 1900 the popular editions of the classics took up the Raimund texts, but the historical-critical complete edition did not appear until the years from 1923 to 1931. It is long since out of print and has also disappeared from the secondhand bookstores. Currently only the fragmentary edition of a Viennese communist publishing house is regularly available in the book trade.

Around the turn of the century the Vienna Raimund Monument in front of the *Deutsches Volkstheater* was unveiled with a prologue by Ferdinand von Saar. The story of that monument bears final witness of the miraculous element in Raimund's story. For, after forty years, "for traffic engineering reasons," they moved the monument from its place to a neighboring public park. If it had remained where it originally stood, it would have been destroyed by a bomb that tore open the front of the theater during the Second World War. Thus it continues to exist, just as Raimund's dramas continue to exist in the Austrian theater repertoires. He has long since moved up to the *Burgtheater*—but how? "A Raimund for new realms. Everything quite 'authentic,' and for that very reason so shabby. If 'Poverty' had existed among the allegorical personnel of Raimund's plays, in the *Burgtheater* she would have appeared suffering from hunger in brocade, and with a beggar's staff from the most elegant studio for the arts." (Alfred Polgar) Raimund was also included in the Salzburg Festival, but in the process his work was radically distorted by an unscrupulous adapter. His posthumous survival has not been spared the conflict that governed his life. He is loved and misunderstood, underrated and overrated, admired and abused.

In his honor the city of Vienna built a Raimund Theater in the sixth district, where he was born. In

November 1893 they ceremoniously opened the theater with *Chained Fantasy*. A quarter of a century later they played *The House of Three Girls* there en suite for years.

It is a great pity about him.

JOHANN NESTROY

or

FLIGHT INTO THE SUBURBS

"Because I take the thought at its word, it comes."
(Karl Kraus)

"The man has an intolerable perspicacity! That should really be strictly forbidden; it is a disruption of intellectual property when one sees through somebody that way!"
(Nestroy)

"And he preferred to appear smaller than he was, rather than swelling to monstrousness."
(Grillparzer about Mozart)

"The substance of a work is that to which a bad work reduces itself."
(*Valéry*)

"And none of it's true! And none of it's true!"
(Nestroy)

JOHANN NESTROY

There are three genuine Austrian dramatists, and there are three completed Austrian stage plays. The completed Austrian stage plays are *The King of the Alps and the Misanthrope*, *Love Affair*, and *The Difficult Man*. The three genuine dramatists are Wolfgang Amadeus Mozart, Johann Nestroy, and Karl Schönherr.

The dramatists, you will note, are not identical with the authors of the completed plays. The plays "happened to" the latter. Only roundabout ways to the theater were open to the dramatists: the musical theater, the suburban utility theater, the dialect theater. The three dramatists are nevertheless-dramatists, the three dramas are nevertheless-dramas.

Few great dramas are written in Austria, and that is not because Austria's climate is unfavorable to the theater. On the contrary: the actor and acting are especially important here. Not great plays, but serviceable plays are written. Above all, roles are created.

In the great conflict between work and interpretation, between what and how, the how dominates in Austria. The interpreters are not servants of the work; rather, the work serves them as an inducement, often only as a pretext to present themselves. In other places works of art are produced and the interpreters reproduce them. In Austria the interpreters produce themselves more than anything else.

The language of the Austrians is also important with regard to the question of Austrian drama. In all of its gradations it is too similar to High German to live a separate literary life of its own; but it is too different from High German to enter literature in its raw and natural form. Austrian prose and lyric poetry must overcome resistance, must wrestle line for line with the tension between the regional and the absolute. In fortunate circumstances, this striving to attain the mainstream from the periphery inspires masterful prose and lyric poetry in the German language. The lines of a character in a scene, however, can hardly survive such a clarification process. One way or the other, when they leave their country of origin, they become artificial; they are only of legitimate greatness when they remain at home. That is the case with Raimund's characters, Schönherr's peasants, in Schnitzler's Viennese prewar quintet, in Hofmannsthal's stylized shorthand, in Nestroy's stylized explosive mixture of authentic dialect and adapted literary German.

Thus Nestroy's flight into dialect may unconsciously have been partially determined by the knowledge that the dramatist who is born in Vienna can express himself perfectly only from the suburbs—that the price he must pay for literary greatness is restriction to the narrowest sphere of activity, the blessing and the curse of not being translatable, even into German.

Not only the two "Viennese classical authors" are wronged when they are viewed again and again as the unit "Raimund and Nestroy." Annalists and observers favor such combinations for the sake of convenience; they pervert coexistence into togetherness, where only temporal and national proximity are present, but by no means an identity of spirit, of style, of specific meaning. Like "Corneille and Racine," "Bach and Handel," "Haydn and Mozart," and "Schiller and Goethe," "Raimund and Nestroy" is also a very deceptive false interpretation. At home in the same Vienna, belonging to two succeeding generations, even though Nestroy was only about eleven years younger, they are children of different centuries. The baroque legacy still lives and works in Raimund; his unattained ideal is classical pathos. He puts man on the stage only incidentally and unwillingly, almost unintentionally, only as an object for higher powers to act upon. For Nestroy it is man, only man, nothing but man, who is the subject. Raimund's *no*, Raimund's question mark is naive, resigned, sympathetic. Nestroy's *no*, Nestroy's question mark is aggressive. Raimund laughs wistfully, Nestroy laughs bitterly.

Raimund, hot-tempered, cranky, cantankerous in his life, is gentle and noble in his works. Nestroy, shy, inhibited, bashful in his life, is vicious in his works. They were both depressive, and both were fleeing from the hell of their inner reality into the orderly legitimacy of theatrical and dramaturgical activity, where the protagonist and author can form the world at his own discretion, and is master of events and their course. But Raimund, the workman, fled upward, toward what was for him the unattainable goal of the "higher spheres." In that he resembles the lyric poet Josef Weinheber who had to leave secondary school, and of whom it was claimed that his poems in the standard language were "attempts to make up for not having graduated." Similarly, Raimund also repeatedly wanted to reconstruct through literature the education that he lacked. But Nestroy came down from above; Nestroy consciously reduced himself and reached his goal.

It is no accident that Raimund was born in the suburb of Mariahilf, Nestroy in the heart of the inner city. Raimund, the son of a lathe operator, was a confectioner's apprentice; Nestroy, the son of an attorney, attended secondary school and almost completed his university studies. For Raimund and Nestroy, escape led away from these two decisively different points of departure.

For Nestroy it also led not to the writing of plays, but to acting. A second condition fulfilled by the two of them, a very Austrian one: they came only in a roundabout fashion, relatively late, to the production of stage plays, neither of them as a result of an inner calling, but each because he needed usable material. Both wrote only plays in which they appeared. It was no different with Shakespeare, with Molière; but in Raimund and especially in Nestroy, the contemporary world also saw above all the actor. As late as the 1870s, Bauernfeld noted: "The same may be true of him as of Raimund: Nestroy cannot be performed without Nestroy."

Yet a third commonality, and again one that is especially Austrian: Nestroy, too, thoughtlessly married a female colleague and was soon divorced and burdened with the consequences of that situation for the rest of his life. Could it be a basic prerequisite for the Austrian fate, a pre-condition that one at first privately establishes, in order to become productive as a result of it: to fail at love, to suffer in marriage?

Nevertheless, the life of Johann Nestroy, the principles and character of his creations are radically different from those of Ferdinand Raimund.

In the beginning there is the actor, equipped with a remarkable singing voice. At the age of twenty-one he debuts as Sarastro, then accepts engagements outside of Vienna, plays serious and comical figures in plays, and sings great opera roles.

The fact that Nestroy played the piano, that he appeared in public as a pianist at the early age of thirteen, is mentioned only in passing by the biographers and remains on the periphery of the appraisals like

Raimund's violin playing and Raimund's natural ability as a composer. In Vienna, unlike other places, music is not an unusual activity, but a kind of second colloquial language.

At the age of thirty, the singer-actor is still hardly recognizable as a future author. At first he assisted with minor dramaturgical tasks, making a role palatable for himself, adapting a Berlin farce to the Viennese locale. While still in the secondary school, he wrote a historical drama, *Prince Frederick of Corsica*, then gave up that form of production. In Graz he wrote and acted in some plays, the first of which had the characteristic annotation on the theater program: "It is part of the current fashion in Vienna that artists of both sexes, for whom benefit performances are held, are the authors of their own income-bringing plays." This occurred in 1828, five years after the benefit performance actor Raimund had out of necessity also paid homage to the current fashion. This first play, *Banishment from the Magic Kingdom; or, Thirty Years in the Life of a Scoundrel*, awkward, laborious, and recognizable as characteristic only with the greatest attentiveness, already employs the supernatural framework only as a disguise for the portrayal of extremely mundane happenings that are thoroughly conventional but extremely real. The scoundrel, his depravity, and his amorality are presumed to be natural; regret, reform, and redemption at the end occur dutifully and less credibly.

Nestroy comes to Vienna, and the crossroads at which he now finds himself is definitely not the dilemma of having to choose between the author and the performer, but simply the question: singer or actor? One version traces the decision back to the higher salary offered by the popular *Theater an der Wien*. It might be more probable that Nestroy's voice had suffered and therefore suggested the transition to the stage play.

Nestroy sang the roles of Pizarro and Fernando in *Fidelio*, the Figaro roles of Mozart and Rossini, also the role of Basilio in *The Barber*, also the Count in *Figaro*, the roles of Don Juan and Papageno, the role of Kaspar in *Der Freischütz*, and parts in operas by Rossini, Grétry, Cherubini, Méhul, Boieldieu, Krettzer, and others. In *William Tell* he played Gessler and Walter Fürst, in *Maria Stuart*, the roles of Burleigh and Paulet, Lionel in *The Maid of Orleans*, the ghost of Hamlet's father, the doorman in *Macbeth*, Just in *Minna von Barnhelm*, Pantalone in Schiller's *Turandot* adaptation, Lancelot Gobbo, Gianettino Doria, Lerse in *Götz von Berlichingen*, and Gottschalk in *Käthchen of Heilbronn*. Before he finally established himself in Vienna he sang or played a total of 450 roles, including the roles of Raimund's Longimanus, Tutu, Florian, Nachtigall, Wurzel, and Rappelkopf. In September 1831 he appears again for the first time in Vienna. From now on the repertoire is prescribed, no operas, no more serious stage plays, but abundant singing and pathos on the detour through the parody, and music, of course, in all the plays of the popular Viennese genre: songs, political ballads, duets, ensembles, opera quodlibets, finales.

In May *The Evil Spirit Vagabond; or, The Slovenly Threesome* has its premiere. Nestroy had become dramatically productive under the sign of the "scoundrel"; his breakthrough occurred under the sign of portrayed slovenliness.

The Vagabond is Nestroy's most popular play. In the truest sense it is inexhaustible. It has resisted filmings and adaptations of many kinds; it established the fame of its author with his contemporaries and accompanied him through his life. In the year of his death, as the shoemaker Knieriem, Nestroy appeared on a Vienna stage for the last time. The success of the novelty *Vagabond* a century and a quarter ago is understandable and explicable; its elementary success through the years, however, is mysterious. As a matter of fact, *The Vagabond* is a very bad play.

Nestroy's first giant step into immortality simultaneously symbolizes the great step of Vienna classicism from the realm of magic to the earth. Just as Beethoven's *Eroica* boldly and resolutely throws the traditional slow introduction of the symphony overboard and replaces it with two chords, here the fairy-world framework is shattered and has become a trivial prelude. A carelessly and casually sketched "Prologue in Heaven," a supernatural pair of lovers who are hardly even really present, two fairy children whose union is made dependent upon the probation of three mortals, and we have already moved from the frame to the middle of the picture. The three slovenly journeymen autonomously dominate the action, even when they hit the jackpot with the help of Lady Luck. The vagabond, the title figure, is not a player in the piece that is named after him, and the higher powers participate only very indirectly in the action. We see a genre painting of the simple life on the country road, in the tavern. We see Leim, the first of the three journeymen, quickly and quite undramatically obtain his master's daughter; we see Zwirn, the second one, living in great style as a parvenu, completely without any action. The third, most important journeyman, Knieriem, has entirely disappeared from the action in the second act. The finale before the big intermission is a grand, parodistical opera quodlibet without any visible motivation. In order to bring it about, an Italian family of three must appear solely for that purpose, and solely to justify their presence, a scene with Italian-German language difficulties must take place. In the third act the three come together again, without Zwirn and Knieriem being ready to give up their slovenly life. The plot becomes muddled and obscure. The triumph of evil is obvious and is suggested only very superficially, dutifully, with an almost embarrassing, demonstrative carelessness in a completely unbelievable last-minute reform:

> "...the world still stands, and we stand in the middle of it with our absurd family."..."Domesticated and industrious—that's the only way you can continually enjoy life." *Dance begins. With the appropriate group and illumination with Grecian fire, the curtain falls.*

From many standpoints, this *Vagabond* is a thoroughly unsuccessful play that disregards the laws of theatrical effectiveness, curiously lacks the elements that promise success, exhibits no tension, no continuous plot, no developed love story, and does not present the great comic character in the second act. *The Vagabond* is also definitely not "authentic Nestroy" and lacks his great satirical aggression as well as his genial, linguistically creative dialectic. Finally, *The Vagabond* is never presented in its original form, but flogged and played to death; traditional improvisations and staged jests about the original form are lodged in many of its stratifications. What we see, even in an authentic *Vagabond* production, was only partially written by Nestroy. How do we explain the effect it had on contemporaries and its even more puzzling effect on later generations?

It is the great *no*, the great question mark that triumphantly fights its way through all the inadequacies; it is the advance notice of what is heard articulated in Nestroy's later comedies; it is the Promethean protest against the higher powers. You can do what you want with us—we shall remain what we are! We do not intend to improve ourselves, to purify ourselves; we are inaccessible for what is reasonable. In Zwirn and Knieriem slovenliness triumphs: "They don't do anything but work, eat, drink, and sleep—is that any kind of life?" Zwirn asks, then decides to run away with the next best "obliging servant," and is inaccessible for all rational remonstrances. He cannot "stand the good days." He confesses: "I have an anxiety in me, a fear—in a word, brother, I can't stand it." He is offered the means "to settle down permanently and respectably somewhere," on the condition that he become "industrious, upright, and diligent." And he leaves the play with the answer: "I can't stand that." *Walks off.*

The temptation, with the reverse omen preceding it, also approaches the shoemaker Knieriem in similar fashion, and he responds: "It is not worth the effort because the time is too short. In a year the comet will come, and after that the world will end anyway." They try to persuade him to accept money, a sedentary life, and diligence. In response he has only one request:

Knieriem: If you'd like to give me a twenty, so that I can go to a tavern.
Peppi: What for? You get everything much better at our place.
Knieriem: Madame, you don't understand. At home, the best drink doesn't taste good to you. You have to be in a

tavern. That's the pleasure of it. There the worst brew has the best taste.

And he sings the comet song: "There is no longer order in the stars...," next to Raimund's carpenter's song the other great Viennese workman's song about destruction. Here, too, the end is anticipated, but as an inducement, in order to make the time until then bearable, and to spend it without regard for categorical imperatives. In the sky and on the earth everything is in confusion; a locally apocalyptical vision is conjured up, whose refrain is: "So we all are so filled with fear / No matter what, the end is near," but this revelation about the end of the world is presented in a cheerful ländler rhythm, with an almost yodellike finale:

...the end is near, near, near, near, near...

Apocalypse in three quarter time, like the "Everything's gone" of *Augustin*, the first Vienna waltz.

For punishment, Zwirn and Knieriem are banished "into the abyss," where the entire company of evil spirits awaits them. With that the plot would be ended meaningfully; then two pages before the end, Amorosa, a powerful fairy, guardian of true love, applies for the souls of the "two loose fellows" and intends to exhibit them "reformed and happy." The closing apotheosis of industry and family happiness is a concession, among other things, to the censors; it cannot influence the basic mood. Virtue loses its competition against vice, two to one. Yes, even Leim, the carpenter, who has entered the harbor of marriage and respectability, is a driven man. One must only understand how to read the text: Leim has broken out of his secure existence as the hopeful suitor of his master's daughter and gone on the road because of a stupid misunderstanding, "over hill and dale, without a 'God preserve you,' and without everything else... It's all over for me, I have nothing left to hope for. I just go along, for as long as it has to be." He, too, is oppressed by fear and anxiety: "...I look like a jolly fellow, but all that is only on the outside. Things are really wonderful inside me. When I drink, I think that every drop is poison—when I eat, death eats along with me—when I leap and dance, inside I feel like I'm with my own corpse—when I see a comrade who has nothing, I immediately give him everything, although I have nothing myself, because in my thoughts I am continuously writing my last will and testament."

What a threesome, the melancholy of the carpenter, the tailor's anxiety, and on top of that the shoemaker: "If I weren't drinking away my vexation, I'd have to become addicted to drink out of pure despair." Slovenliness in three forms as self-protection against the hell of existence, and it would be a rewarding undertaking to devise an Austrian typology of character, and to divide its objects into the three basic types of the Leim person, the Zwirn person, and the Knieriem person.

We now know why the second act seems so weightless and formless. It shows the fulfillment. Leim obtains his Peppi; Zwirn is a wealthy man and as such has no tangible, portrayable experiences of any kind; Knieriem is invisible and later sums up Lady Luck's blessings: "I made a trip along the Rhine—they have very curious wine cellars there..." There is nothing else to say.

And as if to correct the impression that the positive ending of the play could create, Nestroy wrote a sequel to the successful comedy, *The Zwirn, Knieriem, and*

Leim Families; or, The Day the World Ends. There, right at the very beginning, the fairy children who were lovingly united at the end of *The Vagabond* are already unhappily married; when we encounter Leim for the first time, he is engaged in a violent argument with his wife Peppi. His first sentence in the play is directed to her: "You are and remain a rotten woman." During the further course of the play, he wants to get a divorce. To be sure, this play also ends with engagements, but Zwirn and Knieriem remain as they were; the world is not preserved from destruction—with reservations, it only "continues to exist, just until it ends."

The success of *The Vagabond* does not come from the jokes, nor the fabulous motif of wish fulfillment by heaven, nor from the delightful image of three poor fellows who become wealthy. *The Vagabond* radiates skepticism, bitterness, and fatalism, but presents them in a placidly farcical, cheerful guise; man, as he existed prior to the revolution of March 1848, saw himself on the stage; Austrians saw themselves confirmed in turning to the present without regard for the future. This, their clinging to the profane, objective pleasures of eating, drinking, and dancing, which is often misinterpreted as zest for life, *joie de vivre*, but which deep down inside hides only fear of the future, fear of self, is not preached by Nestroy, but only presented as a parable of his own escape into acting, as an expression of his great, comprehensive negation of all values.

He had unconsciously woven together the colors in *The Vagabond* to form a picture; now he becomes conscious of them, now he himself will deliver the interpretation more and more explicitly.

However, he will not write dramas until the day he dies. You see, what happens on Austrian stages is—and not only in Nestroy's works—much less drama than simply theater in general. It is not a matter of an author putting a vision down on paper, to be realized as adequately as possible by an art institute; it is a matter of theatergoers enjoying themselves with actors for an evening. For that a text is usually necessary as a catalyst for the encounter. Nestroy wrote such texts. Above all, he wrote his own roles. He worked in a thoroughly conscientious, well-informed, painstaking, carefully designing, intricately elaborating manner. He filed, rejected, improved, and was upheld by real understanding of stage rules. But he took his materials from where he found them; they meant little to him. Once he wrote: "As long as one carries the cover of his soul, his little bit of body around with him..." Nor are his plots anything more than covers, a little bit of body, carried along by the soul of the play. The soul is always Nestroy, Nestroy as actor, viewed superficially, but inseparable from him: Nestroy the satirist, the thinker, the man with power of expression, the great man who always says *no*.

Nestroy's texts and their message, characterized by Leopold Liegler as the "running fight of a spiritually wounded man," necessarily require this form and no other. The explosive power of his pessimistic aggressions is so enormous that they must be localized in harmlessly conventional, intellectually inadequate stories of clauses in wills, bets, greedy conservators, and dictated engagements, in a world of banal confusions, shams, intrigues, and accidents, in order to be conceivable at all. What Nestroy says to us is so bitter, so provoking, so bad, that it needs the comedy form and the *deus ex machina*: the fortunate turn of events at the end, from the mechanics of the farce, in order to be playable and acceptable.

Nestroy very consciously despises and neglects his plots, even though he does not withhold the meticulousness of his handicraft from them. He illuminates them dramaturgically, in order to expose them to laughter; he includes them in his comprehensive negation. ("So the situation has occurred again so soon? No, so many uncles and aunts must die each year, simply so that everything turns out well!") He takes nothing seriously except his satire. That is the origin of the secular misunderstanding, the confusing of subject and object that Otto Rommel, the great expert and rescuer of Nestroy's works, formulated: They hold the satirist "responsible for the evil that he castigated." (August Strindberg's: "Shakespeare cannot be held responsible for people's cruelty.") Nestroy views man ruthlessly, mercilessly in his entire dubiousness. He flees from his knowledge and experiences into the world of the apparently detached, cozy farce; in front of Nestroy the misanthrope he places a comic actor of the same name. He hides from literary history in the suburban dialect play that is committed to transitory actuality. Once again secondary and primary things are confused beyond recognition. Austrian self-portrayal again, in its entire classical misconception: the demonic, prophetic, and universal in an impersonal, apparently cheerful, seemingly singing form. (Karl Kraus: "...one of those rare authors who are unknown to the many who are familiar with them.")

Of course all Nestroy plays end well. But that must not deceive us. For the positive ending usually consists of one or more marriages, and Nestroy leaves no doubt about what he thinks of marriage, this "mutual institution for the embitterment of life"—this publicity attached to a love pact... Placard of the sweetest secrets, this inadmissible exhibition of a flower with an epitaph tied to it." Nestroy finds "something insulting in this official orgy of love invested with the name *marriage*." He calls—and he always speaks on his own behalf when he speaks of marriage—marriage "a tragedy in any case, because the hero or the heroine must die, otherwise it doesn't end."—"Marriage was invented, of course, so that you can't do anything about it anymore, if you regret it; if there were no regrets, love would really be enough." A portion of a long monologue that was included in the clean copy, but then deleted, reassesses the concepts of happy and unhappy love: It is not happy love that is "the true delicacy of the soul, but unhappy love": "They call that love happy, which has as its goal what is often the greatest unhappiness, a marriage."

That is Nestroy's great theme, with variations in every key, presented with an abundance of parables:

"You have probably already experienced it often, when you have gone to bed very tired and exhausted, on your arm that way, the position is divine, you are in heaven—now: If you remain in the position for just two hours, then everything hurts. You can't stand the divinity, the heavenly becomes unbearable. Just never in the same direction—and that's just an arm."

"Creation once tried its hand at drama and wrote a comedy, *Love*, and the play turned out so well, general applause and approval—then blinded by success, creation wrote a sequel to it: *Marriage*, and just as it always is with sequels, the interest was no longer there."

In *The Vagabond* there were still three individuals on a private path leading through the world to different stations. The mature Nestroy departs from the sphere of his small, conventional, superficial conflicts in monologues and satirical songs, and generalizes; "the human being," "the world" are objects of his meditations, "life" and "death."

Life is "never worth eating up life to preserve your life.—What do you get out of this fifty to sixty years of gasping for breath?"

Life is "a ticklish picture; you sketch the thing quite beautifully, then make a mistake in the execution. Then you have to deliver the bungled work to the pitiless powers, and then you never get it back so that you can revise it."

Life is "nothing but a death sentence that is passed on the day of your birth and then stayed indefinitely."

The world is "terribly rough; the only one who can give an opinion about it is the person who often walks around on it barefoot."

Man is "the masterpiece of creation, and you have to pay tailors until you are completely impoverished, just so that you can properly hide the masterpiece."

A human being is "much too little, if he is nothing but a human being."

Man is "the being who occupies the top step of creation, who even pretends to be in the image of God. But God probably does not feel very flattered by that."

As one can see, creation is included in the aggression with relish. Not to exist would be desirable: "I always say, we could judge it much more easily, if we had never existed."—"I should actually be angry with my mother because she gave birth to me. My God, she meant well. The fact that it turned out badly is another story. I never should have come into reality. As long as I was still a dream of my father, an idea of my mother, I may have been a very charming idea. But so many ideas have this about them: When they come into being, they develop miserably."

People's relationships are often portrayed with cruel mercilessness. The bride says to the groom: "I'll torment you to death so that I'll soon become a widow." A widower characterizes his widowerhood as "happiness." Another one praises the mourning crepe: "From this crepe a peaceful future flowers for me." The doctor complains about his patients: "By my soul, I'll kill them all!" Nothing is excluded from the general negation; only occasionally in the late works are certain reservations regarding authentic human contacts—friendship, for example—avoided, but concerning that it had previously once been said: "If I come into the world again—anything—just no friends!"

But not just the villains or schemers are put down, some in distorted caricatures, some in the merciless directness of critical derogation; no, the so-called good people in particular are also affected by the aggression. "There are very few evil people, and yet so much mischief occurs in the world; the largest part of this injustice must be blamed on the many, many good people who are nothing more than good people."—"We are honorable, good-natured people," says Blasius, the son of the wealthy soap-maker Grundl, to the poet Leicht in *Neither Laurel Nor Beggar's Staff.* "You'll see. When your play is staged, everyone will go and boo it down, but only out of uprightness and goodheartedness."

Nestroy had one of his greatest successes, even with his otherwise negative critics, with *On the First and Second Floors,* for there the authentic, hearty "folk play" appeared to be successful. Even here, however, one must only look more closely to ascertain that not only Herr von Goldfuchs, speculator and millionaire, his villainous servant Johann, and the unscrupulous landlord Georg Michael Zins seem extremely problematic, morally speaking, but also the upright, honest, the "honorably-minded, good-natured," poor Schlucker family. Adolf, the good man's son, loves Goldfuchs's daughter. Mr. Zins loves her too and offers the Schluckers money to send Adolf away. The suggestion is immediately accepted; they even take advantage of the opportunity to brutally reveal to the poor Adolf, without any reason, that he is not a real son at all, but only a foster son. But then comes the message that Adolf's father, whom they believed to be dead, is alive and unspeakably wealthy. With renewed vigor, the previously so badly treated outcast is given the title "Herr von Adolf," and then when Mr. Zins is fully justified in protesting that they must keep their promise and demands that they get rid of Adolf, the moral indignation of the Schlucker family boils up: "There he is, the seller of souls who wanted to make us sell Adolf! Our foster son isn't for sale at all! If we had ten foster sons like him, we wouldn't give up any of them!"

Not the evil human being, but simply "the human being" as human being is to blame for the condition of humanity—("I believe the worst about everyone, even about myself, and I have seldom made a mistake in that regard")—and in the highest court it is the world order, creation; on the dock of the accused appears: fate.

In his continuation of *The Vagabond*, Nestroy has some divine beings turn to Fate, "who controls destiny," the "mighty spirit of the higher regions," begging for help for themselves. He "is supposed to steer toward our purposes everything that will happen on earth."

Clouds float down; stretched out on a throne of clouds asleep, Fate comes down from above.
Stellaris: Mighty spirit!

Fate:	Who disturbs Fate in his most important business?
Stellaris:	I, your nephew, dared to do it. Let me tell you in what matter we need your help.
Fate:	I know everything. *Stepping forward, to himself:* I don't know anything at all, but I am much too lazy to listen to the whole story. It is something splendid to be Fate. I do nothing at all, and in the end everyone says, whatever happened, Fate did it.
Stellaris:	May we hope!
Fate:	Yes, yes. Go ahead and hope!

Fate takes his place again on his seat of clouds and falls asleep, while his seat rises with the other clouds... Stellaris, Fortuna, Brillantine, Hilaris, and Mystifax look thankfully up at Fate, as he floats upward.

Yes: "It is really a luxury for Fate, that he slings arrows; one can tell by his dispensations anyway, that he didn't invent gunpowder."

In another, almost unknown piece Fate becomes the subject of a great satirical song that treats the revolutionary era's belief in progress ironically:

"As a bad ruler for his kingdom, Fate is second to none / Nero and Louis the Fifteenth rolled into one"... "Nothing is settled and nothing's assessed / It's all nicely postponed for eternity's test"—with the refrain: "Fate is not the right thing for our time."

During the same period another satirical song comes into being (in *Mortal Fear*) with the Promethean vision that the "three kingdoms" of the earth, the mineral kingdom, the plant kingdom, and the animal kingdom, rebel against heaven: "By my soul, heaven must now be in mortal fear."

A political analysis of Johann Nestroy's world view belongs to this treatment no more than a discussion of his theatrical genius. But his relationship to language must probably be discussed. Nestroy did not invent enjoyment of puns and wordplays; he found it, like all the externals of his dramas, prefigured in local tradition. Raimund, too, plays with words and with the language, but comparison of the two apparently similar men reveals the enormous distance between two temperaments and two intellects.

Raimund's barometermaker says: "I can't be dirty at all, for I am a wealthy man and accordingly a fellow who has washed himself."* Nestroy's junk dealer (old-clothes dealer) Damian says: "Dealing in old clothes is really a shabby business; you have nothing to show for it, except possibly an elbow when you put something on."

For Raimund, time is "a true corporal who strikes you as years go by. In the beginning it has a little rod made of nothing but May flowers. Every year it sort of gives you a soft tap; you enjoy that, and you jump around like a little foal. Later it comes with a broom made only of roses; there are already thorns there. Gradually the roses are beaten off; then comes the hazel switch. Finally it comes toward you with a boom, just lets it fall, and it's all over."

For Nestroy, time is "the tall journeyman tailor who receives all the alterations to do in eternity's workshop."

*The figurative meaning of the original: "...quite a fellow."

Nestroy's relationship to language is fanatical obsession, delighted oppression by a fullness of images, associations, ambiguities. (Karl Kraus: "...linguistically wanton humor in which meaning and word catch, embrace, and hold themselves clasped together to the point that they can neither be separated nor distinguished from each other.") But he never plays just for the sake of playing; the word is always included perspectively in the image for the sake of the idea. He has complete mastery of the language, which in turn holds sway over him with its magical power. He is "the first German satirist in whose writings language reflects about things." (Karl Kraus) He discovers the word, and in his word language discovers itself. This dimension is decisive for Nestroy's greatness, but at the same time also for the problems connected with evaluating him appropriately. It makes him a classical author, but simultaneously also an almost unknown one. The legitimate question of just what the destructive spirit takes seriously, and where in Nestroy's works one can find the necessary counterweight for parodistic situations that are not taken seriously, is sufficiently answered with the reference to the author's spirit that is reified in his language. But it is that very language that makes him untranslatable, as well as hardly intelligible and difficult to read outside the narrow confines of his homeland.

He would certainly have been capable of using the standard literary language; for him it is not a vainly courted beloved, as it is for Raimund, rather it grants his request when he wants it: when he says of the genius who has become bourgeois, that his fashionably "tied necktie strangled any independence," when he has a character give this answer to the question of his father's profession: "...he is engaged in a quiet, lonely business, in which rest is the only business; he lies bound by a higher power, and yet he is free and independent, for he is his own destroyer—he is dead," when he reasons as follows concerning stupidity: "...it is a rock that stands there unshaken, even if an ocean of reason slings its waves at its head. Thoughtlessness has often been chased away by the soft breath of love, even more often by the raw storm wind of knowledge; even vice has not seldom fled from the light of a better conviction. Only stupidity has barricaded itself behind a firm bulwark of obstinacy, even plants the pointed palisades of malice upon it during an attack, and thus stands there invincible."

But Nestroy does not want to and cannot be content with one linguistic plane; he needs the tension between many nuances of the standard language and the dialect, which occur next to and mingled with each other, even in the speeches of the same figure. Most of Nestroy's sentences stand in invisible quotation marks; that is why they are so difficult to speak (that is why there are so few satisfying Nestroy productions, and the authentic Nestroy style can hardly be completely realized.)

Nestroy cannot do without the dialect because he gains from it a world of unexplored images, and because his ecstasies of association must also be fed by it. He has to use the dialect word *Millimadl* for milkmaid and let the dialect sound of the word for cow, *Kuah* (in the Viennese dialect acoustically identical with *Kur* [in *Kurfürst*]) resonate along, in order to say: "That's more luck than when a milkmaid gets a prince elector [versus: 'cow prince']." He uses the double meaning of *z'sammführen* ('bring together' and 'run over'), in order to invent the wonderful dictum of the "drunken coachman Chance": "...how he brings people together [versus: runs over people]." But neither can Nestroy do without standard German, because it lifts the reflections out of the dialect environment, and also because it exposes the big words and elevated phrases as such. "I have to say it now, Madam, the thing that has been billowing within me for I don't know how many years. You are the idol in the sacred grove of my feelings... Ha! Shatter now, you kneecaps! Collapse, pettifogger! A human being cannot endure such bliss while standing up!"

Declarations of love are made absurd by the very fact that they are expressed in the literary language; the ends of acts and plays are also usually robbed of their persuasive power by their unmistakable conventional casualness: "All: Yes, let this day be a festival of joy!" —"All: Long live chance!"—or: "All: The lovers now are brought together and the wedding feast begins, we see. Slyly mated, that is how love wins its greatest victory."

The key to the nature of the artistic phenomenon Johann Nestroy is his passion for play, expressed most fiercely in his play with words, but also very literally in his passionate, almost manic yearning for the theater and for card games. When Raimund had become a prominent dramatic author, he quit accepting engagements. Nestroy remained with the theater and went there every evening, even if he was not appearing, even in his summer home Bad Ischl, even in Graz, where he lived after he retired. On the stage, "the devil gets into him," declared his director Carl, who, on the other hand, characterized him as a "poor little thing outside the theater."

The form of his private life was also like his dramaturgical forms, his obligatory frameworks for action and those that did not matter. Johann Nestroy was unpretentious, shy, inhibited, unobtrusive, quiet, kind, helpful; he was highly educated, erudite, informative; he was defenseless, fearful, and depressive; he is described as "honorable, reliable, well-behaved." Speidel calls him a "good, law-abiding, inwardly gentle person." He was a convinced and passionately centralistic Austrian patriot with authentic reverence for the ruling imperial house and deepest skepticism toward rising nationalism. ("Can you be hungry for beef when you consider that the oxen come from Poland and Hungary, and that they therefore have also picked up something of the disease that rages there—called 'nationality fraud' by the political doctors? Can you appreciate pork, when you consider that pig breeding specifically comes from Hungary? When you eat lamb, doesn't a bite of it swell in your mouth when you think of the lamblike patience with which they let them tear down the imperial eagle in Pest...," he wrote from Graz to a friend in Vienna a year before his death.)

After the shock of his catastrophic marriage, he soon found an energetic, domineering life's companion. With her he shared *de facto*, if never *de jure*, a lifelong unhappy marriage. His personal weakness of will sought this stability and, once it was found, desperately sought little, secret chances to escape. The beginning and ending of one of these episodes have come to light. It begins with a letter that is probably one of the most peculiar love letters of all time, signed with a code, addressed to an unknown woman whose name and address Nestroy had a servant find out. The writer assures a young woman, "to whom I assign more than normal value," that she is "charming and interesting to the highest degree and the object of his most fervent wishes." He does not believe that she has noticed him, although he, who "spends no evening without attending the theater," has seen her repeatedly. "...one is, of course, usually overlooked, when one, although perhaps armed with some rights to conquests, presents himself at his spouse's side as a marriage cripple."

"In my opinion," it then goes on, "pretty young ladies, no matter what their life's circumstances may be, should never implicitly reject a quietly favored friend whom they have made happy, and who is therefore thankful and discreet, and even if they should become married, after the honeymoon a secret friend of that kind might be useful."

Precise suggestions for a meeting during a drive through the Prater follow. A handkerchief at the open window of her automobile will "be the sign that will make me extremely happy, the sign that you, if you find me worthy of your favor, accept the opinion that I expressed above concerning secret liaisons."

The handkerchief was visible at the window, the liaison began. As a supplement to the spirit of his works, its initiation demonstrates the complete disillusionment of Johann Nestroy, who wrote "love" only in quotation marks and could see a woman only as an object of wishes. After a year and a quarter the relationship ended; the reason for it was not threats or extortion, but the "most disgraceful invectives" of "the subject" against Nestroy's life's companion. A letter to two friends establishes point for point the conditions of the separation, very generous payments of money, then only a few other lines about a portrait that will be given back, and about letters that are to be destroyed. "Otherwise, there is nothing else to mention. J. Nestroy."

After his return to the Viennese stage, Nestroy still played more than four hundred roles, thus not only roles in his own plays by any means, and he was successful as a guest performer on plays in the monarchy and in Germany. He also parodied two Wagner operas and

Hebbel's *Judith*. In 1858 he brought Offenbach's operettas to Vienna, and in 1860 he created the role of Jupiter in *Orpheus in the Underworld* in German. When he stood on the stage for the last time in his life, he played the boy Willibald (*The Bad Boys in School*), a role that he created at the age of forty-six and played a hundred and two times, finally at the age of sixty-two in Graz, two and a half months before his death. He also played the boy Natzi in the early work *Eulenspiegel* into the last years of his life.

Of his own sixty-seven plays, most of which were long enough to fill an entire evening, fourteen were very great and thirteen were extraordinary successes. Others were dropped immediately after the premiere. During the last two decades of his life, twenty to thirty of his plays were constantly in the Viennese repertoire.

When he had died in Graz and been buried in Vienna in the Währing cemetery, where Beethoven and Schubert rested—the funeral procession lasted for an hour and a half; the citizens of Vienna stood side by side along the entire way—much more had died than an infinitely popular actor. But for the Viennese, all that had been much more had died with the actor. Nestroy's plays disappeared, faded into oblivion. Only twelve of them had been published, even those were soon no longer available. For twenty years the lasting renown of the actor obscured the wealth of what he had portrayed. The dramatist Nestroy was also dead. Friedrich Hebbel wrote of the "Augean stables that Nestroy left behind," of his "poisonously immoral farces." In 1867 the suggestion that a street in Vienna be named after Johann Nestroy was rejected.

The change announced itself in 1881, when a Nestroy week was celebrated on the occasion of his eightieth birthday, and was expanded to a cycle during which twenty plays were performed on forty-eight evenings. But in 1886, the surgeon Billroth still had to ask a student with good connections to the theater to search for a copy of the *Judith* parody in the *Carl Theater*, and to have it copied, because he wanted to give it to his friend Brahms, a great Nestroy admirer, for his Nestroy collection.

In 1890/91 a first edition of the collected works appeared, published by Vincenz Chiavacci and Ludwig Ganghofer. After the thirty-year term of copyright ended, volumes of selected works began to appear in 1892, but a true renaissance was still not perceptible. Literary history kept quiet about Nestroy or negated him. ("Nestroy's cynicism arises from...inherent meanness... He was able neither to construct a plot nor to sketch real characters." R. M. Meyer, 1906—"...with his folk plays, which in their best parts are dependent on Raimund...Nestroy misused his not insignificant talent in an unscrupulous manner, in order to appeal to the most ordinary taste of the broad audience." Alfred Biese, 1910—Nestroy's education "was not even sufficient to give him some certainty in the use of the German language." Hans Sittenberger in the *Jahrbuch der Grillparzer-Gesellschaft*, 1901).

In addition to such total misjudgment, there were also, of course, isolated authentic statements of appreciation. ("His devastating derision could rise momentarily to the greatness of a Swift." Ludwig Speidel, 1881). And even while he was alive, a prophetic observer had written: "In Nestroy there lives a true Shakespearean spirit, humor and wit; an authentic folk poet, and I am convinced that the future will confirm my verdict, and that he will be given a distinguished place among the dramatic nobility of Germany." (Prince Friedrich Schwarzenberg, *Tour Book of a Retired Servant of the Country*.)

The great and authentic turning point did not come, however, until 1912, the fiftieth anniversary of his death. Karl Kraus, who had already appropriately noted his hundredth birthday in *Die Fackel*, gave the memorial lecture "Nestroy and Posterity" on May 2, in the sold-out Great Hall of the Music Union, which was subsequently published in *Die Fackel* and soon afterward also appeared as a reprint and in 1922 in the anthology *Untergang der Welt durch schwarze Magie* [The Decline of the World through Black Magic]. ("If art...is the distance that lies between something seen and something thought, the shortest route from a gutter to the Milky Way, then there has never been a runner like Nestroy beneath the German sky."—"Art is that which outlives the material."—"...because he wrapped his dynamite in cotton and blew up his first world after he had made firm their belief that it was the best of worlds...")

The other Viennese newspapers, challenged by Kraus, honored the date, which they probably otherwise would hardly have noted appropriately.

With unseemly delay, in the years from 1924 to 1930, the large fifteen-volume historical-critical edition of the collected works was published by the Schroll publishing company, in which the most important Nestroy expert next to Karl Kraus, Otto Rommel, was able to use the most significant manuscripts and documents before they were thrown away without having been cared for and protected. Meanwhile that edition has been out of print for a long time, as has the excellent six-volume edition of the *Collected Works*. Nestroy's letters, which were not published until 1938, were the victim of politics and never really entered the book trade, which is presently able to offer Nestroy's works only in the selection of a communist publishing house.

Since 1872 there has been one, quite insignificant *Nestroygasse* in Vienna, and since 1932 a *Nestroyplatz*.

In 1929, on the square opposite the *Carl Theater*, where Nestroy had acted so often, a monument had been solemnly unveiled. The monument was carried away in 1942 to be melted down. It was found again in 1946 in a foundry, severely damaged; it was restored but not put in a fitting place. Rather, it was sent into exile. Since 1950 the Vienna Nestroy monument has been in the courtyard of the Cumberland Palace in Penzing, as if purposely hidden and removed from the city's consciousness.

As late as 1923, Felix Salten noted in *Die Neue Freie Presse* "again and again, that today this once so exemplarily original dramatist has withered away in his most important elements," and as late as 1958 Walter Höllerer ascertained in a painstaking, but misunderstanding essay about Nestroy: "Nestroy's literary importance should not be overestimated."

However, the tragic, very Austrian, almost total absence of any indicated and adequate statement of appreciation, the neglect of dutiful care and attention vis-à-vis a great legacy could not hinder a return that is without precedent in the history of the theater. Made possible by the two editions published by the Schroll company, promoted by experts and interpreters with almost apostolic passion, this Nestroy renaissance has not been limited only to the few "classical" comedies, but also includes plays that were short-lived and unsuccessful in their time. Since 1945, in addition to *The Vagabond*, *He Wants to Do It for Laughs*, *The Talis-*

man, *The Disrupted Man, The Girl from the Suburbs, On the First and Second Floors,* and *Unexpected,* the following have been performed and broadcast in Germany, Austria, and Switzerland: *The Confused Magician, Miller, Charcoal Burner, and Furniture Mover (The Dreams of Rind and Stone), Eulenspiegel, The Two Sleepwalkers, An Apartment for Rent..., The House of Temperaments, Happiness, Abuse, and Return, The Fateful Shrovetide Night, The Dyer and His Twin Brother, Love Stories and Marriage Matters, Railroad Marriages, The Spice Shop Threesome, The Protégé, Freedom in the Sleepy Village, The Lady and the Tailor, Mortal Fear, The Old Man with the Young Wife, My Friend, Little Field, Secret Money, Secret Love, Theater Stories, Just Be Saucy, In Vain,* and the one-act plays *The Journey in the Steam Car, Over There—Over Here, The Bad Boys in School, Earlier Conditions,* and *Chief Evening Wind.*

An even century had to pass, in order to bring a suburban Austrian actor gradually closer to fitting respect as "the deepest satirical thinker whom the Germans had after Lichtenberg" (Karl Kraus), the "greatest German comedy writer, to all intents and purposes" (F. H. Mautner), as "the only great comedy writer not only of Austria, but of the Germans" (Otto Stoessl), who "always hits the timelessly valid human prototypes found in the targets offered by the times" (Ernst Křenek).

He had no illusions, he was skeptical toward any greatness, including his own. He was always ready for the worst. Posterity is on the point of refuting him by confirming him.

FRANZ GRILLPARZER

or

FLIGHT FROM GREATNESS

"He throws himself down from the throne."
    (Blanka of Castile)

"It does not hurt at all to be missing. And I do not believe that anything better can happen to people like me."
    (Schnitzler: *The Puppet Master*)

"...to strive halfway toward half a deed with half the means."
    (Fraternal Strife in Habsburg)

"...in a word, after some convulsions of desperation a person deteriorates into a quiet listlessness of sarcasm, where one reflects about everything and on the other hand finds everything acceptable."
    (Nestroy)

FRANZ GRILLPARZER

In Vienna, an unattractive suburban street and a less significant plaza are named after Nestroy, an unattractive street after Raimund; a street in the fashionable city-hall district is named after Grillparzer.

Raimund's monument is dignified, but simple; it presents the poet with an allegorical figure. Nestroy's monument, not of stone but bronze, shows the poet, and only him, and not very attractively; a "personified cramp in the calf," a Vienna cabaret quipped as early as 1935.

Neither monument was erected until about seven decades after the respective poets died. Grillparzer's monument, unveiled only a decade after his death, presents in marble detail the poet and his works; in pretension, size, and loving placement, no other author, no composer or painter can compete with Grillparzer in the cityscape of Vienna; the empress Maria Theresa surpasses him in fullness; the empress Elisabeth in the same public park seems to be an unacknowledged, plainer companion piece.

To this day, Nestroy and Raimund are stepchildren of the book trade. There are innumerable Grillparzer editions of every caliber.

A Raimund Society exhibited modest activity, and "after a twenty-year hiatus" it published two slender almanacs. A League of Nestroy Admirers has a Vienna address, but did not answer an inquiry concerning its activities in recent years.

The Grillparzer Society, founded with great aplomb in 1890, published numerous comprehensive and instructive yearbooks and endowed the once coveted Grillparzer Prize that was conferred upon Wildbrandt, Wildenbruch,

Hauptmann, Hartleben, Schnitzler, Schönherr, Unruh, Werfel, Mell, Hochwälder, and others. After an interruption occasioned by the times, it has been active again since 1949. It continues to edit yearbooks, organizes and patronizes performances and readings, and exhibits again and again, promoted and promoting, symptoms of its presence.

Literature about Raimund and Nestroy is deplorably meager. The literature about Grillparzer is incalculably extensive. In newer and newer formulations and argumentation, the claim is announced and authenticated that Franz Grillparzer was a great writer, a classical author, a man of equal rank with Goethe and Schiller. In these occasionally passionate pleadings, the testy tone is conspicuous. It is not pondering and discerning judges who raise their voices, but attorneys and defenders. Against whom do they defend Grillparzer? Against their own subconscious better knowledge?

True greatness needs no advocate. True greatness also endures criticism. Discovery of weaknesses of Goethe or Shakespeare is not an undermining but a confirmation of their greatness. To this day—and peculiarly today more than ever—earnest criticism of Grillparzer, calling his greatness into question, is an undertaking that borders on high treason, *lèse majesté*, and blasphemy in Grillparzer's homeland. Any serious, thus critical examination of the works of the writer Franz Grillparzer includes risks like those of criticism of a dictator in a totalitarian state, or criticism of Richard Wagner in the vicinity of the villa *Wahnfried*.

Appraisal and fame are subject to changes and are exposed to coincidences and injustices. But worldwide fame is an elementary phenomenon; it can only be ascertained, not demanded. Like César Franck and

Gabriel Fauré, like his countryman Anton Bruckner in music, Franz Grillparzer is a regional occurrence, a local specialty, subject matter for Austria's schools, mandatory subject for Austrian stages and Germanists, a "classical author for more mature youth"—"having arisen primarily out of Austria's need for a classical author" (Karl Kraus). Grillparzer's path leads from biography directly into the reading anthologies, while detouring around Olympus. Monographs, biographies, and scholarly studies change that fact no more than do numerous translations. Yes, it may even be that the special inclination of scholars and essayists toward Grillparzer can be traced back to the constantly renewed striving to realize the wish image of his authentic greatness through new consideration of the subject, to discover the dreamed-of Grillparzer in what is present. This phenomenon was described unsurpassably: "...we think we recognize that the man must have been very much greater than can be suspected on the basis of his works. In part, the unique charm of his works seems to lie in the fact that they make us notice that they are a long way from expressing everything that is in them. Thus they always awaken a new desire for contact with them—next time, we believe, they will entrust to us their most secret meaning. They never quite do it, and we finally grow accustomed to it and are satisfied with a lovely suspicion." (Berndt von Heiseler)

Everything that determines Franz Grillparzer's image has long since lain clearly before us in great detail, obscured only by the wealth of commentators and eulogists: the works, the fragments, the diaries, plans, notes and letters, life documents, and the testimonies of contemporaries. In so doing, we look at a good dozen stage plays, but we see, just as we saw with Ferdinand

Raimund, only one single authentic tragedy: Grillparzer's life. We know of two narrative works, but only Grillparzer's life story has true greatness: the story of his illness that we call his biography, which caused him to strangle his own greatness in incomprehensible self-alienation, strife with himself, in senseless self-hatred. Internally as well as externally, he had every opportunity for fulfillment as an author, as a human being, as a man; it took a lifetime of more than eighty years for him to undermine its realization. He was a tough, unwavering fanatic of self-destruction. He even fled from the often considered blessing of suicide, in order to remain a sorrowful witness to the great futility of it all until the very end. "To accomplish the utmost—but in a way that it cannot become visible...whoever wants to know once and for all just what it is, the Austrian fate—here...you hold it in your hands!" (Berndt von Heiseler)

The "struggle with the demon" is not only the leitmotif of this life. Menace, exposure, disintegration, despair, and the unbearable tension between the inner and the external world accompany any creativity as the prerequisite for all greatness. What Grillparzer confesses, fears, and screams could be in the diary of almost any genial or geniuslike loner: "If I should ever get to the point of...writing down the story of the consequences of my inner condition, you would think you were reading the medical case history of an insane man."—"If ever a person could say without being stupid: *I no longer want to live*, I could do it now."—"Attacked by tormenting thoughts, as if ambushed by dogs, I do not know where to turn... I spent my youth in this strife; my old age will end in it."—"I am withering away, specifically from within, which is the worst way."—"The fact that I am not capable of creating—and a dismal feeling shows me the awful reality that I will never be able to create again—that drives me like a hunted animal." Suffering is a prerequisite for creative greatness; it is the purchase price for the work. But Grillparzer pays the price and still owes us the great work. He does not form his life in the word, he does not master it; the prerequisite replaces creative effort.

> "The muse's goodwill has come to an end,
> And you've grown tired of striving?"
> I practice a toilsome art, my friend,
> The art of present-day living.

A god gave him the power to say how he suffers, but he does not say it in his works, but rather in diaries, epigrams, conversations, letters that he often (like Franz Kafka) does not send and chooses only as a form of monologue, of self-portrayal. An author who shies away from the god-given means to master inner distress, who saves detached occasional writing for personal things, cultivates the epigram excessively, and occasionally ventures with his unattractive lyric poetry into regions that remain closed to the regular dramatist (this perhaps specifically because he did not view lyric poetry as his form of artistic expression: "...just as it was my habit in general to take refuge in lyric poetry only as a means of self-relief, and that is also the reason why I cannot pretend to be a real lyric poet").

It is not Franz Grillparzer who speaks from Grillparzer's dramas, but a figure whom he has shoved in between himself and the material. In the drama his nature is not expressed directly, but revocably, in a detached, subdued manner, with all reservations; his drama, which for him was a notorious form of expression, cannot realize any authentic, experienced expression the way the poem of the non-lyricist "Incubus" does, which formulates the tragedy named Franz Grillparzer better than any essayistic commentary:

> ...And if I once had success,
> And could break through the stress,
> Free with the intellect's might,
> Through, to the form, to the light:
>
> Under my hand it takes form and it rises,
> And what was once dead puts on life's living guises,
> A picture that breathes, it stands in its place,
> All filled with the spirit of builder and space;
>
> So then with a cunning remark he steals in,
> And from my own work he greets me with a grin:
> "'Tis I, master, I, and my house here you raise,
> See, futile your work, and so futile your days!"
>
> I shuddering see, bewitched by dismay,
> How my own self revolts against me here today,
> And cursing my work wish myself in the ground;
> There tormenting me will he also be found?

We will cite some other testimonies against the overestimation of Franz Grillparzer and have some overestimators to criticize, but the chief witness in the case of Grillparzer against Grillparzer is Grillparzer himself.

Let us pause for a moment and remember the great theme of the evidence being presented, the common thread of these observations, the image of Austria acquired from its artists. We remember the Vienna cliché, the cozy, idyllic fragrance that rises simply from the word *Biedermeier*. We compare with it what we have previously learned about Schubert, Raimund, Nestroy, and Grillparzer—and we have now already reached the new firm point from which we will have to view everything Austrian up to and including the present day: the fate which, arising out of the environment but also in equal measure from the inner core, refuses realization to the possibilities, the secondary rails that cross through the main line, flight, forced or voluntary (and usually both), from real fulfillment.

One aspect of this tragedy, demonstrated again and again in each individual case, is the great misunderstanding of the others. Where they rebuked Schubert for acting like a Viennese, a visitor to Vienna in the summer of 1831 observed that Grillparzer was a real Austrian, but found in him a "melancholy that was unusual for Austrians," as if this were surprising and not obvious; and even the countrymen themselves—we remember Bauernfeld—participate in the misunderstanding.

But we know:

Austria—that means: nearness of death, surrender, failure; it means: futility, being unappreciated, underestimation of self; and a great secret dialogue goes around among those who have been afflicted with the fate of being Austrian through the centuries. A key word to the understanding of Grillparzer, "There is something in me that says, it is just as unseemly to exhibit naked what is inside, as what is outside," will be varied responsively in Hofmannsthal's only authentic and direct work, *The Difficult Man*: "The simple fact that one states something is indecent. And viewed more specifically...there is almost something impudent in the fact that one dares to experience certain things at all."

Egon Friedell views "flight from reality" as a characteristic weakness in Grillparzer—disorganized retreat from facts to ideas, supremacy of thoughts over deeds, even over words.

> Shadows are the goods of life,
> Shadows of its joys we view,
> Shadow words and wishes, deeds,
> Only thoughts are really true.
>
> And the charity you feel,
> And the good things that you do;
> And no waking but in sleep,
> When you rest beneath the dew.

it says programmatically in *Life Is a Dream*. Grillparzer had been asked to write a new text for Haydn's *Emperor's Hymn*, when it could no longer praise "Emperor Franz." The text he presented was not accepted and was also not very usable, but in those eight lines Grillparzer had already unconsciously written an ideal text for an Austrian national anthem based on Haydn's melody.

"Only thoughts are really true" according to Grillparzer, and: "In this country they always acted—and sometimes to the extent of the greatest extremes of passion and its results—differently than they thought, or thought differently than they acted," in Robert Musil's *The Man without Qualities*.

"I would like to be able to write a tragedy in thoughts," Grillparzer notes in his diary at the age of eighteen, "it would be a masterpiece"—and three years later, with an almost Nestroylike wit, as we will not find it in any of his other works: "Inside my head it looks like Hungary. An abundance of raw materials, but

In the middle of the Ottokar drama is the embarrassing, melodically inserted hymn of praise to Austria, at which the Austrian audience traditionally retrogresses into a school class and obediently applauds. And the line that always triggers the applause also grew out of the great Grillparzer retraction and is not even grammatically complete:

Perhaps in Saxony and on the Rhine
There are some people who've read more in books:
But what is needful and what pleases God,
The lucid view, the open, proper mind...

Now, what about that?

The Austrian approaches anyone...

And acts? At least gives his opinion, draws the consequences from his lucid view, and his open, proper mind? No, the action only consists of the Austrian approaching anyone...

Has his opinion, lets the others talk!

The Austrian Grillparzer does not draw the consequences, either grammatically, personally, or artistically, from the premise: "But what is needful and what pleases God, the lucid view, the open, proper mind..." He leaves open whether he has it or not, the view, the mind, what is needful, what pleases God; nor does he say what he does and does not do with view and mind—the great, deep, suicidal Grillparzer breach yawns here, right here, between "mind" and "The"—the Austrian Grillparzer approaches any person, any material, any claim, any conflict, any attraction from outside, he does not act, he does not even speak, he lets the others talk, he has his opinion. He resigns himself.

He avoids. He flees from reality into possibility:

> What's possible tow'rs over every vastness,
> What's real reveals itself alone in space.
> *(Recollections of Youth in the Country)*

He sees the end in beginning and refuses to give himself. He describes a desirable woman in many stanzas ("Encounter") and calls himself to order in the last one:

> ...but from the gentle sun
> I back away, my heart with longing glows,
> The little boat, how well it bears the one:
> If something else jumped in—who knows? Who
>   knows?

He watches himself, a hostile brother; he stands in his own way; he destroys himself: "Within me, you see, live two completely separate beings. A poet with the most shifting, yes, hasty imagination, and a man of understanding of the coldest and toughest kind." Neither of the two allows the other to develop itself; each is the incubus of the other, and Franz Grillparzer's most authentic, momentary realization always occurs when he at least breaks through to the expression of this conflict, the external one in a journal entry written during his trip to the Orient:

> Now I am tired of travel,
> If only it would end.

> In hearing and in seeing
> I lose my mind, my friend.
>
> So you want to go home?
> Not there, if you don't mind!
> There life dies out for me
> In that old daily grind.
>
> So where then will you stay,
> When you no longer roam?
> O man with but two strangers,
> And nowhere to call home.

the inner one in the incubus poem or in Jason's confession:

> And I myself have now become my subject,
> Another thinks in me, another acts.
> I often meditate about my words,
> Like those of someone else, and what they mean,
> And when it comes to deeds, I often wonder,
> And try to guess what he will do and what he won't.

or in the closing lines of an epigram:

> ...when one has heard his own death knell
> To walk beside his corpse as well.

with "corpse" taken here in the Austrian double meaning of dead body and funeral procession (Leim in *The Vagabond*: "...when I leap and dance, then inside of me it is as though I walked with my own corpse...").

Unlike Jason, Grillparzer does not feel so idyllically comfortable with this split personality. Astonished detachment does not prevail here, but strife, bitter, deadly strife. Raimund overcame his conflict and elevated it to form in *The King of the Alps*. Like Raimund, Grillparzer was broken by it, but not in a premature end, rather, permanently, chronically, unceasingly, irretrievably. The writer mercilessly tortured and perilously injured the man of understanding, and vice versa. Thus Grillparzer's biography becomes the chronicle of a suicide that was stretched out over long decades.

As a twenty-five-year-old man, the writer with the hasty imagination finished the tragedy *The Ancestress* in sixteen days: "I can say that I wrote the entire play as if in a fever, it came into being in a purely physical manner...," but the man of understanding would "...not have put the play on the stage, because I hated the public so much," and only "—because the situation of my mother and me was so indigent, I thought: 'Well, maybe you'll get something for it!'" Before this elementary physical event, however, he had spent seven years "without the slightest poetic activity." A poet who writes nothing from his eighteenth to his twenty-fifth year!

The writer with the hasty imagination also finished *Sappho* in about three weeks. But before that the man of understanding says: "I found no material, perhaps only because I was not looking for any."

The writer with the hasty imagination wrote the last two acts of *Medea* in two days each. But to blame for the tempo were horrid conditions and the premonition "that the excitement of rage would soon be replaced by the lassitude of discontent." And just as the fever had dictated it to him, he handed over the manuscript in an only semilegible draft, "without revising the play."

King Ottokar's Happiness and Death, written in one month, "almost without corrections," is given to the theater management "in draft form," and even though success finally validates this work, after *King Ottokar's Happiness and Death*, while searching for material for his next dramatic work and wavering between some topics "that were all thought out, and all dramatically planned down to the details, although only mentally," Grillparzer decides in favor of material that he found "perhaps less attractive than the rest." And when the play *A Faithful Servant of His Master* was presented to "enor-mous applause," Grillparzer's "joy at the success" was "moderate, because the play did not satisfy any inner need for me."

No success accompanies the next play *The Waves of the Sea and of Love*, and Grillparzer notes in his journal: "Peculiar the effect that this failure had upon me! In the beginning very unpleasant, naturally, but on the second day an extremely calming feeling soon got the upper hand...my own master again...an introspective man pursuing quiet purposes, no longer taking interest in dreams, but in reality." Thus flight even from the dream!

And while working he had already made the notation: "Decided, to simply quit working with Hero and Leander. This magnificent material has been treated without the necessary love. More in order to do anything at all, than because an inner drive compelled me to create this specific product. Yes, in my irritation about the aversion that I could no longer conquer, and more or less defiantly, from among several subjects I had chosen the very one whose execution demanded the greatest sensitivity."

The man of understanding sets traps for the poet: "That the fourth act bored the audience a little bit was even something I intended."

If we want to criticize the human being and the author Franz Grillparzer destructively, we find no more effective ally, no more credible witness than Grillparzer himself. The term *self-punishment*, coined by Sigmund Freud, intrudes again and again when we consider this wretched life. In every respect he inventively and consistently works toward failure; he methodically prepares for it. The orgies of self-renunciation, denial, despondency, and silence, of morose resentment lack any external motivation; such a thing is occasionally at most an excuse, but never a cause. Like Zwirn in *The Vagabond*, Grillparzer cannot "stand the good days." ("He can't stand it, he says. He would have everything...that his heart desires, and he still can't wait until he's out there again in misery.")

Any failure or misfire, any missing of the mark is his own fault, self-created, his own responsibility. Grillparzer only feels well when he does not feel well; a magnetic, reciprocal attractive force drives him and misfortune toward each other. He is "looking for trouble," and his misfortune is not even meaningful. It has no tragic magnitude, no classical dimension. It is shabby, pitiful, and miserable: he falls from the ladder, down the stairs; while traveling he has difficulties with his passport and with his baggage; he has housing worries, all kinds of illnesses, especially digestive problems (concerning which he expresses himself extensively in letters, diaries, and in his autobiography)—he cuts his finger and writes in a letter: "Thank God, I cut myself while shaving."

In spite of this tendency toward flight from greatness —all the fanatical attempts not to be a poet, not to become a great man—his rise takes place with remarkable, almost incredible speed and intensity.

In his decisive years of maturity he does not write. One day, using a combination from two sources, he internally conceives *The Ancestress* ("...the plan for *The Ancestress* was finished. I was hindered in proceeding to its execution partly by my decision to give up writing dramatic literature forever, and partly by my sense of shame..."). The substance is narrated to Schreyvogel, the secretary of the royal theater, who, "extremely enthusiastic," cries out: "The play is finished. You only have to write it down." But when other family and professional matters surface, *The Ancestress* is forgotten, and Schreyvogel is not visited again. Grillparzer has to be reminded repeatedly, then the text is feverishly and physically written down. Success comes, but no second subject is sought; later, primarily "because of a need for money," *Sappho* is put down on paper in what is again an unbelievably short time and then successfully performed. "The play created an unbelievable sensation," the author himself confesses. And Grillparzer is famous, is translated into foreign languages; Lord Byron prophesies that the hard-to-remember name will be known to future generations. But after the triumph with *Sappho*, Grillparzer writes to Schreyvogel that his condition is the most unpleasant one that he can imagine. "...what hope for a new production lies in this oppressive insensibility? I am almost in despair."

After two more dramatic works—*The Golden Fleece, King Ottokar's Happiness and Death*—Grillparzer is a European celebrity; Goethe receives him more than cordially, invites him to visit, but: "I was afraid to spend an entire evening alone with Goethe, and after much wavering and hesitation I did not go."

Grillparzer writes the speech that is given at Beethoven's grave. Given the sparseness of his output, as a thirty-six-year-old man he could hardly be more accepted, more famous, more celebrated.

Then come *A Faithful Servant of His Master* and *The Waves of the Sea and of Love* with the self-inflicted handicaps and impairments with which we are already acquainted. Concerning the *Faithful Servant* he renders this judgment: "I am aware that while working I changed the plan, and in the process something that breaks the harmony may well have gotten into the parts. I feel my strength dwindling. My heart is deathly sad." A novella, *The Poor Musician*, is begun—it will not be published until seventeen years later—three years pass before the next play, *Life is a Dream*, which is greeted with extraordinary approval; it had already been started thirteen years earlier and had only been set aside because of a ridiculous superficiality during the work on the first act. Four more years pass before the next piece, *Woe unto the Liar*—and at last, this one fails when it premieres, and it is as though this were a desired, expected, induced event, as if it brought welcome confirmation, gave him the excuse to quit at last: Grillparzer gives up, ceases, publishes no dramas, hardly writes anything else.

Two years earlier, when a comedy by his younger colleague Bauernfeld had failed, Grillparzer had "endeavored to help" him "to his feet in the very kindest way." Now, however, he elevates the occupational accident, an essential component of any career, to the great, decisive cardinal point of his life. Twenty-seven years of existence as a writer until *Woe unto the Liar*, followed by thirty-four years of morose, inactive life—but before and afterward fame, honor, the conferring of an order, appointment to the Academy of Sciences, to the upper chamber of parliament, all that on the basis of eight dramatic works. And then afterward *The Jewess of*

Toledo, Libussa, Fraternal Strife in Habsburg, one of which already lay at least half finished in his desk—and beyond that only epigrams, occasional poetry, and the fragment of an autobiography. He stubbornly rejects the promotion of an edition of his collected works. On his fiftieth birthday he says: "I have written things down for twenty-four items of subject matter, and it comes to nothing. What does it matter in the end, if I write another play? It doesn't make me happy. What would make me happy is out of my reach anyway."

What makes him happy? What does not make him happy? He actively brings about what does not make him happy. He finds confirmation in failure. And when we celebrate him, we place ourselves in blatant contradiction to him. For he did everything to be unsatisfactory. His only authentic and effective activity was directed against his own activity. "Never before have I found helplessness, effeminacy, broken will to that degree in a man," Gutzkow notes. "Why doesn't the man make any major decision?" What broke his will? Neither private nor artistic failure are sufficient motives. Nor did Grillparzer die because of Austria, according to Laube; he "had death in his heart from birth," and eerily, this "did... die" is written down when Grillparzer is forty-five years old and will still exist biologically for decades.

Three years earlier, he had written in his diary: "I am forty-two years old and feel like a very old man," and some months later: "The writer G. has died."

He knew everything about himself, and even otherwise infinitely more than he seemed to know. He was ahead of himself and remained behind himself; his dramatic works are only outlines burdened with all the attributes of being half finished, insufficient, written down too hastily, not formed, full of material for the gloomy spirit, so that it grins out at its creator from his own work.

The Ancestress begins with the morose line: "Well, all right! What must, let happen!" and the awkwardly stilted breathlessness of the inserted relative clause seems to be just as thematic as the resignedly autumnal mood of the beginning. An early work?

Years earlier he had already completed a drama, even in two versions, *Blanka of Castile*, and there, too, he had burdened samples of authentic dramatic spirit with incomprehensible linguistic deformities. There a warning is given against "fanning the flames of civil war in the entrails of the homeland." Word order is in provocative disorder there: "And by the nose me let them lead?"—"Then is not quite Don Pedro lost already."—"When fell I then into Don Pedro's arms." Not only the language and plot direction of *Don Carlos* and other things by Schiller are imitated there to the point that they might be mistaken for his work, a copy of Goethe's "Song of the Three Fates" from *Iphigenie* is also included in it:

> ...They're striving and lurking
> To find tempting prey,
> And spinning and working
> Their ruinous nets,
> While awful rings winding
> And carefully binding
> Them threateningly
> 'Round the guilty man's head...

An early work?

The later works are full of such and similar helpless incomprehensibilities. Their abundance makes Grillparzer's works very difficult to tolerate and us very distrustful. When we read Grillparzer's sensible ideas about literature, the confidently mastered, if somewhat dry prose of his letters and papers, and his narrative prose, we think that as the author of works for the stage he consciously played the role of a tragicomical figure, the schoolmasterish, peculiar, awkward, stammering, parodistically ossified, pedantic dramatist Franz Grillparzer —and that he only occasionally penetrated "freely, with the power of the spirit, to light and form."

But the similarities also return in the works of the mature Grillparzer. As she enters, Medea finds the atmosphere to be "So sultry, so heavy," just like Gretchen; Sappho quotes a line from *Don Carlos*, only replacing "times" with "things": "You speak of things that are past," and Rudolf II arouses suspicion of an unseemly relationship between himself and old Attinghausen when he has to say:

> ...United be! The new world comes,
> The aging families are dying out.

The archaic, inadvertently comical accusative form *Blanken* from *Blanka of Castile* is no less comical when the same kind of formulation is applied to produce *Melitten* or even *Sapphon* as similar designations.

The word order remains forced, immature: "Said I it not to you?" (*The Ancestress*)—"Did I him...then tell to sit upon my chair?" (*The Guest*)—"Fall I then, if only they fall too." (*The Argonauts*)—"First my children I will have." (*Medea*)—"How many lovers have you?" (*The Jewess of Toledo*)—"Has your life's every trace been blown away?"—"You like in riddles to express yourself."—"Have you the lock yourself precisely looked at?"—"Had been it in a stranger's hand." (*Libussa*)—"And all the wheels stand still now of this state." (*Esther*)

There are, similarly arising out of the necessity to manage the lines, contractions and compressions that cruelly cripple the flow, the speakableness, and the clarity of what is said: "'nough" (*Sappho*)—"most eas'ly" —"I turn 't down" (*The Guest*)—"'t least" (*Libussa*).

It is understandable that Karl Kraus made marks in the margins by almost every line of *Medea* and *Life Is a Dream*, those, as he called them, "unsightly theatrical works that were composed in the worst, most childishly incompetent haphazard verse," and that for him a few sentences from Nestroy's *Talisman* offset the life's work of Grillparzer, whose lasting renown "would not be justified even by the current"—1922—"lack of literary phenomena that approach his occasional beautiful creations."

But Grillparzer's confrontation with Grillparzer is also incomprehensible; the view of the awkward works from the "occasional beautiful creations," and of the latter from the former.

In a perplexing manner, Grillparzer is occasionally what we call "modern." A sentence for instance, the motto of the story *The Poor Musician*, is drafted entirely in the language of our era: "We cannot understand the famous, if we have not felt with the obscure." From vocabulary to thought, everything here is full of the right spirit. Similarly, again and again we also find beautiful and great and clever things in the dramatic works—many have already been cited—many additional things could be added, from the dying count's farewell in *The Ancestress*:

> Let me, faithful servant, let me
> Once more on the edge of the grave,
> See this wild and tangled life,
> Wild and rough and yet so fair,
> Let me see its face once more.
> All its pleasures, all its sorrows,
> Let me in one last farewell,
> Once more feeling that I'm human,
> Press against this breast of mine.
> One last time, o let me sip
> From the cup so bittersweet—
> And then, Fate, take him away!

to the great political prophecy in *Fraternal Strife*:

> ...not Scythians, Khazars,
> Who once the old world's splendid glory broke,
> Are this our era's threat, not foreign nations:
> But this barbarian from our own womb,
> Who, left unchecked, destroys then all that's great,
> All art and science, government and church,
> And pulls them from their shielded heights above
> Down to his level of vulgarity,
> Til everything's the same because it's low.

But the essence of fatal weakness can even be established in the isolated high point, for example, in the use of repetition—in the trochaically driven presentiment of death in the final act of *The Ancestress*, it is perhaps a legitimate artistic device, but otherwise so often a joltingly breathless makeshift: "O it grows light now, light before my eyes." (*Sappho*)—"What I until now hid from myself, hid from myself, the gods for me rescued." (*The Argonauts*)—"You saw it?—I saw it. Saw how the flame, writhing its way from the golden bowl, toward her—Enough! She saw it!" (*Medea*)—"Because you speak promises without words, and in speaking you contradict the language of your charm." (*Libussa*) It also includes the almost parodistic foresight of Wallenstein in the final act of *Fraternal Strife*, that the war now beginning could last thirty years, which is underscored again by foolish repetitions ("The war is good, even if it lasts thirty years.—Who said that, what's the big idea? And why thirty?—What's the big idea? And why exactly thirty?") and the unfelt, unfinished wordplay: "She did not return to us again, for by disturbing and being disturbed herself, she destroyed* the circle" (*Libussa*).

This is not the argumentatively dialectic demureness of Kleist's verses, whose life, by the way, ended in the year when Grillparzer was just writing his *Ottokar*. It is a dearth of expression that does not become a virtue, that does not manage stressed and unstressed syllables properly and alternately permits a word to have one or two syllables, simply to match the rhythm, even in the central, programmatic key line (*Life Is a Dream*):

> But one thing makes sadness cease,
> One: the spirit's quiet peace...**

It is the vapidly trite, undescriptive usage of the breast, to which, if necessary, we may still permit the dying count to press the joys and sorrows of life; but what should we think of an empty bosom whose poor waves now only occasionally awaken from their brooding rest?

---

*The original contains a wordplay that cannot be translated.
**A two-syllable and a one-syllable version of the same word are translated here with "one thing" and "One" respectively.

What should we think of a breast in which a woman bears the other half of what was longingly beating in the man's bosom—of a melodiousness that swayed in the heaving breast (*Sappho*), of a breast from which duty and right hang (*The Argonauts*), of a glance that throws fire into a bosom (*Medea*), of a breast that is as dark as space (*Woe unto the Liar*), of the spirit that is silent in the breast (*Libussa*), of revenge that sometimes foams up in a boiling hot breast (*Esther*), of a girl who seems to be of an audacious breast and a violent mind—of the spark of will and decisiveness that falls into a girl's heart (*The Jewess of Toledo*), of the seeds of wrongness in the breast of an evil man (*Fraternal Strife*)?

It is the frivolous interjections, the "ah" that recurs ridiculously often, the philistine "well," often the two of them combined: "Did someone call me?—Well, I heard 'Berta'" (*The Ancestress*)—"Well what?—Ah, well, that you came back" (*Sappho*)—"Ah, nonetheless!" (*The Guest*)—"And asked about—well, about the Colchis woman!" (*The Argonauts*)—Gregor: "Woe be unto him who lies!"—Leon: "Well, well!"—"Ah, his daughters… they probably prevent his end" (*Libussa*), and completely incomprehensible as the final line of a tragedy: "Oh well! A faithful servant of his master!"

The unskillful passages in all of Grillparzer's dramas pile up to the extent that one could almost believe they are intentional. Even Rudolf Kassner, one of the great eulogists of recent times, must admit that Grillparzer's imagery "is not always pure, does not taste pure. Bad images occur frequently enough, unseen, undiscerned, tasteless ones." Kassner quotes as an example: "Blood is the red wax that stamps every lie as a truth," and refers to additional examples "of similar stiffness and deformity." And Richard Schaukal arrives at the heart of the problem: "There are 'speechless' writers like Grillparzer who, without creative mastery of the writer's material, language, yes, without an ear for its internal regularity, employ the word only as a conventional and accepted means for the intellectual communication of their ideas, but not as an independent, expressive pattern of original ability to use language."

In our "breast" cavalcade we have already had the opportunity to read some samples that scream for a Nestroy to raise them from involuntary comic effect into the liberating play of language; we intend to and must continue with some other quotes, in order to present the tragedy of a great spirit and the deviousness of his uncritical eulogists as convincingly and clearly as possible: "When the wintery caterpillars of my wishes as golden butterflies around me play." (*Sappho*)—"Intention, friend, is a cautious rider on a race horse fiery, who the deed..." (*Fraternal Strife*)—"There hovered before the eyes of my mind...the image of a flower" (*Libussa*).

We have only demonstrated a few bad habits in Grillparzer's lines with just a few examples. We should also point to the suppressed auxiliary verbs: "Do you practice secret arts, the crimes?" (*The Jewess of Toledo*), to the prefixes separated from their stems: "It can still be warded, still warded off"* (*The Argonauts*), to strangely ludicrous neologisms arising out of linguistic impotence: "female boy" (*The Guest*)—"female walker of the night" (*The Argonauts*), to prosaic expressions in the tragically poetic text: "Don't be mad at me." (*The Guest*)—"Get yourself ready." (*The Argonauts*)—"I greet you.—You, too." (*Medea*)

*The original line contains an improperly separated verb prefix.

Nor can we avoid criticizing some Austrianisms. In so doing, let us say nothing against the tone and nuances of standard German. It does not detract from the nobility of Adalbert Stifter's German, no, more likely heightens it, just as it lends Gottfried Keller's language all its lovely peculiarity. Grillparzer's Austrianisms, however, are not seeds of greatness, but crutches that prop up the meter; they do not come from the strengthening dialect, but from slang. The word *von* [of] is often used incorrectly instead of the genitive case: "when...the young man casts his gaze on a maiden and makes her the goddess of his wishes" (*Medea*), and even in Grillparzer's very central, exposed, Habsburg-Austrian knowledge of self, "striving hesitantly along partial paths toward a partial deed with partial resources" is not the noble house's curse, but "the curse of our noble house," and moreover, the "partial resources" are unbearably encumbered in the next line, "Yes or no, there is no middle way," where the consonance of *Mittel* [resources] and *Mittelweg* [middle way] gets in the way because the words lack any correspondence or antithesis.

Similarly, the Austrian accusative, with its omission of the definite article, is the worst sort of argot. One goes "in woods," and that not even consistently, but only when the meter demands it, so that in Colchis of all places, the memorable line comes into being: "Hello! In woods, you maidens, in the woods!" (*The Guest*). One lays his hands "in lap" (*The Argonauts*), one enters "into pact" with his friends (*Medea*), Wallenstein goes "in war," as does King Alfons of Spain.

In his agonizing loneliness Grillparzer agrees with us completely. "...I know," he says in his diary, "that I do everything clumsily." He is helplessly, powerlessly, impotently at the mercy of his demon of futility, cursed to harm himself in everything, to cooperate in the abuse, the failure of his great intellectual and artistic powers, to have the great cosmic prophecy of the dying Libussa, which encompasses everything from the Garden of Eden to the end of time, begin as follows:

> In Spirit I see a lovely garden
> And in it two people of either sex...

to formulate the stage directions in the third act of *The Argonauts* in language that no village schoolteacher would permit a ten-year-old to get away with: *The inside of the king's tent. The back curtain of the same is such that through the same, without being able to distinguish precisely the individuals found outside, one can still discern the outlines of the same.*

All these points are made, not to ridicule Grillparzer, but to portray and explain him. The attack is less against him, the tragically torn man who did not want to do what he could, and could not do what he wanted, than against his sycophants, from whom he deserves to be protected as much as Austria from the suspicion that Grillparzer was her greatest poet or even a "classical author." Everything considered, he was at best a "delicate, no longer quite viable aftergrowth of Weimar classicism" (Egon Friedell), a second-class classical author. Whoever places him higher is suspect. It is no accident that the first Grillparzer Prizes fell to Wildbrandt and Wildenbruch. All kinds of bearded ones of many eras have seized him. A scholar named Johann Volkelt elevated him above Goethe; Paul Heyse saw in him a divinely inspired tragedian; on the occasion of the fiftieth anniversary of his death, excesses such as the following appeared in Vienna: "With him died the last truly Austrian human being, and Austria's last true soul faded away" (Rudolf Holzer in the official *Wiener Zeitung*), and Hofmannsthal, who published much that is contestable about art and about Austria—for example, the sentence about the "feeling of happiness that issues forth from the music of Haydn, Mozart, Schubert, and Strauss"—thinks that Grillparzer was "our greatest poet," that Austrianness is gathered in his works in an "almost unbroken synthesis." Considering his opinion of Raimund, we already have misgivings when Hofmannsthal sees a synthesis. In Hanover, in a speech addressed to those he called "national comrades," he distorted both Grillparzer and the German language. Even before this fiftieth anniversary, Hofmannsthal had expressed himself about Grillparzer's ingenuously intricate love tragedy *The Waves of the Sea and of Love*, which is lovable for its isolated charms, but already condemned by its inane title alone: "...next to this work, *Romeo and Julie*..."—Juliet is not refined enough for him!—"... seems only like any old tragedy of life, in which..."—In which? In the tragedy or in life?—"in which lovers are ruined." They do not perish, they do not even reach the bottom, no, nothing less than "ruin" will do for him! But let's leave him—a time will come that derogates him as he deserves—let's first just save Grillparzer (Hofmannsthal would write: Grillparzern [accusative case form]) and Austria from his mistaken judgment, as we have to protect Raimund from him. Grillparzer is Austrianness "in an almost unbroken synthesis"? No, Grillparzer is the caricature, the parody, the perversion of Austrianness. His flight is not triumphant and lacks greatness. He is far from the creative Austrian misjudgment, both of self and by others. To be sure, he scorns realization, but neither does he live the possibilities.

Even unfulfillment can become a blessing, even the attempt, the fragment can brilliantly deride the totality; but in Grillparzer's works the halfway, the dull make their mark. His motto is no Promethean "Nevertheless," but a biting "Just not that!" He is probably the most unartistic writer in world literature.

He did not want to be able to; he was not able to want to. In his autobiography he reports that he was an excellent swimmer, but "if they threw me into the water today, I would certainly drown." He also describes a characteristic, but extremely unusual quality of his visual faculty. With his "extremely weak eyes" he could see "only rather hazy images," but once, during a performance of *The Robbers*, he suddenly saw in the actor Devrient "each of his features," he believed Devrient "was jumping into the theater box"—"the distinctness of vision changed to the feeling of approach." And on a second occasion, in the window of a house that lay far outside his visual acuity, he saw at first only "something white," but in the next instant the features of a woman "so similar to those in a portrait that I could have immediately put them on ivory or canvas." In that same way, clearly envisioned features, authentic images also occasionally stand out in his works, but then his strength fails and he is not able to see what he was able to see.

Two words are encountered especially often in Grillparzer's texts; the one is the self-recognizing *hypochondriac*, the other, the *collection*, the concentration, "collection, that bride of the gods, mother of everything great," eternally longed for, wished for, all too seldom prevailing against "dispersion"...

...the mighty planet lever,
That raises all that's great a thousandfold,

And even moves the small things toward the stars,
The hero's deed, the singer's sacred song,
The prophet's dream, the course and rule of God,
Collection did it, recognized its worth,
Dispersion just misjudges it and mocks.
(*The Waves of the Sea and of Love*)

The fact that the so passionately courted collection denies itself to him may be linked in a mysterious way to his relationship to music. As they are for Raimund and Nestroy, musical consciousness and experience are an essential element of Grillparzer's life. As it is in almost every Austrian creative life, the problem of the double talent is also manifest in Grillparzer. In letters and diaries he comments with intense interest on opera performances that are more appealing to him than plays, which he attends far less frequently. He plays the piano, listens to concerts and amateur music played at home, and participates actively in the management of the Vienna Music Lovers. The dying Rudolf II, in many respects a self-portrait, goes with the question "Is there music here?" into the spheres where he is no longer emperor, but a human being—"How sweet it sounds, continues on and on!"

As a very young man he develops great capabilities in improvisation on the piano. "I often placed a copperplate engraving in front of me on the music stand and played the situation that was portrayed upon it." As a thirty-five-year-old he believed that his musical talent was so great "that it even almost overshadowed his talent for poetry." He called the study of music and counterpoint the "means to prevent poetic production." And how deeply the musical element intervened in the poetic is revealed in the history of the creation of *The Golden*

Fleece. The work on the trilogy had been interrupted. Illness, a journey, and the death of his mother had "completely wiped away" the planned continuation that had not been written down, everything that had been "prepared and thought out." His memory failed, but "something peculiar happened." Grillparzer had played symphonies by Haydn, Mozart, and Beethoven four-handed with his mother, and in so doing had thought "incessantly about my *Golden Fleece*, and the thought embryos merged with the notes into an inseparable whole." Then, when he took up the four-handed play again with a different partner, "it happened that when we got to the symphonies that I had played with my mother, they yielded back to me again all the thoughts that I had half-unconsciously put into them when I had played them earlier. I suddenly knew again what I had intended..., went to work, completed *The Argonauts*, and moved to *Medea*."

Perhaps it was a great mistake that he became a writer, perhaps also that within literature he decided in favor of the drama. In that regard, Carlyle says: "Since he lived in a country where they give such great attention to the drama, he let himself be misled to try his own hand at it, but without possessing the basic qualifications for such an undertaking, so that the measure of talent that had been given to him...almost in defiance of his destiny, was forced to write dramas which, although regularly divided into scenes and individual speeches, essentially consist of nothing but monologues, and although swarming with characters, only too often emphasize only one character, and a not very extraordinary one at that...namely the character of Franz Grillparzer himself." In the essay "German Drama Smiths," Carlyle goes beyond that in dealing very thoroughly with

Grillparzer and says, among other things: "...to date we still know of no scene or line by Grillparzer that is anything more than mediocre."

Thus, Grillparzer was perhaps a dramatist; perhaps he was a writer in contradiction with his own internal law, better said: the inner law of his personality may also have caused that contradiction.

What Hofmannsthal calls *synthesis*, and what amazes us as an extreme case of the opposite of synthesis in every imaginable context pertaining to Grillparzer, the "two completely separate personalities," also has an effect on his attitude toward his homeland, toward Austria, toward the Habsburg monarchy. One can call upon Grillparzer as a witness for every pro and every contra (and that has been done extensively); one can make an Austrophile and an anti-Austrian anthology of Grillparzer quotes; and from them one can also produce a contradictory dialogue.

In 1830, Grillparzer, who "loved" his fatherland "to the point of childishness," thought that a republic was better than the "repulsive stability system" that was later defended by Radetzky, whom he cheered in a poem of tribute, although he thought that despotism had destroyed his life, at least his literary life. Twice he begins a welcoming greeting with the line: "I greet you, my Austria," but in his diary he writes: "Therefore, away, away from this situation! Out into the world...in other regions, surrounded by other people, my spirit will perhaps regain a happy mood... Yes, away to Switzerland! Heavenly country!... I want to flee this land of wretchedness...where reason is a crime..." But the old emperor's hymn, "May God Preserve," had sounded wonderful to him when he was still a boy, as a late poem of the almost seventy-year-old man attests:

> ...and now travel-weary, ill,
> Old, but yet with verve,
> Hope and thanks I offer still
> In "May God Preserve"...

He wrote many obsequious patriotic poems of that kind, in every period of his life, an especially awkward "Welcome" for the fourth wife of the emperor Franz, the "magnificent woman," "glorious and gentle," the "exalted, the lovely one": "...for her our lives, for her our blood!" But he also thought: "An Austrian poet should be held in higher esteem than any other. He who does not lose courage under such conditions is truly a kind of hero." Austrian—for him that is "from a civil and political point of view, obviously the very worst thing that one can become." But on the other hand, Austria is:

> ...a good land,
> Well worth it, that a prince should take it on!

The drama about King Ottokar ends with "Hail! Hail!—Hurrah for Austria!—Habsburg forever!" In that "Habsburg forever!" Grillparzer voluntarily and retroactively legitimized and confirmed the very despotism that would destroy his literary life, as he discovered. He legalized that death sentence yet a second time by having Rudolf II proclaim: "My house will remain forever, I know." And Grillparzer was in complete agreement with that, although (or because) he understood: "I would have had to...leave this country early, if I had wanted to remain a poet." There was, he wrote, no "heartier supporter" of the government than he was, but he also said: "The mob that rules us demonstrates an incompetence that can at most be excused somewhat by their stupidity." He calls a colleague criminal because he "who had a name in literature, and justifiably so, allowed and allows himself to be used as the shield bearer of these corrupt and stupid people," but he writes a poem about the emperor's convalescence, through which he "had expected to make an impression on people in high and highest circles."

Immediately after Grillparzer's death, Ferdinand Kürnberger wrote: "While they pull off Grillparzer's death mask, I want to throw out a few words about his life mask... This is Grillparzer's life mask: sent out as a flaming storm to cleanse the air of Austria, he moves across Austria as a small, wet, gray cloud, tinged on the edges by some evening purple. And the little cloud goes down... His strong passion, his great abilities call to it: Send plagues upon Egypt, go before Pharaoh, speak for your people, lead it out into the promised land... But in a corner of his heart the Austrian himself begins to sigh and lament: Lord, send another! I am afraid... Let me rather become Pharaoh's councilor!...Grillparzer's biography is essential to an understanding of the psychology of Austria. They will write his biography in any case, but may the hand wither that does not write the entire truth of it!"

Meanwhile, biographies have appeared in great numbers, whereas nothing has been made known about the withering of numerous hands. However, it is also infinitely difficult to write the entire truth. For, deeply impressed by Grillparzer's fallibilities, weaknesses, and clumsiness while reading and gathering material, a person goes to work and is then still tempted, in spite of the material, to overlook all the negative things, to ignore them in writing, to interpret them away, to prudishly cover up the clumsiness, to excuse and explain the fallibility. Even that is an indispensable contribution to the psychology of Austria: Grillparzer's ambivalence is passed on infectiously, so to speak, to Grillparzer's observers, and the hand, in contrast to Kürnberger's curse, will far more probably wither, if it writes the entire truth, than if it suppresses the same. Complimentary to Grillparzer's self-abasement, a tendency toward the improper elevation of Grillparzer seems to radiate from his image, a tendency that even the writer of this portrayal was able to escape only through fierce discipline. Struck by waves of understandingly forgiving sympathy, he called himself to order and to Kürnberger's categorical imperative, not to harm Grillparzer, but for Austria's sake. In doing that he depended on the help of numerous allies and now intends to use two additional ones to do justice to the novella *The Poor Musician*. The first is Adalbert Stifter, who says that in it "so many strengths of the hero are undeveloped or at strange variance with his introversion." Stifter does not mean to be critical, but in describing the hero, he simultaneously describes the author, who at least partially portrayed himself in his creation. And Franz Kafka thinks that the story "begins in the wrong way and has a lot of mistakes, absurdities, dilettante features, and horrible affectations (one notices it especially when reading aloud; I could show you the passage)." Kafka, making another contribution to the psychology of Austria, is ashamed of the story, "just as if I had written it myself."

But of course this *Poor Musician* is far closer to being a well-wrought narrative than any Grillparzer drama is to being a well-wrought play. The prose is distinctly more polished than his verse, the epic form far more confidently mastered than the dramatic form. But

Grillparzer himself, even here his own enemy, obstructed this way out, confused poetry with literature, and said: "Poetry in prose is nonsense. For that reason I do not like to read any novel, or no more than an occasional one at most." Nor did he like to write any novellas, or at most only an occasional one. And that is a pity. Grillparzer's prose is not very good. But it is better. It, too, is reduced, however, to its mediocre status when confronted with genuine native German, when Adalbert Stifter and Franz Grillparzer meet and such a linguistic encounter even has a real meeting of the two as its subject. In the face of a few hardly substantial, quite noncommittal sentences of Stifter's prose from the *Vienna Salon Scenes*, Grillparzer's complete works shrink to Lilliputian dimensions:

> —the elderly man, who listens to him with a smile and leans back in his chair so cheerfully, as if this were his daily and exclusive occupation, is no less a person than—but I must not mention any names, although his is mentioned as far and wide as German is spoken, and will probably still be mentioned when ours have all faded away, yes, then he will probably stand there even more radiant, albeit more lonely. He has charmed a thousand hearts and lifted a thousand spirits, and instilled into thousands the beautiful, soft stillness of his words.

Stifter is in error here, for he, not Grillparzer's name, should be glorified wherever German is read, and with the noble form of even this fragment, he contradicts its all too modest content. Stifter accomplishes what Grillparzer wants to achieve through hectic drudgery:

collection, the quiet peace of the inner world. Austria is in his camp.

Stifter's prose is harmony of the spheres put into words, sweet analogy to the music of Franz Schubert, as unacquainted with itself as is the latter. Grillparzer, however, knows about himself, knows too much. Unlike Raimund and Nestroy he is not unintentionally and incidentally, but willingly and deliberately a dramatic author who complains about the drudgery of bread-and-butter labor while constantly renewing the pretension of practicing this business as his main profession. And in Austria that is not good. In one of his rare self-confident moments he felt himself to be "just that compromise between Goethe and Kotzebue that the drama needs." He became neither of the two. He stood between them—and between the periods, the generations, between classicism and the nineteenth century. And he projected his intermediate position onto the world. He loved to portray the coming of new eras, to let an epoch end autumnally with some violence if necessary (*The Ancestress*), because it corresponded to his mood. Again and again this autumnal, eveninglike, apocalyptical awareness of life is effective in his works, the superseding of a dying epoch by a violent, wildly confused, new one (*Fraternal Strife*: "The times are bad"), a world-wide knee-strap mood: "In a year the comet will come, and then the world will end," which is a wide-spread Austrian mental attitude, by the way, in literature as in life, proceeding from the assumption: "The world will not last much longer in any case"; but there is considerable variation in the conclusions drawn from it.

And Grillparzer finds not only affirmation in the fact of the impending end. He does not affirm the era preceding it, he affirms the end. In *Libussa*, in a hymnally festive tone he prophesies the rise of Slavism, which must direct itself entirely against his thought and feeling; in Berlin he notes that a cab driver "was wrapped up in Russian fashion in a manner that disgusted me," and adds: "Are you already becoming accustomed in advance to the livery of your future masters?" And he writes an infinitely peculiar poem, "Russia," saluting the country that disgusts him:

> How well I know your threat: you'd bind our hands,
> I know well what you want: the world you lack;
> And yet good luck to you and to your lands,
> Grab hold! Attack! Destroy what holds you back!

Why?

> Not that I'd grant you joyful things or good,
> I hate the customs of such thieves as you,
> I'd like to decimate you if I could,
> If I could crush your adversaries too.

He willingly, almost joyfully accepts the danger, the threat, the challenge, so that the nations will reflect as they once did in the face of the danger posed by Napoleon. What an unbelievably far-reaching affirmation of the negative! How this *yes* to Russia, this *yes* to Habsburg, this *yes* to the enemy, to the end, stands in contrast to the *no* to what is near, to what is nearest!

Grillparzer was a misanthrope: "Who'd not like humans small and fragile be, must keep himself from their vicinity" (*Libussa*), without bringing about reconciliation, at least in his works, as Raimund did.

Grillparzer was also an enemy to God; according to his own statement, he stood with the Lord God "just as two can stand with each other, where one knows nothing of the other."

And finally, Grillparzer was also a woman-hater.

To be sure, "boundless" was how he himself described his "inclination toward love and sensual pleasure." But even here there is internal disunity. "It is peculiar how much these two drives are separated in my heart." He creates all his own barriers to fulfillment. He has women swarming around him, pampering him, and reacts to it with indifference, only to discover later that he is "not capable of love," that he has been "the misfortune of three women."

Again, thought takes precedence over reality. "I think I have noticed that even in the one I love, I only love the image that my imagination has made of her...so that reality repels me when there is the least deviation."

At the age of thirty he becomes acquainted with the twenty-year-old Katharina Fröhlich, whom he will torment for the rest of his life, the "eternal fiancée," whom he elevates above all others with a maximum of closeness, only to the extent that he admits that "of all people" he "hates her the least." For half a century, his suicidal enmity toward man and God celebrates in this union its most disgraceful triumph. It became productive neither in fulfillment nor in self-denial. He is probably the only great writer who never experienced unrequited love, but had every chance for happiness, from which he obtained for himself every imaginable misfortune. He wanted to shift the rebuke to the higher powers. At the end of his love tragedy about Hero and Leander there is the challenging question directed at the statue of Amor: "Do you then promise much, thus keep your word?" But it is not Amor who is guilty with respect to Grillparzer. Grillparzer himself is at fault with respect to love.

There, in his most decisive failure, lies the source and the justification for all his misfortunes.

What a life! What did he make of himself?! What did he do to himself?! What a tragedy, cobbled together out of wretchedness, pettiness, embarrassment, and justified by no higher meaning! It was not a life that failing artistic greatness could sanctify, interpret, or excuse; there was no fulfillment in his works that could make up for his failure in life. Grillparzer lived like a man who fulfills himself only in his works; he produced like one who loses himself to life for it. For the sake of a life, one could indulgently accept such works as conditional, fragmentary, relative realizations, one could bow himself humbly before such a life, if it were ennobled by the permanency of the works. But no affirmation blossoms from Grillparzer's double rejection; in its "vapid evenness" (Karl Kraus), his image, the personification of misfortune and mishap, lacks any dimension. We are perplexed when confronted by the force of such self-abasement, such debasement; we shudder to see the disorganized flight from personal greatness into unpleasantness, torment, pettiness, mediocrity, in a biography that takes its course against better judgment, one in which unpleasantness is provoked again and again, artistically and privately, with nothing short of exact precision.

It is reliably reported that on one occasion Grillparzer and Raimund stood next to each other in front of the monkey cage in the Schönbrunn menagerie and watched the daredevil acrobatic antics of the animals. In admiration, Raimund poked Grillparzer with his elbow and said: "Hey, Grillparzer, that's difficult, you know!" "Does somebody order them to do it?!" Grillparzer responded.

Raimund's demon ordered him to do daredevil acts, to dare the impossible, to "exhibit" himself. Grillparzer's demon hindered him from doing so. Raimund made a monkey of himself and left to us the scene of youth, the third act of *The Spendthrift*, the play about the misanthrope, "somebody ordered" him "to do it." Grillparzer permitted no authority to order him to do what was assigned to him.

The history of the human spirit is a sequence of creative victories and creative defeats. In that history, the Austrian Franz Grillparzer deserves no chapter, but only a footnote in small print, because he did not gain victories and suffer defeats in the struggle against the world, because he fought only against himself, was defeated by himself, wounded himself, and killed himself.

ADALBERT STIFTER

or

THE SWEETNESS OF ORDER

"Sometimes the saying of the holy books occurred to me in connection with him, where the divine figure was supposed to appear on one occasion: it was not in the rolling of the thunder; it was not in the raging of the storm; but it was in the murmuring of the breeze that went along the brook and down into the fruitful bushes."
(*The Confirmed Bachelor*)

"A deep soul ordains itself to sorrow."
(Raimund)

"What is pure and glorious in man is undying and a gem in every age."
(*Indian Summer*)

"In a pipe dream even the caretaker's house looks like paradise."
(Nestroy)

"...for the words are so powerful that they move everything, just as the firm justice of deeds forms humanity. The word is mightier than the catapult..."
(*Witiko*)

ADALBERT STIFTER

Now I intend to write about Adalbert Stifter and have made up my mind to avoid the words *demon* and *demonic* while doing so. On the advice of friends and experts, I did not read the "demonizing" Stifter biography, and I only leafed through the psychoanalytical Stifter portrayal.

I have read little about Stifter, but I have spent many weeks reading Stifter, narrative works, observations, descriptions, letters, and documents of his life. I have spent many weeks, I have spent an entire winter, so to speak, with Adalbert Stifter, and concerning that time I would like to say in words from *Egmont*: "The world has no joys compared to these!"

When I had to report on a premiere of *King Lear* in the *Burgtheater*, and I opened to the description of the visit to the *Burgtheater* in *Indian Summer* for the purpose of quoting from it, I did not want to write my report, but to continue reading.

When I read Adalbert Stifter's prose in connection with Grillparzer, it was already difficult to remain with Grillparzer and not become engrossed in Stifter.

Adalbert Stifter's prose radiates extreme, blessed joy. When he praises *The Poor Musician*, humble and looking upward, the praise towers over its object, lifts the critic high above what he criticizes:

> ...To this external asset of noble form, which can truly be called a virtue in our time, is also added, however, as the animating spirit of the beautiful body, that which constitutes the artistic essence of a work, namely everything that

causes us to place the human soul higher than everything else of this earth, that causes us to appreciate the things, but to love the soul: Such a redolence of the life of a soul is poured out over seemingly very untoward, yes, almost contrary conditions, such that a noble emotion creeps into our hearts and at the end we experience the most soothing moral resolution and a rewarding lift.

Stifter about Grillparzer? Stifter about Stifter!
Before he could become acquainted with *The Poor Musician*, he himself had portrayed an almost identical motif, not in a carefully crafted novella, but in a sketch, not at the height of his creativity, but in year four of his literary existence...

Grillparzer:

...Until at last, five or six hours before nightfall, the individual horse-and-coach atoms condense into a compact line, which, impeding itself and being impeded by new arrivals from every side street, obviously contradicts the old proverb: It is better to ride badly than to walk. Gaped at, pitied, mocked, the decked-out ladies sit in the apparently motionless coaches. Unaccustomed to the continual stopping, the black Holstein horse rears up, as if he intended to proceed along the way that is blocked by the basket carriage in front of him, by crossing over the top of it, which the screaming women and children passengers of the plebeian vehicle apparently also seem to fear. Untrue to his nature for the first time, the rapidly dashing coachman furiously calculates the loss caused by having to spend three hours covering a distance that he otherwise covered in five minutes. Squabbling, yelling, reciprocal attacks against the honor of the coachmen, an occasional crack of the whip.

Stifter:

In the middle of this stream of human beings, like ships amid ice floes, the wagons move, usually slowly, often held up and standing completely still for too many minutes, often, however, when the line of wagons gets breathing space, flying next to each other like glistening phantoms past the more quietly strolling crowd of spectators. Towering here and there above the sea of pedestrians, moving back and forth past the row of wagons, the figures of riders bounce, and the most splendid houses along this street rise calmly from the pressing swarm of people on both sides, and their windows and balconies are occupied by countless spectators, who are there to watch the glistening stream flow past in front of their eyes and to enjoy the splendor and luster and glitter... One would think that everyone in the city had become silly at a quarter to four and was now strolling down this specific street in his or her obsession...

When the thirty-nine-year-old Adalbert Stifter wrote that, he did not yet consider himself to be a writer. To be sure, he had already published stories; the first two volumes of his *Studies* were just then coming out, but in that very year, 1844, he submitted an application for admission to the Widows and Orphans Pension Fund of Creative Artists, signed it "Adalbert Stifter, landscape painter," and wrote in it: "Recently the undersigned has made some small endeavors in writing literature, it is true, but he believes that this should be no hinderance to him, since another member of the laudable organization, Mr. Anton Ritter of Perger, is also known as a writer of renown."

He had reached his mid-thirties and had hardly written anything (like Ferdinand Raimund before him and Peter Altenberg long after him). He did not seriously consider practicing the writing profession at all; he devoted himself to literary endeavor on the side, as an amateur (as Raimund and Nestroy and Grillparzer devoted themselves to music). He was a landscape painter and occasionally sold pictures; he had studied law and natural science and lived primarily on his income as a private tutor. He wrote a little bit, just as he also played the violin and the clarinet and sang, but he had to be forced into a literary career.

During a visit to the home of the literarily active Baroness Mink, a roll of papers protruded from the jacket pocket of the thirty-five-year-old painter and tutor. The daughter of the baroness secretly pulled the roll from his pocket, read it, and cried out, "Mamma, Stifter is secretly a writer; a girl is flying in the air here!"

Then Stifter had to read the novella *The Condor* aloud. The baroness decided that the *Wiener Zeitschrift für Kunst, Literatur, Theater und Mode* would have to print it; the editor printed it and accompanied the payment of the honorarium with the note: "I shall rejoice with all my heart, if you will give me the opportunity to make similar payments very soon and very often."

Seven years later, Nagler's *Neues allgemeines Künstlerlexikon* [New General Encyclopedia of Artists] described Adalbert Stifter as a "Painter in Vienna, a still living artist. He devotes himself to genre painting and is also known as a writer of literature. His stories are of great value." At this time Stifter said of himself: "As a writer I am only an amateur, and who knows if I will make any progress in that field, but as a painter I will accomplish something."

In a statement of his artistic views, addressed to an editor in Augsburg and directed in very sharp words against Friedrich Hebbel, he observed: "Greatness never blows its own horn, it is simply there and has its effect. Usually greatness does not know that it is great, and thus the greatest artists of the world have the loveliest, most childlike naivete and are constantly humble before the ideal that always glows in front of them."

Because the artist Stifter so consciously described the unconsciousness of greatness, he could be accused of coquettishness and arranged, artificial naivete. And yet he acted against his own real destiny, and perhaps unconsciously for that very reason. For thirty-five of his sixty-three years, he ignored it and even banished it to the sidelines—and above all never perceived the true, the entire, the sacredly grand greatness within his writing.

For it is not so much in what is portrayed, however inspired it may be, not so much in what is conveyed, occasionally preached, however uplifting it may be, that the greatness of Adalbert Stifter's prose lies. Above all that lies the presentation in the language. God spoke: Let there be German! And there was German.

The German language is a very late language. German literature is a very late literature. The German language knows no generally compulsory high form that one can acquire by personal effort, that one can more or less approach. Good French, good English are present as a standard and are identical with themselves; despite any individual nuances, the currently better and best English and French will always resemble each other. Better German, best German are different from each other, come into being on the other side of a compulsory standard. Whoever writes masterfully in the German language also creates the language anew with his work. What was once said in a specific way in German is, for that very reason, no longer authentic. In lyric poetry and prose—word for word, line for line—the German language develops before our eyes. The greatness and the peril of all writing in the German language lie in this uniqueness. German literature is a late literature. Lessing wrote its first dramas a hundred years after Calderon, Corneille, Racine, Molière, a hundred and fifty years after Shakespeare. Goethe's *Werther* appeared and established what still remains the living narrative prose in the German language, when Swift was long dead and Sterne had just died, when French prose had already definitively attained its measure and form.

In the true sense of the word, Austria's prose does not begin until Adalbert Stifter. In Austria there had been much theater, much had been built, painting had experienced its peculiar, isolated heyday in the Danube School, but only music had transcended the bounds of the landscape and time to create in Austria its great, pure, highest values. With Adalbert Stifter, the first master of the language attains rank equal to that of the masters of music; in Adalbert Stifter's prose Austrian literature is created in the German language. And when we fit the dates of his life into the great lines, we see how close Stifter remains to the beginnings, and yet how close he already is to us. He was born only a good half century after Matthias Claudius, Gottfried August Bürger, and Goethe were born, thirty years after *Werther*, and died thirty-six years after Goethe, when August Strindberg was nineteen years old and Sigmund Freud and Oscar Wilde were twelve, six years before Karl Kraus was born, ten years before Georg Kaiser's birth, and fifteen years before Franz Kafka was born. He has not yet been dead for a hundred years; he did not begin writing until the fourth decade of his life—what we still preserve as living Austrian prose only began a hundred years ago. Its ancestor and greatest figure was the contemporary of the beginnings and the new authors, who called themselves "the moderns" and still have to pass the great test of transitoriness in our time. How short is the span of literature in the German language; how near they all are to each other and to us!

Beginning and climax simultaneously: Just as in Greek tragedy, as in symphonic music, as in cinematography a new form realized the extreme as it came into being and then never exceeded it, at best equalled it, so also in Adalbert Stifter Austrian prose shared in fulfillment as it has never done since. And in order not to endanger greatness by the consciousness of greatness, this prose had to come into being on the side, next to painting at first, next to the school office later, in a constantly active, but consciously private, unobtrusive, unsensational life. It had to disguise and hide itself and its greatness to the point that posterity completely overlooked it for almost half a century and only began to notice it from a great distance—in the upswing of an unprecedented return whose dates and extent mysteriously remind us of the Johann Nestroy renaissance, and whose limits can still not be measured.

But in order to make greatness possible through the renunciation of greatness, a great sacrifice also had to be made in this life that was withdrawn with dignity. A clear, distinct, almost systematically regular biography shows a blind spot, a dark point. Adalbert Stifter, born in 1805 in Oberplan in the southern Bohemian foreland of the Bohemian Forest, was hardly noteworthy as a child; yes, the project of having him study at the university almost failed because of his "lack of talent." But just as Schubert had learned it "from the Lord God," an early flash of endowment was already visible in Adalbert Stifter the child. Once he told his grandmother and another woman the story of Joseph in Egypt, and the woman cried out: "Ursula, I tell you, the Holy Ghost himself is speaking through the boy."

How infinitely meaningful was this landscape of his childhood! Every walk, every impression, every encounter was so secretly pregnant with his literary future. But how important it also was that this decisive period of his first thirteen years could be lived completely without reflection, and without regard to later literary production, that Stifter was no child prodigy. Later he often visited Oberplan and its environs, but he never lived there again. From the dispassionate distance of time and place he located a fullness, the emphasis of his works there: *The High Forest, The Village on the Heath, The Forest Walker, Granite, Mica, Abdias,* large portions of *Indian Summer* and *Witiko,* and in that respect it may be of significance that Oberplan is not, not yet, the forest, the Bohemian Forest, the mountain range, but lies on the outside, on the threshold, that even seen from the place of his first impressions, forest and mountains are not the immediate surroundings, but goal, mystery, something on the other side.

Then the great step across takes place: Adalbert Stifter travels to the Kremsmünster Abbey, where he will go to school for eight years. And in this journey a great deal is symbolically expressed and anticipated. From the foothills down onto the plain..., "where the Chapel of the Saints stands on the left and a stately mill on the right, the mountains parted, the descending valley ended, and the great spreading plain began. The brook flowed broadly toward the fields and trees, where not far away a silver glimpse of the Danube beckoned to him through the branches and awaited him: the wanderer turned right, walked into the bushes and out of them again on the white road that led out into the beautiful flat fields that were planted with autumn fruits, and which he had caught sight of from above as a fragrant woven ribbon. The firmament of the Alps stood before him again deep in the south—" (*The Forest Walker*).

The Danube waited for Adalbert Stifter. He climbs down to it from the borderland where the German and the Bohemian touch each other, where the arc of mountains continues north of the Danube to the Black Sea, down into the flat region that opens to the east, toward Vienna, where he will begin to write, away from Linz, where he will die on the bank of the Danube. And further south Kremsmünster lies in the foreland of the Alps, on the threshold once more, again at a fruitful distance, like that from Oberplan to the Bohemian Forest.

This "firmament of the Alps" returns as a leitmotif again and again in Stifter's portrayals. It is one of his great themes in ever-changing variations. In Kremsmünster, he writes, "my apartment was...such that when I opened my eyes in the morning, the whole chain of the Alps shimmered into my bed." A few years before his death he wrote of a recuperation stay in Kirchschlag: "From the roof tiles to the snowy mountains, the magnificent chain of the Alps lies in my windows and fills my soul with gentle majesty when I look at it."

In *The Village on the Heath*, "the distant mountains" draw "a pretty blue band around the dull-colored land."

In the prelude to *The High Forest* there appears the image: "The trace of the entire chain of the Alps draws around the sky like an airy fairy belt, until it goes out into soft, hardly visible veils of light in which white spots flicker, probably the distant features of the snowy peaks."

The valley in which Abdias builds his house has "a midday view that is wrapped in the blue which peeks in from the distant mountains."

In *The Confirmed Bachelor* the mountains float "like a blue wreath" behind the young man who is climbing down into the valley.

In *Depiction of a Young Fir Tree* one sees the Alps "hovering outside as distant and fabulous as pale blue, frozen clouds."

"Toward noon we see the friendly blue chain of the high mountains rambling away against the sky." (*Mica*)

And very early in *Witiko* as well, the great combination is there again: "At his feet he saw the great forests, he saw the Inn, the Isar, and the Danube, and on the edge, he saw the mountains and the Alps." And when Witiko later travels downstream on the Danube: "...he came eastward out into the flat land. There in the distance the mountains of the Alps were visible, as Witiko had glimpsed them from the forest of St. Thomas."

In Kremsmünster the young boarding-school student does write poems and even makes awkward attempts at being a storyteller, both, however, without any thought at all of serious work as a writer, no differently than a person who plays music at home or acts in plays with other amateurs. Learning to paint is more important to him here than anything else.

An experience of this period of study may have caused Stifter to realize for the first time that greatness can and should be unacquainted with itself. The students had a poetic assignment to turn in. Stifter had sat over his own work for almost an entire day. Then shortly before the beginning of class, a schoolmate asked him to write verses for him, for he himself had not managed to write any. In flying haste—it had to "be just very simple"— Stifter threw the lines down on paper within half an hour. And this time the professor gave the work of the less "prominent" pupil the first prize, for Stifter had "written a little too affectedly" for him. Thus the less conscious Stifter had triumphed over the carefully polishing one (and in so doing had made a noteworthy first contribution to the discussion of the unsolvable dispute between spontaneous first versions and polished late versions).

It is a moving thought that Franz Schubert could have seen Adalbert Stifter, just as it is strange anyway to trace the contacts of the great life lines. In 1827, in Graz, Schubert attended a Meyerbeer opera in which Nestroy played a role; Stifter saw Nestroy on the stage in Linz and probably also in Vienna, and while on a journey through Upper Austria in 1825, Schubert was in Kremsmünster while Stifter was studying there.

In 1826 Stifter comes to Vienna. Beethoven and Schubert are still alive, Raimund has just become a dramatic author, Nestroy is still an actor and singer in the provinces and far removed from any thought of dramatic production, Grillparzer is at the height of his productivity. But Stifter will not be discovered as "a secret writer" for fourteen years. After spending eleven years in Vienna he will marry Amalia Mohaupt, and one may suspect a connection between these two facts and time periods and posit here the blind spot, the dark point in his biography, the great renunciation of fulfillment.

While a student in Vienna, Stifter had loved Fanny Greipl, a girl in his distant home town. He had courted her, had been turned away by her wealthy parents, and had made several attempts to obtain employment in order to improve the chances for his acceptance. For example, he applied for a position as a professor of physics at the Royal and Imperial Lyceum in Prague. He even passed the written examination in the most brilliant fashion, but then did not appear for the oral examination.

We know this fact only from records that state that "Stifter, Adalbert, candidate for a teaching position from Vienna, among the best in the written examination, did not appear for the oral presentation." It is never mentioned or explained later. And very soon, almost simultaneously, he accompanies the beautiful Amalia Mohaupt home from a ball. She "had greatly aroused his interest during the ball." Afterward she misses her dancing shoes, which she had given to Mr. Stifter, and indeed the shoes are "in the side pocket of his coat, where he has forgotten them until now, and he will have the pleasure of personally returning them to their owner." A witness to the development writes that immediately after his estrangement from Fanny, Stifter "already had a very intimate relationship with Amalia, who clung to him like a bur. How this love came about, and how it developed and continued until they married, I must pass over with eternal silence, for the sake of the two of them as well as my own, *nam taedet mihi mentionis.*"

Later, when everything pertaining to Fanny was in the past, Stifter saw her again, and under the influence of that encounter he wrote her a unique, powerful letter: "...so, as it always seems to go in such cases, I sought in a new relationship the happiness that the old, first one had denied me, and pretended in the face of the feeling of abandonment: now you are loved and happy—oh, but I really was not happy. There is only one, a single love, and after that no other. It was wounded vanity—I wanted to show your family that I did know how to find a beautiful, well-to-do, and aristocratic woman—oh, and I almost broke my heart with the experiment. The closer to marriage I let it come with Amalia, the more restless and unhappy I became... In spite of my deliberate embitterment, you really always were the bride of my heart—you were really always the saint to whom my better inner self prayed"—"...for I did not love her, and if her kiss was to be pleasant to me, I had to imagine that it was your lips...so accept my love again—I offer it to you as a humble gift—and heal my melancholy with kind tenderness." That this plea could not be realized must have been clear to the letter writer, who anticipated that alternative: "If, however, you say that you do not love me, I am determined to endure it, no matter how much my heart aches, and I intend to make only you the bride of my ideas, and I shall continue to love you until the day of my death."

Is it an exaggeration to connect this "eternal bride" to the love situations of Nestroy, Lenau, and Grillparzer, to suspect that here, too, a person created the prerequisites for failure himself, or helped create them, that he more or less consciously entered a situation that separated heavenly and earthly love, in order to be inspired artistically by this conflict?

Stifter married Amalia (who, by the way, was certainly not well-to-do) on November 15, 1837, two years after that letter to Fanny. Fanny had already married the cameral secretary Josef Fleischhanderl from Upper Austria on October 18, 1836. As a result of complications during the delivery, she died on September 16, 1839 with her newborn son.

"Whoever practices art," we read in *Two Sisters*, "must almost be more than human, in order not to be defeated by it." The danger exists that he will be "inundated and destroyed" "by what he gives to others, by which he is more affected than they are."

In one of Stifter's letters we read: "...for where I cannot love, I do not like to live." The fact that he did not like to live made him a poet. Stifter did not love Amalia. And in the years after his marriage and Fanny's death, he practiced the art that destroys.

In his writings there are many references to pain that are addressed either directly or indirectly to his own situation:

"I do not give up pain, because then I would have to give up the divine."—"...through pain one proceeds to greater character."—"Pain, of course, is also sent from God...the dearest angel, who...makes the great, the pure, and the sublime more accessible to our heart than it would have been without it."—"Pain is a holy angel, and through it people have become greater than they have through all the pleasures of the world," it says in Stifter's letters. In *Two Sisters* the narrator says: "My experience teaches me that pain and what we call misfortune in everyday life are actually only an angel for the human being, indeed, the holiest angel, in that he warns the person, lifts him above himself, or shows and interprets for him treasures of the mind that would otherwise be eternally hidden in the depths." And in *Abdias* fate is portrayed at the beginning as "a cheerful flower chain." It "hangs through the infinity of space and sends its gleam into the hearts—the chain of causes and effects." The most beautiful of these flowers is reason...but is not pain, which moves in and out of the human heart, "itself a flower in that chain? Who can find that out?"

Where he cannot love, he does not like to live. He consciously enters the situation that causes him to become weary of life. And in those years he begins to write narrative prose.

In that prose he will report again and again how it came to pass that two lovers did not come together. He will transfigure and sanctify heavenly love, but pay little attention to earthly love, which he will neglect and not mention. Once the floodgates are open, he will produce in impetuously abundant measure, immediately attain maturity and soon the greatest mastery without any detours through the problems of the beginner. In the years from 1840 to 1842 he will present a series of stories that weigh as heavily as an entire life's work—at the age of thirty-five still not an author, at thirty-seven, as the author of *The Village on the Heath, The High Forest, Castle of Fools, My Great-Grandfather's Writing Case,* and *Abdias*, the greatest storyteller in the German language in his century.

The first novella, *The Condor*, is written in first-person form. The chronicler of the unrequited love of a painter for a proud girl is an old man.

In order to be able to exist where he does not like to live, Adalbert Stifter must transfigure his renunciation and justify it again and again. And to measure up to his creative greatness, he must not become conscious of it.

So he gives himself a new law, the "gentle law" that changes the dimensions and relationships.

"I consider the flow of the breeze, the rippling of the water, the growth of grain, the waves of the sea, the greening of the earth, the glow of the sky, the glittering of the stars to be great." He views lightning, the storm, the volcano, the earthquake as smaller, "because they are only the effects of much higher laws." Great is "the general whole," in it alone is "grandness" because it "alone is what preserves the world." And if an individual has perished for this gentle law that is proclaimed in the preface to *Colored Stones* and also referred to as the "law of right and morality" and the "law of justice and morality"—if an individual has perished for the sake of this law, we do not feel that he has been vanquished, "we feel that this underdog has triumphed; delight and a shout of joy are mixed with our sympathy because the whole is greater than the parts, because goodness is greater than death."

The great becomes small in order to be overcome, the small becomes great, in order to make existence conceivable. A new order is created, a new meaning is posited, an entire life is placed on the line in order to justify the sacrifice of that life in forms achieved again and again, and in order to integrate it into a higher order. The renunciation of love, the unpleasant marriage to an inferior woman must become part of a great order, so as to confirm that life. He must believe in that order, he must passionately create it himself to affirm it, he must take it from life and place it in his works, so that it can reflect from the works back into life. He must create the world according to the image that presents it filled with pain and renunciation, and must place that image in a paradisiacal light, using the gift of form and the benefit of legitimacy and the blessing of vividness, so that he can look at it himself and say that it is good.

At one point in the late work *Witiko* it is said of a past era that the nation "became acquainted with the sweetness of order." Stifter realizes that sweetness in his prose, through what he portrays as well as through the portrayal of it. He "had the courage and the strength to lead humanity from world history back into paradise." (August Sauer) In that, and not only that, he resembles his great countryman Franz Schubert.

In 1840 he began to publish, in 1844 he still called himself a painter, in 1850 he became a school superintendent. Thus literary endeavor was almost continuously pressed into the status of a part-time occupation, came into being under the sign of *nevertheless*. The fact that Stifter's greatness and uniqueness were not recognized is understandable, but, very much like Schubert, he was never completely unknown and unsuccessful. With his first publications he had succeeded in the best possible fashion; he was well-known, respected, controversial, and even a kind of fashionable author for a time. (1844: "Adalbert Stifter had the very good fortune to be spoken of by the correspondent of a widely read journal. And now look: since then Stifter's novellas have become fashionable articles that cause publishers to envy each other.") He was a misunderstood genius and actually still is, while at the same time being very well known through the writings of his early creative period, almost all too well known. He continued to paint with enthusiasm and passion until his death. If he had been only a painter, according to competent opinion he would still be seriously taken into account in nineteenth-century art.

He devotedly and faithfully applied himself to his position in the service of the educational system for about two decades, thoroughly creative even in that area, so that one could justifiably regard it as incomprehensible that Stifter's treatises on school policy have still not been appropriately appreciated, for they should have "caused a pedagogical revolution long ago." If the maxims that Stifter also recorded in *Indian Summer* had become more well known, according to an expert in our time, "the education of youth would probably have taken on a form different from that of contemporary practice."

Well-known and undiscovered, creatively active in three ways, open to his contemporaries, accessible to posterity, but mysteriously obscure—and yet his importance as an author is assured in deep levels of consciousness! In 1842, when only a few narrative works and still no books at all had been published by him, he described the total solar eclipse of July 8th in a newspaper article that is the equal of the greatest revelations in German prose. In it he said: "I always thought the old descriptions of solar eclipses were exaggerated, just as perhaps in a future time this one will be regarded as exaggerated." The limiting word "perhaps" betrays his knowledge of the lasting quality of his formulation of even this superficially almost journalistic piece.

In about that year, 1842, we can date the actual breakthrough of the poet Stifter's entire brilliant power, to the extent that with this portrayal of the elemental, the extraordinary phenomenon, as well as in the novellas *Castle of Fools* and *Abdias*, he presses forward for the first time to the limits of what can be said.

Up to then he had initially put his ordering activity to the test with lyrically romantic and idyllic efforts in a first conventional love story of *The Condor*, in the intricate, not really masterfully plotted rapture of the *Wild Flowers*, in a first calmly simple, lonely, well-rounded narrative, *The Village on the Heath*, and in the quietly renunciative glorification of nature, *The High Forest*, early attempts by Stifter to traverse the landscape of his soul and his language, rich in beauty, perfect in their fullness of individual success, but not yet rounded and whole; these first works reflect the world but are not yet the world.

The Condor and *Wild Flowers* are still painter novellas, and for that reason alone they are not completely generalized, are still parts and not wholes. We find a first great success in the magnificently economical love scene of *The Condor*:

> ...their lips melted together there, only an indefinite sound of the voice—and the most blissful moment of two people's lives had come and—was gone.
>
> ....
>
> "This moment," said the young man then, "is the most beautiful thing that God has sketched out for me in my life, but it now seems to me as though a great, long pain were standing behind the great happiness—Cornelia—how will I learn to forget this moment?"

And the first deep resignation at the end:

> ...and far, far from her...an unknown, strong, disdaining man wandered, searching for new heavens for his seething, creating, thirsting, still innocent heart.

"I actually do not hate any man on God's whole green earth," writes the narrator of the epistolary novella

Wild Flowers at the beginning of one of his letters, each of which is given a title in the name of a flower; and at the end of that letter it says: "I know only one thing, that I intend to love and protect all people...for this short existence, as much as it is humanly possible—I must do it so that only some, some part of the tremendous thing occurs to which this heart drives me."

If renunciation was formulated to a certain extent in his own cause in *The Condor*, Stifter here permits himself the dream fantasy of fulfilled love. And as if to call himself to order, a decade later he writes to an addressee in Germany, whom he invites to visit him in Linz, about "an outstanding, beloved wife" with the added comment "the Angela of the *Wild Flowers*," although the model for the idealistically brilliant girl Angela most certainly was not the dull, uninterested, uneducated Amalia, but probably a daughter of one of the numerous aristocratic Viennese families into whose homes Stifter was admitted as a private tutor.

Amid all the foolish rapture of the story, which at one point classifies itself as "romantic," a moment of love is once again a great high point that is perceived with tangibly profound emotion:

> ...but it was not beauty that had its effect just then; for I do not remember a single feature of her face, even when I torture all the nerves of my brain; only the one thing, the whole image lies upon them, as if burned into the mirror of my eyes, and if I close both of them, I always see it floating before me. I cannot say that I love her; for we love only what we know—and yet it is as if she had been my wife on another planet, unnumbered years ago.

Amid the conventional, the dependent, the acceptable and the successful aspects of conversation and portrayal, city and landscape, cheerfulness and reverie, amid much spirit and beauty and traces of future extraordinariness, there is in these *Wild Flowers*, immediately following the cited recognition of heavenly love, a great, although hardly noticeable word that is visibly inspired and summoned forth by it. The letter writer describes a night sitting at his desk by an open window: "The clock strikes twelve, there is no breeze, the spring night becomes ever quieter and warmer; more and more seldom the soft rolling of late carriages comes to my ear from many a dreaming street, and at the edge of my field of vision the first flashes of lightning thirst like fleeting kisses of midnight."

In the middle of what is only good or better, this one "thirst" brings a lightning flash of what Stifter's language will become.

And less elementary, but clearly noticeable if one is familiar with his later works, we very often sense amid the exuberance the message of gentle stillness, of regulating strength, when, for example, we read: "...in the small room the gentle light flowed and sketched the quiet window cross on the floor."

Then, in *The Village on the Heath*, renunciation again, now already on a higher plane, integrated into the great continuance of nature, more concise, simpler, more Biblical, radiating gently, and very orderly.

With "And so, dear reader, farewell!!!" the *Wild Flowers* had ended; and *The Village on the Heath* also begins with a personal address to "the dear reader and listener." Felix, the "black-eyed boy of ten or twelve years" is still "our little friend." But the wild flowers have now risen from the chapter headings in the earth.

And when Felix leaves the world and returns to his origins at the end, externally he has failed, but simultaneously with the irrevocability of his private renunciation comes the desired rain, and it saves the village from destruction. With the inhabitants of the village, Felix lets the wetness of the gently trickling continuous rain "sink through his clothes. He went along and gave thanks with them, and nobody knew what his soft, quiet eyes hid."

For the first time, in this portrayal of the drought, the natural occurrence has entered Stifter's works, "...ever more beautiful days came and more beautiful ones than that," and because greatness is not great, this beauty is destructive, catastrophe threatens—"It was the severest time"—and with the loss of his private happiness, the man who has returned home pays the price for the salvation of his home town through something that is gentle and seems great to him.

From the beginning, the story is governed by the principle of order, the certainty of justice. This assurance includes every futility, every self-sacrifice, even reaches past the collapse of wishes and hopes with the knowledge of meaning: "God, of course, always makes amends for everything, everything, and it will also be good where he sends pain and self-denial."

In *The High Forest* he steps back into the past. There, from the perspective of Stifter's present day, the "gentle reader" is presented with a landscape of the kind that the author, who hides behind the "we," knows from his own experience, an image "like the one that we ourselves carry in our hearts since the time when we were permitted to stroll there and dream a portion of that double dream that heaven gives to every human being once, and usually combined, the dream of youth and that of the first love." Stifter is still not completely free of oppressive personal experience; he still must call himself expressly to order, before he establishes order. But in this story from the time of the Thirty Years' War, which was incorrectly viewed as the high point and chief attraction of his creative work by his contemporaries and many later generations, only the last step toward maturity is realized, not maturity itself. From distant Vienna the author sees his home region. He calls its towns by name, but he places them at a greater, a temporal distance, which he not only contrasts with the present in the beginning, but also emphasizes as the situation develops. ("The house was made of wood, as one can still see them in those regions today."—The tower "had no roof, and its ring walls had no gates, just as it still stands today.") Here the narrator wants to soften—without purposely aiming to do so, of course—the present, his present, from the perspective of the past, by placing the immutability of nature above the human element and transposing the transitoriness of the passions from the past into the present in a comforting manner. A love was unfulfilled, a castle destroyed, but we can portray these things in calm, self-contained beauty—thus, from the perspective of greater distance, our own troubles and futilities become ornaments in the beautiful tapestry of the ages.

Here, too, there is already a great degree of linguistic brilliance: the "little spruce tree that seeks to begin its green life high up in the dark blue of the forest's edge"—"An enormity of loveliness and seriousness floated and moved above the resting, twilight-blue masses." And yet in all the bliss of nature there are still traces of convention, a weakness and carelessness with respect to plot and historicity to which Stifter himself confessed in later years: "With *The High Forest*, as a careless individual I hurriedly wrote the story and then stuffed it into the drawers of my imagination. Now I am almost ashamed of that childish behavior."

But now Stifter has established his own standard. Now it is time that the extraordinary becomes part of his work. It overpowers him almost tangibly in the middle of the story *Castle of Fools*, which again places the past and a castle in a contemporary frame: in pleasant rural cheerfulness and a touchingly straightforward love-and-inheritance story. It has already gone far in its development, with nature and history and all kinds of mystery, when it erupts forth from an old document that the hero reads, no less powerful than all the tempests and fire, water, snow, hail, storm, and war miseries in Adalbert Stifter's entire works: "What I write here is not I—I cannot write me, but only what it did through me." And then an outcry of the self against existence:

> ...what are pictures, what are monuments, what is the story, what are the clothing and the dwelling of the departed—when the self is gone, the sweet, lovely miracle that does not come again?! Help destroy the blade of grass on which his foot trod, help the wind cover the sandy trail where he walked, and help transform the threshold where he sat, so that the world will be virginal again and not tarnished by the dragging afterlife of a dead man. You could not save his heart, and what he left behind was desecrated by the indifference of those who were coming...
>
> ...do not be surprised at this, my pain, because all that I wrote on the many pages above was so cheerful and pleasant; do not be amazed: For I go to meet the angel of my most difficult deed...

Here is the new language and the new dimension; here Adalbert Stifter's self-realization is complete. Here —thirty-six years after Stifter's birth and thirty-five years after Austria's birth through Emperor Franz's renunciation of the title of "Roman Emperor"—here, in the year one of Adalbert Stifter's literary career, Austrian literature begins in a high point of German prose that has hardly ever been attained again and was surpassed only by Stifter himself.

The substance is now insignificant; it will remain so from now on. The substance is nothing, the medium is everything: the language. In a higher sense Stifter's art is art without a subject, because the utterance stands above what is uttered. ("That is why even the substance is so unimportant, if only the individual is able to display his own great inner world by means of it; and that is why it is especially poverty of the inner world that seeks out the greatest possible material and is then cast down by the material every time: for it never knows what the material demands. The great artist trembles in the face of great material..."—he flees from greatness— "...because he gives up hope of attaining its greatness." From a Stifter letter of January 15, 1865.)

Stifter's greatness simply consists of the fact that from this moment on he can display "his great inner world" in the medium of language. And it is specifically in this first overpowering of the mastery of his initial productive years that he repeatedly places the human being in contact with what is greatest, the elements:

Then the description of the solar eclipse comes about: "...it was the moment when God spoke and men listened."

And in the *Castle of Fools* there is the cosmic vision: "...then everything rolls onward—to where? We do not know that. Millions of millions have cooperated to make it roll, but they are wiped out and exterminated, and new millions will cooperate and be wiped out."

Then the powerful *Walk through the Catacombs* of St. Stephen's Cathedral takes place, with its significant introduction that denies all progress, and its finale in the face of the great futility: "They all struggled, acquired, consumed, worked, rose, performed deeds; the thousand arms moved daily, their spirits thought, their hearts glowed with wish and desire or in satisfaction and triumph; their passions boiled and cooled down—now everything is over, and a page of history is all that remains of the mountain of works from their lives, and even that page, with the rolling of the centuries, shrinks to a line, until that, too, finally disappears, and the time no longer exists that seemed to be so tremendous and so uniquely magnificent to those who lived in it."

And then in *Abdias* the unity becomes perfect. The times and places unite, in that Biblical and homeland elements, Orient and Bohemian Forest are encompassed in one grand frame, in that the remote is drawn into the immediate vicinity. As soon as the minuteness and insignificance of the individual's fate has become clear, when compared with history and nature, then that small fate can be portrayed with almost divine love; its happiness and its pain, its yes and its no, its enjoyment and its renunciation, its nonsense and its sense can become one and can have meaning. The order of magnitude is established, and order and greatness now live in what is small. ("God does not have the words *great* and *small*; for him there is only what is right." 1853.)

In the novella *Abdias* this unity is attained, greatness is achieved, greatness that does not recognize itself and wants to be regarded as simplicity, greatness that stands in its own shadow, that bestows peace and legitimacy even upon confusion and the chaotic through the grace of inspired portrayal; its goal: "to portray the immeasurable in the moderate." (Fritz Novotny)

Like Raimund, Nestroy, and Grillparzer, Stifter also feels the Austrian "The world won't last much longer in any case," but he draws other conclusions from it. He does not help it happen by acknowledging the prognosis; he negates it in his own sphere of activity, by acting as if the world were in order and thereby at least helping to delay the end of the world.

The simplicity of other authors is usually inability with respect to complication and differentiation or the negation of complication and differentiation; Stifter's simplicity is the subduing of complication and does not exclude differentiation. Stifter's light is not negation but the subduing of darkness. Unlike almost all other great men, he does not say *no* to the world; he says *no* to the world inside him, and for that reason says a powerful *yes* to the world. He does not wait until the crowning conclusion of his works to work his way through to acceptance or reconciliation, as the finales and conclusions of acts written by others do before the harmonious end. He is a painter; through narration he can also create pictures that radiate that great harmony as complete units. From the beginning they are characterized by his two favorite concepts: *appropriate* and *harmonious*. He includes chaos in his order by calling it by name. From the beginning, his symphony of fate is in the key of C major. For him, the great struggle and effort are not the work of art's object, but its prerequisite.

In order to fulfill his new, definitive dimension, he must step back, develop objectivity, approach himself anew. Thus *Abdias* begins far away from the world of previous locations that were familiar to him, his Bohemian home, the Alpine landscape, the city of Vienna, in fabulous, unknown, Oriental remoteness, as far away as the "new heavens" are for the "creating, thirsting, still innocent heart" of the hero of *The Condor*.

And no act of narration or identifiable "I" now provides for the relationship between the author and his material. Abdias is not Stifter, or only to the extent that he is Job and that every human being is Job. Abdias is the human being as sufferer, as innocently guilty party; his story is acceptance, it begins in the desert and ends where Stifter's story began. It draws the generality of tragic subjection to the power of circumstances from the timeless distance of North Africa into the familiar vicinity of the Bohemian Forest landscape. It prophetically anticipates Stifter's own fate by denying a man fulfillment in marriage and robbing him of his daughter. Stifter, who was denied the children that he longed for, loved and was very attached to his foster daughter, whose death irreparably wounded him. And again, as in *The Village on the Heath*, nature is there with its double face—a thunderstorm gives the child her sight, a thunderstorm kills the child, but the storm "that had kissed life away from the child's head with its soft flame, had still poured down rich blessings that day on all the meadows, and, like the one that had given her sight to her, it had ended with a beautiful rainbow across the broad morning."

And as the rainbow expresses in beauty the peace between creator and creation, as the elemental event brings destruction and blessing, in Adalbert Stifter the elementary miracle of creative language now binds the things in the world, gives form to what can be said, and touches on what cannot be said.

To be sure, the infinite, mysterious magic, the almost supernatural light, the breathing, blossoming beauty, the harmony that provides happiness and purification in Adalbert Stifter's prose is the message of a great mind and of high art, but its greatest and highest element is taken into and from the language. The German language, incomparably mastered in many lyrical documents and in Goethe's great collected works, is created anew in Stifter's prose, no: it is created, it creates itself, and as is the case with Keller and Gotthelf, who also forge ahead from the periphery to the essence, the overcoming of specific idiomatic obstacles becomes fruitful in the process.

In no way does Stifter deny his linguistic origins; he proceeds from them and remains faithful to them. The Austrian element is a substantial color in his comprehensive spectrum of language. In his works we read that the disc of the moon was "*ober*" [over] instead of "*über*" [over] the desert, that someone reaches around with his hand "as if he were seeking Johanna's hers" [*sic*], we find not only the Austrian term *verkühlen* in place of *erkälten* [to catch cold], but also Austrian dialect forms for the plurals of *day* and *carriage*. A person says "I think on you," the light comes in "by" the windows, one has "a joy" to see somebody, something is left "*über*" [over] instead of *übrig* [over]...and this is not felt to be a mistake, a wrongness, a weakness, but a necessary evidence of the earthly in what is otherwise hardly imaginable perfection.

Stifter literature inexplicably shows little interest in the language as the great ordering power of thought and formulation in Adalbert Stifter's narrative prose, essays, and letters. If Nestroy was "linguistically wanton" in Karl Kraus's formulation, Stifter, in his relationship to language, succeeded in presenting what was denied him as a creature: high, sacred, mutual marital love.

What an unsuspected, new power there is in the auxiliary verb here; and how grand and dignified and autonomously creative the usage of the verb *to be* is: "...an inviting twilight is everywhere among the tree trunks..."—"...rays of sunlight played into the room, so that sprinkled shadows were on the carpets..."—"There were vineyard, flowers, and dwarf fruit trees."—"Where very long days were..."—"Among the tree trunks is ample rank undergrowth."—"One afternoon, when there had again been strawberries for a long time..."—"Owing to the fact that in the library nothing happened, other than that the books were there..."

In this last example, the power of the auxiliary verb in Stifter's works is especially distinct; existence and event are made equivalent; the only thing that "happens" in the room consists in the fact that books "are" there; existence is activated, becomes event, becomes "being there," which, especially in connection with the library, becomes very impressive, as does later the passage of the same novel, *Indian Summer*, in which the narrator, who puts down a book, describes it this way: "I placed the words of Homer on the table." Being is event, word is work.

The word *werden* [will, shall, but also independently: to become, arise] is also often elevated above its accustomed function as an auxiliary: "When the people of the forest had arrived where their enemies were, a battle arose." And the neutral, faceless word *thing*, as well as the well-worn, otherwise hardly weighty word *sehr* [very, greatly, very much]—in Stifter's works they are filled with aspect, weight, and power: "The night, a thing foreign to man ..."—"At that time I thought that grain was also one of those inconspicuous, enduring things of this life, like the air."—"The roses flourished greatly."

Contrary to all practice, the participle is also granted great, almost Latin power here: "Even the juniper pressed closer to this place, spreading itself out..."—"... we arrived in Nussdorf while the sun was still shining ..."—"there stood...a human figure, casting itself up against the glittering water of the lake." Where calmness and passivity are to be expressed, we note that in Stifter's presentation action is portrayed. The figure, although standing, "casts itself up" against the lake. In another instance, in the same, magnificent *Confirmed Bachelor*, an area is described that "lay out across soft hills, generous and beneficent," the moon "lays panels of light on the floors," and where we are already looking at *lie* and *lay*, we also read of people "in whose hands lay the entire situation of that part of the world," we read: "The mountains...became darker and darker and laid threatening, dark, and splintered spots on the lake..."—and from now on we would like to read nothing but the prose works of Adalbert Stifter again and again, for the sake of the word and the fate of the word, and from so doing we would gain the greatest, blissful enlightenment.

Everything is unique here in a double sense: unique in the dimension of artistic expression, but also unique in that any true act of linguistic creation cannot be repeated, is unprecedented, was never there before, and can never be there again. For, what Stifter forms and coins here in his greatness, a greatness that does not know itself, was never said before, is not learned, but experienced, has no model—as it can only occur in German. Flashes of lightning have never "thirsted," they will never thirst again; excepting in Stifter's works, one could never speak of the "inconspicuous, enduring things of this life." German cannot be learned through any course for speakers of foreign languages or hardly even as a native language, for where, if not from God, could one get formulations like: "I saw...that a dense inhabitation conferred something cheerful upon the area"? A student of German will search in vain in the dictionary for the right foreign word for *erteilen*, and will not find *dahinliegen* there at all.

But he who repeats what he has seen here, he who would employ Stifter's somnambulant finds a second time, incorporate them into the linguistic heritage, makes a fool of himself. Anybody following Beethoven, who composes like Beethoven, is an inferior imitator; anyone who builds Gothic cathedrals in the nineteenth century is a commercial artist. The authentic work, and more than any other the German literary work, only lives in itself, as an image, not as a model, should be seen, felt, and admired, but withdraws from emulation.

Thus, especially in works of art in the German language, it is moving for the feeling individual to encounter each great word and sentence and each great figure, because he or she knows that this perfection is specifically found here and only here. Only in the second piece, *Brigitte*, does "the fiery flow of wine sleep and the glistening sight of the metal grow dark, dimmed by the earth." Only in *The Confirmed Bachelor* is the valley in which the foster mother of the hero lives called a "mother valley" in analogy to the fatherland and the city of one's fathers, and even in the same story it is not called the same thing again, but "the maternal valley." Only in *Indian Summer* is the depth so deep that from afar the narrator portrays a place in which "a deep part of my essence dwells." Only in *My Great-Grandfather's Writing Case* does a girl approach of whom the narrator says: "...she carried her pure face toward my eyes," only there does spring consist of the fact that "the warmth confided itself anew in a very lovely way." And only in the still underestimated epic *Witiko* could the mighty, unstoppable nature of an advance in battle become words in such uniquely majestic fashion:

> Witiko's men did not make a sound. Then the horns of the billy goats sounded the one long tone of battle. The men lowered their pikes to a horizontal position and moved forward. They pressed the ground with their heavy boots as they had done on Mt. Wysoka. Arrows and bolts flew toward them. They moved forward. The encounter with the enemy occurred. They moved forward more slowly. Shield and sword and lance and spear and hammer and club were used against them. They moved forward. The green and white and red and blue emblem, the emblem with the feathers and the ribbons, the white banner of the men of Plan with the dark red wild rose, all moved steadily forward, and the large rose-red silk banner was with them. The troops of Rowno and the others moved forward. The riders encountered the enemy, and Sigfrid von Milnet was visible on the white horse of old Peter Roder. The archers shot arrows and bolts the way they shoot the same things at lynxes and martens. The enemies raised a greater cry than before; the men of the forest did not answer; the long tone of the battle rang out. Then, when it became quieter, the blacksmith of Plan raised his

voice, and shouted so loudly that everything else was drowned out: "We're winning."

"We're winning!" the men shouted with loud voices.

Then it was quiet again. The enemies retreated more rapidly; the warriors of the forest moved forward more rapidly, and then the order of the enemies dissolved. They scattered in flight and an open space appeared before the warriors of the forest. The latter fell to their knees.

Then it is often as if the writer is overcome while writing and carried away to the most extreme tenderness in his words; the fact that he is touched in that way is expressed in the wealth of adjectives in which the term for a lovingly observed object is wrapped, for example, horses: "...she loved the beautiful, slender, and magnificent animals that were so amusing and youthful and innocent and obedient," or the water that repeatedly has almost ritual importance in Stifter's works: "His uncle had not offered him any of the wines—Victor also loathed even the wine, but poured for himself some of the water that the same old woman who waited on them replenished every few minutes in a transparently beautiful decanter, and recognized that he had never before drunk such an excellent, fresh, stout, and strong water."

A schoolmaster would probably criticize "transparently beautiful" as a mistake in a German essay. He would certainly mark "but" wrong, which is employed irregularly here, since *to pour* is not the opposite of *to loathe*, and since the correct formulation would have to be: "...loathed the wine and..." or "...poured himself no wine, but water." And yet: What a magnificent sentence this is, simply because of the pregnantly exciting, surprising, unique, unprecedented "but"! One of Stifter's mistakes is worth more than an entire library of the most renowned German prose.

In his passion for the word, in his eagerness to express himself, Stifter was genuinely obsessed. In Hallstatt, where Stifter obtained the idea for *Quartz*, a friend observed his encounter with the landscape: "I still see him before me, as he suddenly stopped in front of the well-known, beautiful rock formation behind the mill in the ash grove and then began to sketch and paint it with words, and continued with this work of speaking until a very lovely sketch lay completed in the writing case of his memory."

The fact that he first became and above all considered himself to be a painter, can be seen as extremely essential and meaningful for his writing, for that is how he developed the technique of sketching and, more important, the ability to let the work arise in its entirety and yet permit a shared tranquility to prevail in all movement and development.

An initial ring of seven years encompasses the bulk of the stories. When the year 1848 begins, four of the six volumes of the *Studies* have appeared. *The Forest Walker* and the first version of *Quartz* have been published; with respect to stories, what will follow later is meager in comparison to what has already been written. In those first seven years (from the middle of his thirties into the beginning of his forties), the novella writer Stifter achieved and demonstrated perfection repeatedly. In those years of his early marriage and the beginning of his career, he was very poor and lived in wretched conditions. His wife was frequently ill; he had to continue to earn money by giving lessons; need and necessity may have been decisive factors that contributed to the astonishing abundance of his creations (he also continued to paint diligently). He himself was—how could it be otherwise?—not satisfied with himself. He tormented editors and his publisher with excessive polishing and correction and late delivery. He strove for perfection.

In *Indian Summer*, he gave voice to a realization that had already been similarly formulated by Goethe and was later picked up by Hofmannsthal ("And yet it has... become completely clear to me, that Goethe's strictest of perceptions is true, and that an imperfect work of art is nothing; that in a higher sense only the perfect works of art, those rare products of genius, exist." "The Poet and This Time").—"What is true for a living human being," it says in *Indian Summer*, "is not true for a work of art in which all parts must be equally beautiful, so that none of them are conspicuous; otherwise, as a work of art it is impure, and in the strictest sense it is not art." Both Goethe and Stifter are mistaken here. They themselves, but few other lyrical works in the German language other than theirs, some painters, draftsmen, sculptors, and architects, and many composers, but no dramatic, no narrative works in the German language fulfill the ideal demand—or fulfill it only to the extent that perfection includes all imperfections, as, for example, an apparent mistake is not one because it appears in a work by Stifter (like an impure rhyme in a work by Goethe). When Stifter and grammar or stylistics contradict one another, grammar and stylistics are wrong.

For, with respect to the highest authority, from which there is no appeal, again and again it is a matter of who says something and not what is said. "The days had grown much longer, the sun was already shining very warmly..." can be written by anyone, could be found in a school composition, a private letter, a pulp novel, but that is not important, for from the trite and the arbitrary, the context itself makes something great that presents itself, when Stifter writes it, simply as the introduction to a sentence that only he could write: "The days had grown much longer, the sun was already shining very warmly, the periods of time in which the sky appeared clear and cloudless became longer than those in which it was cloudy or foggy; the earth yielded sprouts, the trees budded, diligent effort was expended on the rose tree in front of the house, everything was cheerful, and spring had come in all its fullness."

Neither "the sun was already shining warmly," nor "Farewell!" or "I love you" is good or bad in itself, genuine or in bad taste; it depends on whether a tenor or Thoas, king of the Taurians, says: "Farewell," whether the star of an operetta or a girl in one of Stifter's works says: "I love you."

In Stifter's narrative works, love in particular is always especially important, and, with very few exceptions, it is almost always placed in a nearly holy and hallowing light of absolute purity. It seems that with all of his portrayals of loving couples, again and again the writer mentally carries out his engagement and wedding to Fanny, the bride of his ideas. There everything always proceeds quite harmoniously, in a straight line, and is peacefully happy. There the order denied by reality is immortalized in a lasting, exalted form, and the great concept *eternal* also immediately and constantly stands as a quite ernest and undoubted blessing over every serious decisive conversation.

"How I would have loved a beloved woman and adorned her with the beauties that God amassed so abundantly in his world, and that are mirrored in art...,"

Stifter wrote to a friend in June 1836, after he had already belonged to Amalia for a long time. He transplanted the beauties from the world into art and reserved the reflection for his great dream.

He repeatedly caused things to happen in words, things that he had not been able to experience, "the feeling through which the creator holds his human beings," "the feeling that God made so beautiful only in man, his rational friend," "that incomprehensible feeling through which the creator binds the two sexes so that they serve his purposes happily," "the sweet inclination of the two sexes"—

> "...just know this one thing: that I love you more than anything in this world, and that I will love you for all eternity..."

> "...and gladly, gladly give you my heart, and I intend to love you for as long as I live." She paused for a moment; then, however, as if illuminated, she added the words: "I had to say it, because it is so, and because you asked; but now that it has been said, you can depend on it forever."

> I placed my arm on her shoulder and said, "Susanna! For eternity."
> "For eternity," she answered.

> "...and we will live like a brother and a sister who love each other more than anything, anything, whatever this world can bear, and who will remain faithful to each other forever and ever."

"Forever and ever," she said as she quickly grasped the hands that I held out to her.

"Eternally for you alone," I said.
"Eternally for you alone," she said.

I held my hand out to her and said, "Forever, Mathilde."
"Forever," she answered, as she grasped my hand.

"Mathilde, yours forever and eternally, only yours alone, and only yours, only yours alone."
"Oh, eternally yours, eternally, eternally, Gustav, yours, only yours, and only yours alone!"

"So, will you follow me into the house?" Witiko asked.
"I shall follow you into the house," responded Bertha.
"And will you wait there until you die?" asked Witiko.
"I shall wait until I die," Bertha answered.

As the year 1848 begins, Stifter's private, disorganized life is finally and unambiguously organized in words. But now a new disorder sets in, one that deeply upsets the moderation and balance that he has attained: the revolution.

Stifter joyfully and expectantly welcomed the new order that seemed imminent in March 1848. He did not withdraw from his democratic duties, but let himself be nominated as a delegate for his district. He recognized the demands of the day as a high responsibility; in this and the following years he published an abundance of political and pedagogical essays. He willingly accepted the position in the school system, in order to serve the state. But he was almost shattered by the reality of 1848. "Tears of joy glistened in his eyes"—in March 1848—"I shall never forget that radiantly happy expression of a deeply enthusiastic man who had been liberated from a nightmare. We both walked on the embankment. The crowd cheered... Stifter looked excitedly and intoxicatedly at this bustling activity. But hardly had the friends reached secluded streets when a serious mood overcame Stifter... 'The structure is torn down,' he said. 'Who will clean away the rubble now, and where are the men who have the strength and the calling to produce the new structure?'" In May of 1848 he wrote from Linz: "It is a distressing phenomenon that so many who coveted freedom are now themselves assailed by despotic appetites... May Europe soon become firm and orderly in its partially newly won, partially long existing freedom. Otherwise, with the appearance of so many immeasurable forces, we move toward a dismal future..." And in March 1849: "This has been a terrible year!... I once said to Zedlitz: If a movement should break out one day, then may God protect us from the journalists and the professors... Last summer I suffered inexpressibly because of so much that was bad, insolent, inhuman, and stupid, which became brazen and pretended to be extremely great. Whatever was great, good, beautiful, and reasonable in me became indignant. Even death is sweeter than a life like that, where morality, sanctity, art, and divinity are nothing any longer, and every mire and every brutality believes it has a right to break forth because there is freedom now... Illness would have been a comfort in comparison with this spiritual suffering." And in September of 1849: "If I could describe for you only a tenth of what I have suffered since March 1848... When stupidity and hollow enthusiasm, then depravity and emptiness, and finally even crime spread and took possession of the world, it almost literally broke my heart..."

And years later, in a description in a letter we read: "...[I] loved people in general, was (at least until 1848) cheerful like the peoples of antiquity."

The reality of the revolution, the hard actuality of world history had to wound Stifter deeply, even if, especially if he dreamed of a change in things. For reality, of course, robbed him of his dream. In Austria realities always have an especially difficult time. Grillparzer also favored the revolution and hardly recovered from the shock of its actuality. "Only our thoughts are true," and for that reason what is externally true has to confuse our thoughts. Stifter, too, like Grillparzer, places thought above everything—the fantasies that "appear in such sweet form" that "one has the superstition that on paper they will also be that lovely and free." If what is written is already "so cold, empty, and awkward compared to thought," how severely the real must clash with what is imagined!

All eminent Austrians were shocked by the events of 1848, even if they had previously longed for a change—only Bauernfeld remained on the side of the revolutionaries. But even Nestroy had known: "...so many ideas are like that: When they are born, they develop miserably." As a satirist and critic, he was predestined to be a partisan in the cause of freedom, but he reacted like Grillparzer and Stifter. "Nestroy knows where there is danger. He already hears the ravens of freedom that are black from printer's ink... And instead of reproaching religion for the preachers he prefers to reproach the enlightenment for the journalists and progress for the popular scientists." (Karl Kraus)

Called to suffer and fail and renounce greatness, the Austrian prefers to become the victim of a hostile rather than a friendly trend, or subject to a hated rather than a desired one. But either way he is destined for defeat; he wants to dream his dreams and must therefore exclude any form of fulfillment.

As a school official, Stifter had the opportunity to make a new, great sacrifice. Even his life in the service of pedagogy was one of renunciation and unfulfillment. For, the gloomy reactionary tendencies that powerfully emerged anew in the 1850s strangled all of his promising plans and formulations for the renewal of the educational system.

First a new cycle of seven years almost passed without important narrative accomplishments. The change of locality (the move from Vienna to Linz), his politically caused depression, activity in his work, his manifold journalistic and essayistic production—all these things caused what had gone on before to appear finished and past, to be a first stage that he had transcended. To be sure, for the rest of his life he will continue to write new stories and revise, add to, and collect old ones—but one that at first promised to become not much different from the others now expands and gains substance. Previously novels had often been planned; now, developed from a novella that had originally had the working title *The Old Steward* and then *The Old Bird Lover*, appearing for the first time in writings of the year 1848, something that was conceived as an addition to the collection *Colored Stones*, "the book that I would like to call *Indian Sum-*

mer," comes into being. On June 9, 1853 Stifter wrote that he was "almost finished already," but the conclusion of the first volume was not sent to the publisher until February 29, 1856, and then on September 12, 1857, after having worked with the material for almost ten years, Stifter reported to his publisher: "Today, at twelve o'clock I wrote down the last word of *Indian Summer*."

In contrast to everything that he had previously written, Stifter was satisfied with this work: "...you see, I am pleased with the book in the proofs, which has never happened to me before."

Even more than all other stories by Stifter, *Indian Summer* transcends the external story substance, is, so to speak, dematerialized narrative literature. In every respect, one can use passages from *Indian Summer* itself to characterize and praise this most beautiful and sublime novel, for example: "There is also a uniformity that is so sublime that it seizes the entire soul as fullness and encompasses the universe as simplicity," or the discovery that music, painting, sculpture, and architecture are bound to the same substance, "they must more or less struggle with this substance; only literature has almost no substance any longer, its substance is the thought in its broadest meaning; the word is not the substance, it is only the bearer of the thought, as, for example, the air carries the sound to our ear. Literary art is therefore the purest and highest of the arts."

It was always Stifter's longing to free himself from the material, from the compulsion toward action and its composition. In *Colored Stones* he tells a story "in which nothing unusual occurs, and yet that I could not forget." He creates a new version of the novella about the two sisters, which, as Franz Glück notes, destroys the actual theme, resolves tensions formulated earlier, nullifies the meaning of the plot that is defined by the action, and requires the writing of a new introduction noting that "not a simple story" is presented here, "but even less...namely, the condition of a family."

This revision falls in the period of the preparatory studies for *Indian Summer*, which raises the abandonment of the active, the occurring, the event to the level of the sublime, certainly within the mysterious context of generally Austrian timidity and skepticism with respect to all actuality, and the Austrian contempt for the event and its subdual in word, in thought, in dream, and in play. And here we also find again the great parallel to Franz Schubert. Just as they reproached Stifter for his lack of action, they criticized Schubert's inadequate "expositions" and did not notice that for both of them the apparent lack means the attainment of higher, highest, lonely accomplishment. Goethe's and Stifter's demand for perfection is met here; differently than in *Faust* or in the works of Shakespeare, which are "nevertheless" great and heavily burdened with imperfections. Unlike what we find in Austrian works in general, which achieve greatness by way of detours, as in many of Goethe's verses and many of Schubert's musical works, "the sweetness of order" is very immediately alive here.

In *The High Forest* we read of an old man; the author compares him with a ruin, "now only still illuminated by the gentle evening sun of goodness, like a silent Indian summer after heavy, noisy thunderstorms." Later in *The High Forest* we find the sun of Indian summer, " so pure, so warm and inviting, that his heart yielded itself faithfully," and the "peacefully quiet splendor" with which the Indian summer had come over the forests.

In the novel *Indian Summer* the first occurrence of the great key words is quite casual and inconspicuous, but not without meaning, when the bird lover portrays the life of the birds and following the "period of work, like ours during the adult years," concludes with the words: "Toward autumn there is a time of greater freedom again. Then they have, as it were, an Indian summer and play for a while before they leave." This occurs at the beginning of the many hundred pages, and only shortly before the end does the concept return in three important places. Looking back on his life, the baron says of his unfulfilled love for Mathilde: "So we experienced in happiness and constancy what was more or less an Indian summer without a summer preceding it." Then it says that the baron wants to continue to manage his house in the same way until his death so that he, as he says, "can enjoy his Indian summer to its end." And the father of the hero and narrator intends to do like the baron and "also have an Indian summer as he did."

Not autumn and not farewell, but the decline of the mature years, the most intensive fullness of existence glows from the work that Stifter writes around the fiftieth year of his life. It conveys tension of a peculiar kind. For, every individual scene, every turn of events, every observation could stand in another masterful novel entirely as it is, as an introduction to the incidents and entanglements that otherwise appear in all other narrative prose and through the development and resolution of which narrative literature finds realization, or as a resting point between them. The reader, without finding personal justification for it, inwardly waits for the harmony that is spread out before him to be—as in every novel—disturbed, interrupted, shaken, for "it to become exciting," but he waits in vain, and this tension before and above and beyond all the usual tension is no less intensive and is more sublime than any other.

From beginning to end, *Indian Summer* is verbalized peace before the storm that is banned from the events; it is order that does not have to be restored at the end because it was indestructible and undisturbed from the beginning. The dismal and evil and hostile things are not glossed over nor denied, but they are not permitted to enter the portrayed world. Twice they are touched by a sidelong glance. We read: "An indolent conservator, deceitful business friends who made questionable demands, and an unfortunate court case that arose as a result created for our mother a situation in which she had to struggle with worries about our future." And in another place—especially important for the understanding of Stifter—marriage is discussed: "Not all, not many relationships of this kind are happy." Stifter's "exposition" limits itself to these two voices of opposition. The rest is harmony, expressed in the language of *Indian Summer*: harmony, harmonization, a concept that we already find occasionally earlier in Stifter's works ("... that he lived the healthiest of lives here and attained the greatest age possible for the harmony of his body's elements." *The Forest Path*—"...and then dressed himself as harmoniously and suitably as he had learned to do in the meticulously clean home of his foster mother." *The Confirmed Bachelor*) and which also recurs here as primary and orientation words in the adjectives *harmonizing*, *suited*, or *consonant*: "...that everything in the rooms was put in order with the greatest cleanliness, beauty, and harmony."—"...at an earlier time I would not have used words to put the beauty and harmonization of these things in the right light at all..."—"...that her dresses were far more simply made and adorned than those of the other women, but that they were far more harmonious and of more noble character than one finds otherwise."—"She had no jewelry on at all, not the smallest piece, although her body really would have been so suited to precious stones."—"Below the roof there is a wall of a similarly dark color, in which there are windows at consonant intervals."

There are two great, moving high points in the calmly peaceful portrayal, and they are more moving than any ever so powerful external event in other narrative prose:

The mother visits the house in which her young son lives, distributes gifts, then calls her son.

> The young man stood up and walked around the table to her. She took him amiably by the hand and said, "What still lies there belongs to you. You asked me for them long ago, and for a long time I had to withhold them from you because they were not right for you yet. They are Goethe's works. They are your property...
>
> "...The books are not new and beautifully bound ones, as you perhaps expect," she continued. "They are the same Goethe books that I read with joy and with pain during so many hours of the night and so many hours of the day, and which were often suitable for bringing me comfort and peace. It is my Goethe books that I give to you. I thought they might be dearer to you, if, in addition to the contents, you found the touch of your mother on them, rather than perhaps only that of the book binder and the printer."

The scene, which continues on, has infinite greatness and consecration; it overpowers us, even more than the fateful encounter of the hero with Shakespeare in the description of a performance of *King Lear* in Vienna's *Burgtheater* ("...the most beautiful words that were ever written about that tragedy." Gustav Landauer), and just as strong as the portrayal of his being overwhelmed at the sight of an ancient statue that he has already often seen but only completely recognizes when he has reached the status of higher maturity:

"Why didn't you tell me...that the statue standing on your marble staircase is so beautiful?"
"Just who told you that now?" he asked.
"I saw it myself," I answered.
"Well, then you will know it all the more surely and believe it with that much greater firmness," he responded, "than if someone had made a claim about it to you."
"I believe, namely, that the image is very beautiful," I answered, correcting myself.
"I share with you the belief that it is a work of great importance," he said.
"And why have you never spoken to me about it?" I asked.
"Because I thought that after a certain period of time you would notice it yourself and consider it to be beautiful," he answered.

The natural occurrences of attentive encounter with great art, however, are only crucial points and not the main subject of the novel. Here, art in Stifter's sense is "described as an ornament of life, not its goal." The goal of mortal life is rather "the fulfillment of all of his powers for suitable activity in making himself and others happy."

A single "situation," in its traditional, literary, technical meaning for the narrative form, occurs very late, in the next to last chapter, and is placed in the prehistory that is only now repeated as a "retrospective." It is a single, soft, hardly noticeable, subsequently retroactive endangerment of the general order, a single open question posed by the reader, which the old host and bird lover Baron von Risach answers for the narrator, the young Heinrich, by telling about his first meeting with Mathilde, their separation, and how they later met again, thereby clarifying all of the relationships of the main characters to each other. And at this critical point in the private "plot" we read the key sentence: "Love is everything."

In *Indian Summer* Stifter again tells his own story, of course, better said: he presents his dream again, but this time clarified and purified on two levels: the story of the young and the story of the mature Adalbert Stifter. The young narrator Heinrich wins the love of Natalie, completely without storms and passions in the regularity of harmonious development, a fulfilled dream of the union of two beings. But his mentor and host, Baron von Risach, lives in a mysterious relationship with Mathilde, Natalie's mother, and tells in retrospect about their love, engagement, disunion, and separation, and as he does so, the deep reason for the relationship's failure remains strangely open, for the "No" of Mathilde's parents seems to be only an excuse, not a cause. Biographically, however, this baron definitely has similarities to Stifter himself. At a mature age, those whom we may view as ideal images of Stifter and Fanny, both widowed, calmly acquiescent, have found each other in the contented Indian summer of suitable activity, in the mutuality of educational effort with regard to Mathilde's son.

> ...rang out...Mathilde's voice, which said, "As these roses faded, so our happiness faded." She was answered by the voice of my host, which said, "It did not fade, it just has a different form..."

And among these very sparse events that are placed hesitantly and carefully before the reader, life occurs, personal life in the regularity of its everyday course. The special thing about *Indian Summer* is the very fact that it tells nothing special, that it does not reproduce exceptions but the rule, on an elevated social plane and in the elevated environment of the conversations, which, however, are also not disputes and not contradictory, but reciprocal utterances that confirm each other and continue harmoniously with "What you say is so right" and "When it comes right down to it, you are perfectly right." Roses and cacti are cared for; birds are tended and observed; works of art are collected and studied; jewelry and pieces of furniture are constructed and restored; they read and eat and change clothes; they show their guests the house, the garden, and the agricultural efforts; they take trips; they talk about all this and other things as well; they visit each other, give each other gifts, and do nice things for each other. To reach the central locale of the proceedings they come from the city (which is Vienna) and from the high mountains (which can be recognized as the area around Hallstatt and Mt. Dachstein). The city and the Alps also offer many motifs and scenes for the events that calmly, intimately, and steadily follow their course. Nature and art open themselves to the same loving solicitation, are recognized and investigated. In the parts, as in their sequence and combination into a whole, great, sacred order is presented. Even the elements are pampered. In earlier works the catastrophic, the extraordinary had often been presented in Stifter's narrative prose, danger and its conquest, the drought in *The Village on the Heath*, the falling ice in *My Great-Grandfather's Writing Case*, the hail and the fire in *Mica*—in *Quartz* the wintery glacier was an enemy, even though it was conquered. Now nature is pacified; the same Dachstein glacier, when climbed in *Indian Summer*, has become a friend; the encounters with it and with the blooming *cereus peruvianus* are just as heavy with meaning as the encounters with Shakespeare and Goethe, the recognition of ancient beauty, and the preservation and restoration of a Gothic altar or old furniture that Stifter calls "devices." What happens in the carpenter's shop, how a painting comes into being, how precious metals and stones are most suitably integrated to form jewelry, what color the facade of a house should be painted in conformity with its style—all this moves the characters of the story and the readers, too, who are put in an extremely good mood corresponding to the fine, calm flow of the high prose. The triumph of morality is exemplified as it is transformed into words; order is established through the process of describing it, the world is created in the fact that a creator sees that it is good.

Stifter himself suspected how far beyond what he had previously achieved he had gone in this new round of creative work: "This book has a future, and someday, when the *Studies*, which were for their own time, have become passé with the passage of time, they will be purchased because of *Indian Summer*.

For the most part, the contemporary world remained skeptical, in many cases even ill-disposed. Hebbel sneered at *Indian Summer*, other people misunderstood it. Eight years after it appeared, a second printing was delivered, but because it could hardly be sold anymore, in 1877, after Stifter's death, a shortened edition appeared, and it was not until 1919 that *Indian Summer* was again published as a book in complete form, although in 1879, in an often-quoted passage, Nietzsche included the novel with Lichtenberg's aphorisms, the first book of Jung-Stilling's life story, and Keller's *The People of Seldwyla* among the few works of German prose ("if we disregard Goethe") that would deserve to be read again and again.

Misunderstanding and lack of understanding, however, have also remained faithful to the novel ever since its glorious return. Once again Hofmannsthal pushes his way into our field of view; concerning his essay about *Indian Summer*, Karl Kraus correctly observed that it belonged "in a reader of warning examples, because German youth can learn more from such writings than from the paragons of German prose." And if we recognized Stifter's linguistic genius in the use of *lay* and *lie*, we see the opposite in the man of letters who was unjustifiably considered to be a great stylist, in whose hands abstract branches lie and upon whom formulations of a moving world are based ("very important branches of administrative service lay in his hands at times"— "two great formulations of the German mind are included in *Indian Summer* and based on the world that emerges in it"). And it is not only the world that moves, for Hofmannsthal the moments also move ("In such a long period of time, a moment usually approaches a work of literature, in which it dies.") But Hofmannsthal's snobbish aestheticism is still gold (albeit low-carat gold) compared to the senseless psychoanalysis of Stifter by a certain Winterstein, who shall not be spared from proper disparagement through quoting him: "Heinrich's interest in the history of 'Mother Earth' is derived from the urge to study his mother's body. Even the desire to climb high mountains, of which Heinrich speaks, has its subconscious motivation in his strong bond to his mother."—The argument between the old man and the young man, concerning whether or not a thunderstorm will sprinkle his house, attains a deeper meaning in the light of this interpretation: The father calms the son with respect to his fear of castration.

Friedrich Gundolf should also be mentioned here briefly, but no less irritatedly, in whose opinion "the emotional scale never transcends the tones of home and family" in *Indian Summer*.

Parallel to the work on *Indian Summer*, Stifter had pursued all kinds of historical novel projects that he had originally intended to develop first; but it was very significant that in the declining years of his life and creativity, in what amounted to four times seven years of literary productivity, the two great, lonely monuments *Indian Summer* and *Witiko* were written in that sequence.

When he has completed *Indian Summer*, he can begin his own Indian summer, which, only occasionally enlivened by travel, brings a final decade of special emptiness, loneliness, grief, and disappointment, the deaths of his foster daughter and his niece, illness and physical decline, and a gradual fading from public literary consciousness. Stifter becomes eccentric, a pedant; his pets and cacti replace his associations with friends. But what *Indian Summer* had poetically prepared can now radiate from the work into his life. The faded love, the marital transfiguration in the farewell to summer is now transferred to Amalia. With moving, passionately painstaking effusiveness, Adalbert Stifter bestows all tenderness and thankful dedication upon his wife; from the twilight, light falls on the day that is ending, from the autumn, light falls on the summer; thanks to this retrospective power of illumination, the past appears idealized and transfigured. Stifter consciously creates a final chord of marital bliss of such infinite harmony that he himself probably begins to believe in a symphony that is "in tune" with the coda.

When *Indian Summer* appears, he has one decade left: the decade of the novel *Witiko*. In *Indian Summer* the special part of human life, the immediate present, had been put in order, and in *Witiko* the great order can be expanded to things in general and the distant past of the twelfth century. The historicity from which Stifter suffered can be illuminated by a look at its origins. Conflicts and struggles are sanctified by the governing limits of clarified presentation. In *Indian Summer* little had happened; in *Witiko* many things happen, everything happens: confused, terrible, painful things, and yet they are brought to light and incorporated into necessity. Until now it had been as Johannes Aprent, the faithful friend of Stifter's late years, had portrayed it: "He hated everything that was muddled and confusing. He wanted to see the governance of moral law, and where he was not able to catch sight of it, he most preferred to turn away his gaze completely." But in *Witiko* the muddled and the confusing is woven into the governance of moral law; chaos, clearly portrayed, viewed from a great distance as if from above, is no longer chaotic.

The High Forest ended with the destruction of a fortress. *Witiko* ends with the very great sentence: "In later years he enjoyed an additional great pleasure when his son Witiko began to build a fortress on the crag of the crooked meadow that now belonged to Witiko's tribe." It is the same fortress.

The fact that in reality it was built almost five hundred years earlier and in Stifter's time had been a ruin for more than two hundred years remains unimportant; in words it is first destroyed then built twenty years later. The word causes it to be resurrected and preserves it over and beyond actuality.

Stifter can include in a visualized past everything that he wishes for his own time and the future. He makes his peace with history; he reconciles and connects the times and the nations. In the summer of 1848 he wrote: "We should forget everything that has happened and accept even the Czechs—who create such difficult times for us as a result of blindness and misjudgment—as brothers, when they approach us again and receive our concession of all their customs, habits, and language, as they should permit the German who is isolated among them to live after his own manner."

Stifter accomplishes this reconciliation in *Witiko*, for in the novel there is no difference between those who speak German and those who speak Bohemian. There is a common language for all of them, and literature has gone back to paradise, to the condition before the erection of the tower of Babel, and in the dismal present points with what it draws from the past into an ideal future. No matter how much Germans and Czechs continue to rage against each other, the blindness and misjudgment is transitory, the reconciliation in *Witiko* lasts and stretches beyond them.

The stream of narrative in Stifter's early and middle works now expands to an ocean, powerfully moved by ebb and flow and storm, of course, and yet resting in itself and its endlessness. The conversations are no longer bilateral speeches that complement each other in the service of the same idea, they are expositions in question and answer, the measuring of opposite points of view. Over all this stands the power of the word, the speech, the urge to describe and through description to preserve, to remove from transitoriness.

This striving fulfills not only the author, but through him his characters as well. Experience, in a higher sense, only becomes real when it has become language. When two lovers find each other again years later, their conversation is the eternalization of their first encounter:

"I wanted to see you," said Bertha, "and when I had seen you, you were dear to me."

"And when I had seen you, you were also dear to me," said Witiko. "We were two children."

....

"And because I was dear to you, you spoke to me?" asked Witiko.

"Because you were dear to me, I spoke to you," answered Bertha.

"And because I was dear to you, you went to the seat stones by the maple trees with me?" asked Witiko.

"Because you were dear to me, I went to the seat stones by the maple trees with you," answered Bertha.

"And sat next to me on the stones," said Witiko.

"And sat next to you on the stones," Bertha said.

"And you were so dear to me," said Witiko, "that I would have liked to sit and talk with you forever. Today you are dressed as you were then, Bertha."

"It is the same clothing that I was wearing that Sunday," answered Bertha, "but the little black skirt has become a little shorter on me."

"Everything is the same to me as it was at that time," said Witiko.

The language of the account has a new form of greatness. It no longer luxuriates in unique creative innovations; it has also rid itself of almost all traces of the specific regional idiom and has attained the status of impeccable mastery. After finishing this book, one must die—just like Duke Sobêslaw in its beginning, who says "that he only wants to know what is happening, and that he will then die." Just as the elemental catastrophes of the stories had been recognized and affirmed as the workings of a higher law, so now the ups and downs of power and dominion are expressed in battles, military campaigns, sieges, negotiations, and peace treaties, and viewed as the workings of higher forces, as a part of the great, unknown plan. In a grand, epic panorama Stifter portrays how the young Witiko gradually enters the historic proceedings, how he takes sides, how he helps to put the situation of his country in order, to create a just status with the help of weapons, and to defend that status, with the help of weapons, against new threats—just as every young person always thinks that in his neighborhood only this or that condition would have to be produced, in order to secure permanently what is good and better. Then, however—and this significant component of the Witiko novel's greatness has been viewed as a mistake in the novel by critics who have misunderstood it—then, however, Stifter feels that his illness does not leave him much more time. On the face of it, he hurries perceptibly with its completion, but only in that very fact does he give the epic its true meaning and rhythm, its greater equilibrium.

Witiko, born in 1118, appeared before us as a twenty-year-old, and the contents of the account comprise about fifteen years of his life and the history of his country. The work has three volumes with a total of eleven chapters. When the last chapter has begun and we no longer have even a hundred of the several hundred pages before us, the tempo changes radically; the material is no longer presented, but summarized. In the same paragraph the story moves from the year 1154 to the year 1155, on the following page we are already in the year 1156, and four pages later in the year 1158. In that the specific changes to the general in that manner, the idea is expressed that nothing can be purified and ordered definitively, that flow and ebb and storm will continue, that part of the very nature of order consists in its being temporarily established ever anew, again and again, as if it had permanence. Witiko's youthful service for the just cause is integrated into the man's knowledge of the progress of history in this fashion: "If revenge is exercised against revenge, then a third revenge will be exercised against the second, and a fourth against the third, and that goes on until everyone in this hall no longer lives, until their grandchildren and the grandchildren of the grandchildren no longer live. So it was in ages past, and so it will be. But we arm ourselves for everything that is necessary."

In the final chapter two and a half decades are appended in a tenth of the pages that were reserved for about a decade and a half, and to view this particular apparent disproportionality superficially and primitively as the storyteller's "panic at closing time" is more accurate and true than a superficially conciliatory conclusion that resolves all tensions would have been for this particular novel. For just as novels can come to an end with engagement and wedding, while human problems cannot, so the regularity of history cannot be abolished for the sake of finale and exit. Where the happy upshot of *Indian Summer* was the fact that love never ends, the discovery of *Witiko* is: World history never ends.

But how Stifter's great prose and ordering mind are able to lift the stormy, the violent, the small, and the common into the sphere of distinct processes! He does not idealize as much as he apportions. From a distance he looks at flow and ebb and storm and says: ocean. Because the things that he describes were completed a long time ago, they can be complete. And since we know that in the twelfth century they may not have consistently proceeded in such a soft and gentle and well-tempered manner, and nevertheless accept them willingly in this presentation, the conclusion suggests itself to us that when viewed from a distance and from above, even the small and common acts of violence of many a later era are governed by meaning, moderation, and order.

In *Witiko* everything is as it should be. Arguments for and against alternate with each other, great ceremonies proceed in perfect regularity, visitors come when the owner of the house is at home, people with appointments find each other at the right time, there is eternal, magnificently harmonious motion, like that of the stars in the sky, in the great circle of politics and strategy as in the small, private circle. People come, speak, eat, spend the night, say goodbye; visits are followed by return visits. People give gifts to each other, they show each other their houses and yards, they carefully prepare everything that is planned for days to come—and it is specifically this small, private sphere, with its urgent attention to the unobtrusive, the unsensational, to the day, the very thing that is only background in other novels but foreground here, that makes the novel *Witiko* so unique, because above all, this, of course, is the primary component of life.

In another context Stifter once saw "general history" as "the pale total picture of individual history, in which only love is omitted and the shedding of blood is recorded. Yet the great, golden stream of love that has come down to us through the millennia...is the rule, and we have forgotten to pay attention to it; the other thing, hate, is the exception to the rule, and it has been written about in a thousand books." (*My Great-Grandfather's Writing Case*)

In *Witiko* the rule is rehabilitated, "general history" is glowingly colored by the great stream of love that is directed not only toward human beings, but also toward animals and everything inanimate; a thousand-and-first novel makes up for everything that a thousand books before it left out.

And once again—how could it be otherwise?—the landscape is also very visible: the "high forest" that Stifter had to visit from Oberplan as a boy, which had long since given way to civilization, but which he now brings into his vicinity, giving it as a present to himself and his first landscape—the Moldau River is there and the Danube and Bohemia and Moravia, the cities Vienna, Prague, and Nuremberg; and if ever an individual, a later writer came up to the standard of "the words of Homer," it is achieved in this great epic that does not consciously dabble in antiquities, but simply proceeds at the measured pace of the rigorous comprehensive report:

> On that day, the men who wanted to move were also prepared. There was Christ Severin, the wool weaver, with a maple staff, his bundle of food, and a sack for the spoils, Stephen, the wagon builder, with sword and spear, his bundle of food, and the sack for the spoils, David, the carpenter, with sword and battle axe, his bundle of food, and the sack for the spoils, likewise Paul Joachim with a spear, Jacob with spear and sword, Tom Johannes, the fiddler, with a spear and a large sack for the spoils, in the same way Maz Albrecht with a maple staff, then Peter Laurentz, the smith, with an iron rod and an iron club, then Urban, Zacharias, Lambert, and Wolfgang with maple staves, Gregor Veit with sword and spear, then many of the young people and farmhands who could be spared. They were wearing coarse, gray woolen clothes, had boots with large iron-plated soles on their feet and thick felt hoods on their heads. Raimund, the laborer, had asked to go with Witiko, and Witiko had consented. Because Witiko had explained that he would ride at a walking pace, the men said that they should remain together and walk beside him. Witiko considered that to be a good idea.

A great didactic work concerning the active life and legality, a hymn about democracy with all of its riches and its challenges, a saga of the rise of a noble heart, *saga* in the normal sense and in the literal meaning that Stifter gives to the [original German] word when he writes at one point: "...the saying* arose that there... would be a great hunt," *saga* as "what is said," what is spoken and comes into existence through the word. It was not understood, but rejected and ignored by the contemporary world. It was not appropriately perceived by posterity, has still not been discerned in all its dimensions, was out of print for half a century, not resurrected until the edition published by Insel in 1921, underestimated and disparaged even by the Stifter apostles and apologists Emil Kuh, A. R. Hein, Gustav Wilhelm, Otto Stoessl and others. (Adalbert Horicka, collaborator in editing the collected works, 1911: "...this novel shows us the writer already on the wane... It is only proof that at the end of his life the decrepit man roused himself once more to take on a larger work, without, however, coming close to achieving what one could expect of him.") All the more important are the scattered opposing voices, the first being Johannes Aprent, then later, among others, Rudolf Pannwitz, Franz Hüller, the editor of *Witiko* and author of the introduction to the collected works, Albrecht Schaeffer, Felix Braun in the foreword to the Insel edition: "Like an enormous high mountain range his final work towers above everything done previously...as a new writer, Stifter created his first historical novel, the only valid one of our literature," and Berndt von Heiseler: "*Witiko* is a holy book."

*Both *saga* and *saying* are translations of the German: *Sage*.

The great work first appeared in three volumes in 1865, 1866, and 1867 respectively. On January 28, 1868, Adalbert Stifter died. In 1865 he had been forced to retire. On the application for his retirement appeared the confidential note of an influential friend and supporter, who alluded to an incurable disease.

A few years earlier he had complained that because of his official duties and his many other offices and activities, "on many days" he had "not even enough time to die." Now he had the time. Perhaps he had very consciously sought the excessive activity and taken it upon himself in order to have no time to die. Perhaps he also needed the excuse, the appearance of insufficiency, the unfulfillable dream of writing as a profession, in order to practice it. Perhaps the unfulfilled wish for leisure time was the father of greatness. While completing *Indian Summer*, in a letter he complained about the frictions and interruptions that impaired his work and mood: "Perhaps they will read this letter someday and feel sorry for the children slain in the womb; then it will be too late, as it was too late for Kepler, who also lived in this accursed city of Linz, and as it was too late for Mozart." Reasoning à la Grillparzer...but was it too late for Mozart? Was it not something complete that Mozart left behind, like Schubert, like Stifter?

In full possession of his leisure time, as a professional Olympian, Stifter would probably have filed, changed, improved even more intensively, would probably have produced more versions, but not more works, would have strived for perfection so consciously that he would have made it questionable. With the two great novels he left behind only one, albeit meticulously crafted version of each. Nor did he revise *Indian Summer* for the first new edition. The novellas, however, exist in two or more forms and raise once again the gigantic and unsolvable question of the first and original version, a question that plays off the creator against himself.

The great problem can be illustrated in a small example. In *Depiction of a Young Fir Tree* we find the eternal image of the distant Alps again. "Only on very clear mornings, when rain approaches and the region is not covered by any tinge of haze, but things lie there in mournful clarity, in the southeast the Noric Alps float out above the narrowest band of forest, as distant and fabulous as pale blue, fixed clouds," the first version reads. But the new version says: "On a morning when rain approaches and the air is so clear that you see things not colored by haze, but in their simple naturalness, in the southeast you occasionally catch sight of the Noric Alps above the narrowest band of forest, floating out there as distant and fabulous as pale blue, fixed clouds."

Who would want to decide which version is the "authentic" one? Beyond that question, this example is instructive because of the change from the "mournful clarity" to the "simple naturalness."

Stifter called himself to order and no longer permitted himself to see the "mournful clarity" of things. His path as a writer leads from mournful clarity to simple naturalness. But from there the path goes no further.

What one could look at from the last bend in the path after *Witiko* is shown by the fragment of an autobiography from the last years of his life. It was found in his literary estate and touches the uttermost limits of what can be said:

>...Far back in empty nothingness there is something like bliss and delight that penetrated my being, seizing me powerfully, almost destroying

me, something unlike anything else in my future life. The characteristics that I remember are: it was brilliance, it was turmoil, it was below. This must have been very early, for it seems to me as if a high, wide darkness of nothingness lay around the thing.

Then there was something else that went softly through my inner world and soothed me. The characteristic is: There were sounds.

Then I swam in something that waved up and down. I swam back and forth; I became softer and softer inside, and then I became as if intoxicated, then there was nothing more...

The plan was not carried beyond a few pages, could not go any further. One may repeat what was said about Schubert: He "would have gotten a hundred years ahead of his time. That could not be; and so he died."

After *Witiko* no new great work is conceived; instead, *My Great-Grandfather's Writing Case* is rewritten and expanded in a fourth version. Stifter probably feels that he can no longer produce anything new, so he intends to renew something older, and elevate a work from the cycle of the *Studies* into the world of the novels. The work is interrupted by the writer's fatal illness. What may have been the last sentence he wrote ends with: "...follow him joyfully to the altar." On this page 164 of the manuscript Johannes Aprent wrote: "Here the writer died. The editor of the literary estate."

In those last years Stifter "changed beyond recognition." The "formerly so friendly, fresh, and full face was dark yellow, sunken, aged, and his body had lost its stately fullness." He travels to Karlsbad to a health resort, to recuperate in the maternal mountains. From there he writes his wife tenderly grateful, Indian summer letters: "I love you now far, far more than when you were a twenty-two-year-old, radiant, indescribably beautiful girl..." He has put the things of the world and the human condition so completely in order that he can now also put his life in order. And from there he writes his last prose piece, not narrating, but reporting, "From the Bavarian Forest." There the Bohemian Forest is portrayed one last time. One last time he looks at what he has described as on the very first day, passionately "sketching the landscape with words," the "dense, unbroken, beautiful forest," Lake Plöckenstein, Seewand Mountain, Mount Plöckenstein, Dreisessel Mountain, and "as the crowning feature of the whole, the chain of the Alps from Pinzgau to the Schneeberg in Lower Austria, in the most delicate, serrated blue." For pages the report immerses itself in the landscape where the three lands, Bavaria, Bohemia, and Austria touch each other. Then the actual process begins: a final conjuration of the elements, a snowstorm, "a natural event that I had never seen, that I would not have thought possible, and that I will never forget as long as I live," and the overcoming of great resistances until the return home, illness, and recovery thanks to the "heartfelt love of all those who are in my home."

At the age of twenty-four, Stifter had already sung about this region, the land that was "their home":

> ...O you lovely land, you land of marvelous forests!
> Take me in one day, when my hair is fading gray,
> Harbor me there in your shadows, tend me in my old age.

> One day when the Lord calls me away from my work:
> I shall look once more around at the mountains and then
> I'll lay down my weary head to eternal rest.

The circle is closed, the day's work done, the mountains have been viewed once more. But death is not a gentle lying down at the first call of the Lord.

Stifter had "conditions of agitation and anxiety" that caused his Karlsbad landlady to voice the opinion that they had to be careful that he did not harm himself. He himself reported about these spells: "...at the moment they are there, I always think that something terrible is coming." Visitors who "found him to be very cheerful and talkative" in Kirchschlag, above Linz, four months before his death, nevertheless thought they noticed that "a deep grief must be tearing away" at his life.

He died on January 28, 1868. In the parish death records "hectic fever following hardening of the liver," and on the death certificate "hectic fever as a result of liver atrophy" are given as the cause of death.

He received the last rites, and a Christian burial was not denied him.

New research concerning his fatal illness, undertaken by Viennese doctors in 1959 on the basis of letters, expert opinions, reports of friends, and extensive, previously unpublished notes in a diary intended for the doctor, entitled *My Condition*, establish that in all probability Stifter did not die of cancer of the liver, but cirrhosis. Certain neuropsychiatric symptoms of such a liver insufficiency have only recently been investigated. Among other things they include a disorientation with respect to time and place.

It is certain that before his death Adalbert Stifter inflicted a wound on his neck with a razor. The family doctor was called, who sewed up the wound and stopped the bleeding.

The suspicion that Stifter committed or attempted to commit suicide was voiced for the first time in 1892, in the biographical description of the *Allgemeine Deutsche Biographie* [General German Biography]; successively versions of hanging, slitting of the wrists, and stabbing in the heart with Mrs. Stifter's sewing scissors appeared.

In the Stifter biography that A. R. Hein wrote much earlier but did not publish until 1901-1903, it says:

> In the night from the 27th to the 28th of January 1868, the terrible agony increased with such stunning power, that the raging torture confused the writer's mind. As if gripped by sudden insanity, in an unattended moment—the clock had just sounded one o'clock in the morning—with trembling hands he reached for the little table in which his razor was kept, seized it, and inflicted a terrible cut on his neck in the frenzy caused by the unbearable pain. A dark stream of blood gushed out and flowed over the bed linen and the pillows. When Mrs. Stifter entered the sufferer's room again a few moments later, she found her husband wheezing and wrestling with imminent death.

Among other things, the time given in this portrayal is inaccurate; it is ascertainable that the wounding had already occurred in the night from the 25th to the 26th of January. Since Stifter was later given the last rites, he must have been conscious. An "original correspondence from Linz" that appeared in Vienna on January 29, 1868 in the evening edition of the *Neue Freie Presse*, dated January 28th, was not taken into consideration by A. R. Hein. It reports that the writer "although unable to speak since eleven o'clock last night, was completely conscious until the moment of his death early this morning."

Hein's portrayal is also suspect in that it quotes incompletely and therefore misleadingly from a letter of the mortally ill writer to Aprent: "The doctor says it is about over, and then everything will suddenly be fine..." The following sentence, left out by Hein: "...it was the same with my wife"—Stifter's wife had recovered from an illness a short time earlier—shows that Stifter did not long for death, but for recovery. Thus, "it is about over" does not refer to life, but to his illness.

In Hein's papers material was found that only became available to the biographer after the printing of the biography and that he did not take into consideration. In particular there is a statement that Aprent, certainly an authoritative witness, made about the alleged suicide long after Stifter's death. He asserted "that this malicious rumor had no basis in truth." He "was nothing less than infuriated about all this baseless gossip. The stimulus for it was perhaps the fact that according to Aprent's very definite statement, a few days before his death Stifter attempted to shave himself. Sitting in bed, thus in an extremely uncomfortable position, the attempt not only failed, but Stifter's already unsteady hand directed the razor so adversely that he injured his neck and bled profusely! Through the application of an adhesive plaster the actually insignificant wound was closed and the bleeding stopped." That was what Aprent said, and he added that now, twenty years after Stifter's death, he "did not have the slightest reason to say anything different from what he knew with certainty." Mrs. Stifter, whose feelings should have been considered under the circumstances, was no longer alive at that time.

With cirrhosis of the liver, there is no question of unbearable pain. A. R. Hein, who had plenty of opportunity to question all the relatives, friends, and other witnesses, both orally and by letter, and who pursued his first-hand research thoroughly, bases the material in his portrayal only on the statement of Maria Rint, the daughter of the sculptor who made Stifter's death mask. The girl, who was still very young at the time in question, heard "under the seal of confidentiality" about the wound on his neck and probably quietly passed on the suicide version. She may also be the source for Hein's declaration that a "heavy strip of paper" had to be placed "over the coagulating blood of the neck wound" before the death mask was made.

If the suicide version is accurate, it is probable that everything was done to cover up the truth. But it is just as conceivable that they wanted to maintain silence about the harmless wound in order not to inspire inappropriate rumors, and that it was this striving for discretion itself that caused the rumors.

It is conceivable that the temporally disoriented patient attempted to shave himself during the night. And it is rewarding for commentators of every caliber "to unfurl" a life and a personality anew from the perspective of a terrible end, and to see the entire harmony of moderate integrity dissolved, destroyed, and negated in the dissonant final chord.

Let the researchers continue to develop and establish their versions and play them off against each other. It is certainly interesting and informative to receive information about the end of a great man, but it is unimportant whether or not Stifter, who had been suffering from an incurable disease for two years, wanted to end it all two days before his death. More significant than all the extensive studies about the wound on his neck are three sentences of Johannes Aprent's account: "On the morning of January 28, after the sick man had lain there for some time without any sign of consciousness, he opened his eyes once more and they were filled with tears. Then they closed forever. But the most cheerful smile, which did not yield to the rigidity of death until the following day, lay on his countenance."

If Stifter had died on the 24th of January, he would be as complete before us as we must and intend to see him, without regard to all the question marks surrounding his last days. His death is a matter for the researchers and not for literary criticism, but he should remain protected especially from feuilletonistic excesses. (Martha Karlweis: "Steadfastness for the sake of emphasis suffers the precipitate delivery of the deed of all deeds: murder... Buried peasant childhood breaks forth: How does one slaughter an animal?")

Stifter is also interesting enough without an interesting death—and whoever does not find him interesting should leave him alone. Stifter would also be no different at all, if the short, not very meaningful novella *Confidence*, which was written in 1846 and not included in the *Studies*, had never been written or if it had been lost. This novella contains the statement: "We all have a tigerlike disposition, just as we have a heavenly one, and if the tigerlike one is not awakened, then we think that it is not there at all and that the heavenly one simply dominates. That is why we judge the characters of stormy periods so unjustly, because they acted in an ill condition, for example, one of fever, but we do not find these prerequisites in ourselves and therefore impute their actions to our healthy condition, and thus do not comprehend them." This statement has often been quoted and used as evidence for what is enigmatic and hidden in Stifter's nature. But Stifter continues: "The great man...resists the awakened tiger and does not permit him to rend...," and that alone is significant. We do not need the novella *Confidence* to recognize that Stifter knew just as much about human nature as about inanimate nature; nor did he leave any doubt about that in his other works. In his efforts he gave a great example of resistance that is familiar with the tiger but turns away from it and overcomes it through the declaration of loyalty to the sweetness of order.

According to the testimony of a friend, he had "died long before they buried him." Writings that he left behind appeared and were not noticed. Two years after his death, the grave in the Linz cemetery was marked only by a simple wooden cross. In February 1870 they published an appeal for a collection for a dignified tombstone. The obelisk was completed in November 1871, but because of a lack of money the committee was unable to fulfill the widow's request that the grave be surrounded by an iron fence. To be sure, in August 1868 they unveiled a memorial plaque on the house of his birth in Oberplan. In 1869 there was a *Stifterstraße* in Linz, and soon after that another one in Budweis; and in 1877 the first Stifter monument stood on Seewand Mountain. But after the death of Amalia Stifter, when his estate was auctioned off in 1883, because of minimal interest paintings, drawings, and manuscripts by Stifter, as well as valuable relics from his personal possessions passed into indifferent hands at unbelievably low prices. Manuscripts in which nobody was interested went to the writer's family and were given out as souvenirs a page at a time to visitors of the Stifter house in Oberplan.

The turnaround did not begin until the copyrights expired thirty years after Stifter's death: Numerous editions appeared—by 1906 there were already twenty—a Stifter archive was established; in May 1902 the beautiful Stifter monument in the city of Linz was unveiled. Since 1903 there has been a memorial plaque on the house in Linz where he lived and died, and a Stifter monument was also erected in Oberplan in 1906. After many incidents, however, the monument in the Türkenschanz Park in Vienna could not be unveiled until 1919, although a "preparatory committee" had already met in 1904. One after another the authorities had rejected requests to set it up in the Rathaus Park, on the Elisabeth Promenade, and at another place in the Türkenschanz Park.

The leading role in undervaluation and disregard, however, was reserved for literary criticism. In a 320-page *Leitfaden der deutschen Literatur* [Handbook of German Literature] by August Kurz, which appeared in 1872, three lines are devoted to the "original nature painter" Stifter. In six lines, Adolf Stern's *Geschichte der Weltliteratur* [History of World Literature], which appeared in 1880, reproaches him for "transitory adherence to small things, aversion to portraying unique characters," and a "style in which inner falsity is counterbalanced by affected boredom." Rudolf Gottschall's *Deutsche Nationalliteratur des 19. Jahrhunderts* [German National Literature of the 19th Century] (1892) calls Stifter banal and unpoetic in fifteen lines (after fourteen pages about Börne); in eight lines the *Deutsche Literaturgeschichte* [History of German Literature] by Vogt and Koch (1897) states that the "bourgeois" Stifter lacks "all the passion that is really necessary to the poet, as well as the compelling soul in general." The new edition of 1914 repeats this characterization. The German literary history by Georg Witkowsky, which was intended for teachers and published in 1912, criticizes in the "currently very overrated Adalbert Stifter" the fact that he is "only a painter of small things, flat in his feeling," and lacking "warmth in his portrayal of human beings."

In the introductions to new editions, such opinions were only gradually countered by other voices: Gustav Wilhelm, Felix Braun, Otto Stoessl, and others. Stifter literature and Stifter research also gradually began to be effective, yet it is as if trouble and adversity passed from Stifter's life to his continued existence after death.

The story of the great edition of his collected works and the first Stifter biography are evidence of a fateful tragedy that has continued to make itself felt beyond the grave, almost to the present day, as though true greatness must not only prevail against resistance in life, but also fight against concentrated reversals of fortune in the face of unquestionable approbation. Alois Raimund Hein, who was born in 1852 in Vienna as the son of a railroad engineer and died in Vienna in 1937 as a retired middle-school drawing teacher, became acquainted with Adalbert Stifter's works as a young man, visited all of the Stifter memorial places, published articles about Stifter, began working on his Stifter biography as a twenty-four-year-old man, and had contact with Stifter's publisher, Stifter's widow, and his contemporaries in Vienna, Linz, and Bohemia. In 1878, however, Stifter's publisher Heckenast died and thus shattered the hopes for the planned publication of the biography in that year. Thirty publishers that Hein approached refused even to consider the manuscript.

It was not until the years from 1900 to 1903 that the *Mitteilungen des Vereins für die Geschichte der Deutschen in Böhmen* [Reports of the Society for the History of Germans in Bohemia] published the work in installments. In 1904 the biography appeared in an expanded and revised version that was published by the society; the edition was limited to 600 copies. The poet biography series of the Reclam publishing house published an excerpt of it in 1913—in 1916 Karl Kraus called this publication "probably the only decent new book in the Reclam collection"— but the sales of the unabridged work did not make a new printing necessary. And in spite of the enormous increase in interest in Adalbert Stifter, in spite of the absolute disappearance of the first edition after the First World War, the attempt to publish a new edition of the biography on the basis of subscription was not undertaken until 1931, and it failed because of the low number of subscribers. Thus the standard work remained a bibliophile rarity, and the public was deprived of it. Ten years later the publisher Walter Krieg took steps to print a new edition, gathered illustration material, and sent the printer the text that Gustav Wilhelm had completely revised. In November 1943 the plates for the illustrations were destroyed by bombs. Soon afterward a bomb hit Gustav Wilhelm's apartment in Vienna and destroyed irreplaceable treasures of originals, autographs, the galley proofs, and the biography manuscript. Soon after that bombs destroyed part of the paper stored in Mainz. The rest was destroyed in a bombing raid on the Düsseldorf freight station. It was not until 1951 that Walter Krieg was able to publish the classical work in two volumes, after Otto Jungmair had been forced to carry out the editorial work again from the very beginning.

The large historical-critical edition of the *Complete Works* of Adalbert Stifter has, however, not yet been completed. Edited by August Sauer, the first ten volumes appeared between 1901 and 1916 in Prague. After the creation of the Czechoslovakian Republic, the continuation was ensured with the greatest of difficulties, so that in the years from 1920 to 1939 fourteen additional volumes could be published in Reichenberg. The editors were replaced; toward the end of the Second World War the bombs on Vienna and Brünn had destroyed all of the material: manuscripts, galley proofs, and printed copies of the missing volumes. Only years later did a copy of each surface again, as if by a miracle, so that a new printing at least became conceivable. Volume XII/1 appeared in Graz in 1959; volumes XIII/2 and XXV are still pending. With that, after six decades, what is by nature an already long outdated complete edition will finally be available. The East Berlin Academy, in cooperation with the Prague Academy of Sciences, is planning the modern complete edition of Stifter's works to which our official generation, which has the responsibility for it, has given such insufficient attention.

To be sure, for a long time now there have been Stifter societies and Stifter associations here and there, the benevolent, active Stifter Institute of the State of Upper Austria in Linz, Stifter memorial rooms in the Beethoven House on the *Mölkerbastei* in Vienna. In September 1954 the erection of a Stifter bust, which had been planned for almost two decades, took place in the Regensburg Valhalla. During the sesquicentennial commemoration of Stifter's birth in 1955, the Austrian Ministry of Education established an Adalbert Stifter Medal for outstanding literary accomplishments, and the State of Upper Austria funded a literary Adalbert Stifter

Prize. The editions of his works are numerous and have also made the original versions, which have been cared for by the outstanding Stifter expert Max Stefl, accessible to the readers. Up to now, however, in spite of every intensive effort, it has not been possible to determine clearly the situation of the Czechoslovakian Stifter Archive with its treasures.

In 1945 the Stifter monument in Oberplan was tipped over, and the Stifter House and the Bohemian Forest Museum were plundered and ravaged. The high forest around Lake Plöckenstein has been cut down. A large reservoir has flooded the "Heart of the Moldau" and the heart of the Stifter landscape and made it unrecognizable in the very place that Stifter immortalized in two oil paintings and in *The Forest Walker*:

> ...there is a legend that the devil, who did not like it when the Hohenfurt Abbey was built, and who was in danger of losing many souls who are edified there, devised the plan to use the waters of the Moldau to drown the pious fathers who dwell there. For that purpose he chose a night in which he intended to bring together at this one place all the stones that could be found in the area, and build a wall, so that in the narrows between the mountains the water would swell to a lake, which he would then suddenly release onto the holy building by opening a gate. But he took too many small stones that lay around on the surface of the mountains, and had to go back too often, which would not have been the case if he had taken the large ones that were integrated into the earth. Thus it occurred, as he was busily carrying stones, that a cock suddenly crowed, a

pale morning light appeared in the sky, and the angels up in heaven began their early prayers. Then he had to go away and leave the thing as he had it. They still show people the place in eternal memory of it, and you can clearly see how he could not have completed his work and that the fragments now lie in disarray upon each other. That is why there are so few stones on the surface of the earth in the entire area, and on some rocks that lie at the bottom of the Devil's Wall, in spite of rain and wind that have washed over them, you can also still make out the horseshoe mark that was stomped into the hard stones and has remained there. The fathers dedicated the place and the entire area to the Moldau, so that in the next night he could go no further and could not go on to do such a thing anymore at all.

Today the stone blocks with the mark of the horseshoe are flooded. The Devil's Wall towers over the lake as a warning to those who, despite the legend, would let "such a thing" occur to them again. The area is desolate, abandoned by its inhabitants. The forest has withdrawn itself further into the past and into the eternity of preservation through the pictures and the words of the literature of the "greatest Austrian writer next to Raimund, in spite of Grillparzer" (Richard Schaukal).

Stifter probably knew what test period lay before his attainment of immortality. He prophesied: "With *Witiko* people will not understand me until a hundred years from now." *Witiko* appeared in 1867. Thus some years, even though no longer all too many, remain until we completely understand the greatness of Adalbert Stifter.

JOHANN STRAUSS

or

THE TIME OF THE OPERETTA

"...just as the opera composer cannot lack insight into poetry, in order to distinguish the bad from the good, so that his art is not wasted on what is poor."
    (Goethe to Eckermann)

"Do you know any merry music? I don't!"
    (Schubert)

"Strauss played the violin like a god,
And the people dined poorly."
    (Raimund)

"Everything is cozy here... We sing and make music and go to the theater and to Strauss, and with him we stick our heads in the sand of our coziness."
    (Theodor Billroth)

"But every power is bound to a powerlessness."
    (Eduard Hanslick in the obituary of Strauss, the younger)

"Happy he
Who'd not see
What can never altered be."
    (*Die Fledermaus*)

JOHANN STRAUSS, SON

There is no merry music. There is no merry art. Life is serious—how then can art be cheerful?

Tragedy can be predominant or intimated, it can be evaded, it can be overcome; but where it is negated, art does not occur.

Art may say *no* or *yes* to life, but even the affirmed, the accepted life remains serious and tragic. All cheerfulness is bitter, all gaiety aggressive and painful, all joy of life a *nonetheless*. And just because art must find an end, a final chord, a final sentence, a final group, it cannot be jovial; for only the tragic, never the positive conclusion is final; only that point is final from which one cannot continue; only hopelessness is final, never the hope of a way out that shows a direction but no goal.

Final is the work that has separated itself from its creator; the artist becomes final in his work. Every work is a portrait—of him who created it, and all the more similar to him, the less he thought about expression and self-portrayal in creating it, the less consciously he intended to create something, the more clearly he simply intended to work, to practice his profession.

You cannot portray the joy of life, you can evoke it through presentation, in the listener, the reader, the observer, and in your own soul. And in the process it remains unimportant whether the content of what is portrayed is merry or tragic, melancholy or pleasant.

Johann Strauss, the father as well as the son, practiced his profession and wrote notes, and that not even as a primary activity. In both cases, the phenomenon named Johann Strauss did not consist in a composer of that name, but in the union of the personae of an orchestra leader, a violinist, a concert master, and a festivity organizer who, among other things, also composed brilliantly. The artistically productive element gradually moved from the sidelines into the center of focus, but in principle the respective careers and the fame of the two men named Johann Strauss would also have been conceivable and hardly less sensational if the two of them had produced no compositions—as would have been the careers and the fame of the brilliant actors Raimund and Nestroy without the production of their own plays. The fact that neither Johann Strauss had to compose primarily gave them the freedom to develop themselves very naturally as composers, without any burdening responsibility. Both Johann Strauss's were highly praised as violinists; both were also admired as directors. Even at the height of their fame as composers, both played for dances, but also zealously and painstakingly performed works by Mozart, Beethoven, and the contemporary opera composers. Both were what we would call modern or progressive and existed entirely within the general musical world of their time.

The extraordinary and unique thing about the natural event called Johann Strauss is its duality. Twenty-one years apart, almost identical processes occur:

When the father wants to become a musician, he has difficulties with his family. As a very young, approximately twenty-year-old beginner, he withdraws from the circle of his opposing player (Joseph Lanner). He then has his own orchestra, triumphs over his opponent after the initial rivalry, begins to compose because the practice of his profession demands it, becomes world famous as a violinist, orchestra director, and composer, and dies before his fiftieth birthday.

He did not invent the waltz, but found it already in

existence; he developed his own form and made it more socially acceptable.

He not only played for dances but placed the great classical music and important works of his notable contemporaries on the program, even the "moderns" Berlioz and Meyerbeer. In the concert that featured the premiere of the *Radetzky March*, Beethoven's *Leonore Overture* was also presented. Strauss was admired by Franz Liszt and Richard Wagner, revered by Mendelssohn, Cherubini, Auber, Halévy, Adam, and Meyerbeer, and honored by European rulers and royal courts.

The younger Johann Strauss has difficulties with his family when he wants to become a musician. As a very young, approximately twenty-year-old beginner, he withdraws from the circle of his opposing player (Strauss, the father). He then has his own orchestra, triumphs over his opponent after the initial rivalry, begins to compose because the practice of his profession demands it, becomes world famous as a violinist, orchestra director, and composer...

He did not invent the waltz, but found it already in existence; he developed his own form and made it more socially acceptable.

He not only played for dances but placed the great classical music and significant works of his important contemporaries on the program, even the "modern" Wagner, whose champion he became; as early as 1848 he played music from *Tannhäuser*. Liszt, Wagner, and Bülow admired him, Brahms, Bruckner, and Gustav Mahler revered him, European rulers and royal courts honored him.

In neither case was composing an end in itself or the intended goal when they selected and practiced their profession.

Johann Strauss, the father, was a member of the orchestra of the brilliant violinist, director, and composer Joseph Lanner, when the latter said to him: "Strauss, see that you think of something," when a new waltz was needed. That is how he began to compose. (Strauss, the son: "...that my father accidentally discovered his talent for composing.")

Johann Strauss, the son, did not begin to compose until his first public concert was set and he felt compelled to compete with his father in every respect.

Whatever contemporaries said about the father could have been said about the son a generation later: "In his waltzes there ferments and boils, sizzles and foams, sings and effervesces a bond-bursting fullness of melodies that slings one cork after another into the air like the half million devils of champagne."—"...this Mozart of the waltz, the Beethoven of the cotillion, the Paganini of the gallopade, the Rossini of the medley..."

Robert Schumann wrote: "The masters be praised—from Beethoven to Strauss, each in his own way."

Hector Berlioz wrote: "We still do not sufficiently appreciate the influence that he had upon the musical sensitivity of Europe as a whole..."

In 1838 the *Theaterzeitung* wrote concerning the then thirty-four-year-old Strauss, Sr.: "His fame flew across the world faster than the tempo of his gallopades...the North Americans speak of Strauss and his music with enthusiasm... This glowing charm of composition, this stimulating fire of execution have caused even Paris, the proud world city whose applause is regarded as the highest reward for that art, to pay tribute to the Viennese waltz player... He possesses the rare, praiseworthy artistic ability to create tone poems that the common man can understand and the educated man can enjoy."

Eduard Hanslick praises Strauss, Sr. as an interpreter: "In his modest garden productions one could hear much better performances of good instrumental music, than in many festival concerts with high-sounding names." In Bülow's opinion, Strauss, Jr. was one of the few colleagues for whom he could have undiminished profound respect: "...the likes of us can learn from him! He is a genial director in his little genre... Something can be learned from Strauss's style of presentation for the *Ninth Symphony* as well as for the *Pathétique!*"

In his obituary for Strauss, Sr., Hanslick lamented that in a short period of time Vienna had lost its best director in Nicolai, its most witty critic in Dr. Becker, and its most gifted composer in Strauss, Sr. And fifty years later, in his obituary for the son, he wrote that at his grave one must "repeat the lament that with him the most original music talent had passed away."

Whatever was said or written about the father could be valid for the son. In Hector Berlioz's obituary: "with Strauss Vienna lost one of its most beautiful adornments," and a Vienna obituary: "Strauss is the most popular musician in the world. His waltzes captivate the Americans, they resound over the Great Wall of China, they rejoice in the African bivouac, and a Viennese lady acquaintance of mine wrote me a short time ago, how deeply moved she had been when she stepped on Australian soil and a beggar used a Strauss waltz to ask for alms." (*Ostdeutsche Post*, November 28, 1849).

An almost mirror-image identity of two careers of a father and a son with the same name, where the second career repeated the first following an interval of about twenty years, careers that during their lifetimes realized for the first time in the history of the arts what we now call world renown. Until the advent of cinematography in our century there was no living individual who could generally be assumed to be well known on all continents. There may have been melodies and songs, but not names of composers that were present in the consciousness of their world; and even today it is more likely to be the interpreters than the creative individuals who are known as individuals to the world, right down to the Australian beggar, with the exception of the personnel combination of creator and interpreter, who, very much like the double phenomenon Johann Strauss, began to practice his craft entirely without claim to immortality and greatness, and in so doing certainly became the most popular artist of all time up to now: Chaplin.

He, too, entertains, but is sad. He, too, may evoke joy of life, but at the core of his being he is depressive, resigned, endangered.

Johann Strauss, both father and son, played dances for the world, but they were nondancers like Franz Schubert. Once, when Johann Strauss is in an especially joyful mood, a letter, in the most extreme expression of his happy state of mind, says that he would like to joke, laugh, leap, "even dance," although "the last would probably be very difficult" for him.

It is one of the numerous macabre ironies in connection with the life of the older Johann Strauss, that he became "Strauss, the father" for posterity, and yet did not want to be a father, apparently very literally did not, as one can gather by placing the wedding date, July 11, 1825, next to the birth date of his son Johann on October 25, 1825.

And the third decisive relationship in their lives, the relationship to their profession, was no less encumbered. When Johann Strauss, Sr. devoted himself to music, he had to prevail against the opposition of his family, but not of a father, for the latter had committed suicide soon after the birth of his son. When the situation then repeated itself with Johann, the unwanted firstborn son of the unwanted marriage, the father was just as merciless as his own stepfather had been at the time, although the son of a celebrated musician would certainly have been spared the bitterest difficulties of beginning. How he must have suffered in his musical existence, that he wanted to save his son from it! "That will not happen to me again!" was his attitude, although he proudly rated his son Johann's musical talent very highly. A father-son conflict like the one in Franz Kafka's family, but without the patriarchal triumph of the superior father figure, more closely resembling the Oedipus situation.

The conflict shatters the family, it dissolves. Johann Strauss, Sr., highly extolled, wealthy, idolized by his homeland and the world, leaves home. He descends into a shabby, dull companionship with an attractive milliner and has with her five children who will sink into anonymity. He cannot forgive his wife for making him the father of a second Johann Strauss. And when the latter has nevertheless become a second Johann Strauss against his father's will, his father lives only another five years and dies, not yet fifty, in the wretchedness of a small, dark apartment, although his music has conquered the oceans and the Great Wall of China. He dies because of his children: his child, the daughter of his life's companion, also brought him the fatal scarlet fever.

This happens in a street named *Kumpfgasse*, originally called *Kumpflucken*, that even today seems very obscure and hidden and deeply sad, and the sound of this street name, like the name of his life's companion: Trampusch, makes the dullness, the lightlessness, the shabbiness of this end very clear.

They wept for him, consecrated him in St. Stephen's Cathedral, played funeral marches that his colleagues composed for that specific purpose; all of Vienna mourned for him, a fifth of the population participated in the funeral procession, but he died in the bitterest affliction, left alone, poor, and miserable. They found his body on boards in the completely empty apartment that had been hastily vacated by his life's companion. She had taken the children and all of their movable possessions with her.

But the mother, who lost her Johann Strauss, made a second Johann Strauss of her son, when the latter reached the age at which she met her Johann Strauss.

Joseph Lanner, the brighter, more friendly man, also left his wife and children and spent the last years of his similarly very short existence with a life's companion, the butcher's daughter Marie Kraus.

The failure of Raimund and Nestroy in marriage, the breaking away from the family to join a life's companion was repeated in the lives of Strauss, Sr. and Lanner.

The grandfather had departed from life when his son had come into the world. The father left home when his son chose his father's profession. Johann Strauss, Jr had no children. He had only a mother and was infinitely deeply bound to her. He probably never completely overcame the shock of the father-son catastrophe.

Before and after the catastrophe, however, the father was filled with restlessness; as if fleeing from himself and family life, he traveled as much as possible on concert tours to Hungary, Germany, Belgium, Holland, France, and England. If we sense that he does not look at all like a Viennese, it is true in this case; he is small, pale, with a high, protruding forehead, nervous, agitated, irascible, tyrannically energetic, yet at the same time hypochondriac. Wagner called him the "nerve demon." In 1833, Heinrich Laube reported from Vienna about the third figure in the triumvirate, of which Napoleon was the first and Paganini the second member: "They will ask you, I said to myself...the generation of the future will ask you: 'What does Strauss look like?' The man is quite black, like a Moor; his hair curly, his mouth melodious, enterprising, pouting, his nose blunt. One can only regret that he has a white face, otherwise he would be a perfect Moorish king... He also directs his dances in an authentically African manner; his own limbs no longer belong to him when the thunderstorm of his waltzes has broken loose...then the fat is in the fire."

In a somewhat lame and strained tribute on the occasion of the centennial of his birth, Richard Strauss called Strauss, the son, "the laughing genius of Vienna." Neither the son nor the father can separate themselves from the triumph of thoughtlessness in cliché that presents them as cheerful, carefree, joyful, and epicurean. Not only operettas and films, but also the biographers share in the responsibility for the false image. One must only present the unadulterated life's documents of the two Johann Strauss's in order to recognize that even the romantically idyllic Viennese Biedermeier period and the world of its balls and festivals, like the saturated middle-class mentality of the second half of the century, were acquainted with the demons and tragedies and the desire for self-destruction that existed even in the pleasurable realm of the "dancers and violin players." In spite of his illness and breakdowns, Strauss, Sr., who had a weak constitution, drove himself and his musicians from concert to concert in Vienna, on tours from city to city, in flight—from what?—from Vienna, from his own people, from himself, in an unconscious desire to take himself to the grave? Following a brief period of youthful pranks, no trace of tenderness, of love, of real enjoyment in his life has been passed down to us, only the tough, passionate energy with which he—for what?—excessively pursued his musical activities while paying no attention to several collapses.

"Twitching with liveliness" while playing music, skillful in the organization of his contributions and tours, especially gifted as an arranger of large-scale, sensational events, he is "modest in his personal dealings—silent, attentive," thoroughly skeptical with regard to his own greatness. When a controversy breaks out because an effusive tribute to his artistry causes a protest, in a letter he writes one of the few characteristic statements in his own cause that have been handed down to us: "I did nothing to make them call me an artist, which I have never claimed to be." He played music, arranged, composed; he played the violin—when Lanner expanded his quartet to a small orchestra, the first violinist left his chair, and in so doing began a tradition (that of the directing "standing violinist"). He worked quickly, sometimes hastily, when he composed; he worked very energetically and fanatically when he rehearsed and directed. But otherwise he did very little and lived modestly. Because he was so busy with playing, there was often hardly time to write music or even to arrange carefully. In his early years he wrote no scores, rather he sketched a piece and then immediately wrote the part of the first violin. After that, Philipp Fahrbach, his flutist and assistant wrote the flute part, Strauss the second violin part, and Fahrbach the viola part. The first and second clarinet, the first and second horn, and the first and second trumpet parts were then produced in similar fashion. And while Strauss then wrote the drum part, Fahrbach copied the first violin part, and the orchestra material was finished. Sometimes a piece was written down only an hour before the beginning of the ball and played without a rehearsal.

He did nothing and desired to do nothing but "make music," restlessly driven by the compulsion to hold his own against a rival, first against Lanner, then, after the latter had died in 1843, immediately against his son, who made his debut in 1844. Recognized by the world as the king, in Vienna he exercised autocratic rule for only a year.

Like Raimund and Nestroy he created his works only as material, as bases for his successful activity as an interpreter; like Raimund in many and Nestroy in all of his works, he also often took foreign material into his works, citing, propagating, parodying, transcribing. Many of his pieces became popular, like many pieces by Raimund and Nestroy, but the creative act always occurred without a special view to anything beyond the present; they wrote for concrete occasions, not for the editions of their complete works.

Very soon after their triumphant activity, after their absolute double rule over Vienna and the world sovereignty of Strauss, Sr., Lanner and Strauss were forgotten, still present only as names and no longer in their works (like Raimund and Nestroy in the decades following their deaths). Of Lanner's work, only the *Schönbrunner Waltz* lives on, of Strauss, Sr.'s work, only the *Radetzky March*. Everything else lies in the shadow of the cultivation of historical concepts like "Lanner and Strauss" or "the waltz dynasty." Popularity had already passed by the creations of Lanner and the older Strauss in the seventies of the previous century. Soon there lived only a march and not a single waltz written by the great reformer of the waltz who conquered the world for that dance.

Numerous pictures of Strauss, Sr. have been passed down, among others the well-known, moving engraving *The Cashier of the Silver Café*, which shows Strauss next to Lanner and in front of Raimund. But if we attempt to visualize a figure, in spite of all the pictures and caricatures and the numerous descriptions, we will not really be able to see and experience him as clearly as we are perhaps able to see Raimund and Nestroy, or Haydn, Mozart, and Schubert.

Johann Strauss, Sr. remains in indefiniteness, seems more like a historical concept without content to whom no figure corresponds. That situation may be connected with the disastrous identity of name, the incomprehensible disappearance of his works from musical consciousness—the function of "Johann Strauss" had passed on from the father to the son. But it may also arise from the epithet "the father," for the image of the demonic, young, gypsy star of concert and ball is not that of a father figure. Any one of his other functions would be more characteristic than the very one that we allocate to him: the role of the father. And he is also the "elder" only by virtue of his birth date, not according to his image, for we see him as a thirty and forty-year-old man, while the "younger" Johann Strauss has impressed himself upon our consciousness in the numerous patriarchal pictures of the seventy-year-old.

Above all, however, Johann Strauss, the father, is still completely at home in that prehistoric age of music that still does not distinguish in our minds between the creator and the performer. The work is still primarily an occasion for performance without a complete life of its own. Bach wrote for his students and his congregation, and for that reason he disappeared for a century after his death and was known only in name. Haydn wrote for the concerts of his royal patron; for their contemporaries, Mozart and Beethoven were at first interpreters, as were later Chopin and Liszt. Music was written for concrete occasions and to order, just as people compose today for films or cabarets. The previous century was the first to gradually develop—parallel to the figure of the director—the figure of the professional, more or less exclusively composing composer, who, while writing his works, does not think of certain houses but turns to the "world of music." It may have been Franz Schubert's tragedy and blessing that he, who only composed from the very beginning, without assignment and without a patron, never overcame inconspicuousness. And it was certainly the tragedy of the older Strauss that he was printed and published and posthumously even deemed worthy of an edition of his complete works, but that the private and public dances constantly needed ephemeral novelties and still did not recognize any classical works in the present-day sense.

Johann Strauss, the father, was a king and a favorite of kings, but he lived anonymously and degraded; he continued to play concerts in gardens and cafés and popular nightclubs, in *Das Grüne Tor*, in *Der Große Zeisig*, in *Das Odeon*, at the Hernals church fair—he composed for the "noble students of law at the College of Vienna" or the "noble students of medicine" when they held their balls at *Der Sperl*, for the "noble officials of the Kaiser Ferdinand Northern Railway" on the occasion of the Northern Railway officials' ball in the *Sophien-Bad-Saal*. He remained in the everyday world and did nothing during his entire life to cause "them to call him an artist." In the face of his greatness he withdrew into the *Kumpfgasse* to Emilie Trampusch. He had affected the world like Paganini, lived like a busily occupied orchestra leader, died like a dog, and been buried like a king. It is certain that he was very sad all his life. He had conquered the world like Alexander or Napoleon, but after the death of the conqueror the world empire fell apart, and unlike the situation with them, the great victory parade hardly left visible traces behind.

For twenty-four years, from the twenty-first to the forty-fifth year of his life, Johann Strauss, the father, had played in concerts and composed. Then he died.

For eighteen years, from the nineteenth to the thirty-seventh year of his life, Johann Strauss, the son, had played in concerts and composed. Then he married.

Up to that point the careers of the father and son had been spectrally identical. Here the parallel ends, right in the middle of the century that was later once called the "century of the waltz" and lasted from Joseph Lanner's birth (1801) to Johann Strauss's death (1899).

Johann Strauss, the father who did not want to be a father, dies after about two decades of fabulous advancement—Strauss, the son, marries at the end of the second decade of his likewise fabulous advancement and will— not counting a short, unhappy intermezzo—remain a son all his life, but not the son of his father. In a wife he seeks the mother to whom he is so deeply attached, and in the middle of his life he marries a singer who has already said farewell to the stage. The statements concerning how much older she was than he vary from one year to five, seven, nine, and sixteen years; she was probably about seven years older. Strauss, the son, did not want to become a father either, but in spite of that fact he did not want to forgo having his wife be a mother. When he married her, his first wife already had two daughters and at least one son; his second wife remained childless; his third wife brought a daughter into the marriage, who, moreover, bore the name Strauss. All of his wives mothered him, dominated and commanded, and had a strict hand in all professional matters. The intermezzo of his second marriage, the attempt to be a husband to a girl instead of being adopted by a widow, failed after four years. The husband failed, his wife left him for another man.

From the moment of the first marriage on, the composer leaves the personnel union of violinist-director-composer. Now he composes with purpose and consciously. Two hundred and sixteen opus numbers in the eighteen years from 1844 to July 1862, two hundred and thirteen in the thirty-seven following years to 1899, of those the first third, seventy-six works, in his accustomed style; in the eight years until autumn 1870 only isolated dances and marches—but from 1870 to 1899 not even fifty opus numbers of independent individual works, the remainder, from opus 347 to opus 479 only music for operettas.

Johann Strauss, Sr. had never thought of combining his music with words, much less with drama. Until the thirty-seventh year of his life, entirely in accordance with his father, the second Johann Strauss also gives no thought at all to the theater. The submissive son of his mother-spouses is forced to produce dramatic music; he was an operetta composer against his will and spent the second half of his life, which lasted seventy-four years, in vain attempts to prove to those around him and the world that he was not suited for the production of dramatic music, that the theater was foreign to him, and that they should finally cease to make such unreasonable demands upon him. Johann Strauss, Sr. perished miserably in a dark side street; Johann Strauss, the son, no less miserably in feudal, palacelike villas.

Just as unique as everything else in connection with the double phenomenon Johann Strauss is the duality in the creations of the son. Unique and otherwise unattained is the wealth of inferior material that he produced during his second, married existence. No genius ever even came close to producing as much useless music as this one, who could never do enough to himself in terms of self-punishment, self-abasement, and self-denial, who always sought and found ways to prove his lack of aptitude as a theater composer—in the middle of these proofs, however, very near the beginning, as the third of sixteen works for the stage, he fails with *Die Fledermaus*, justifies not only half but all of his life, and includes in its failure all the greatness and all the disputability of the "Vienna operetta," which it simultaneously creates, brings to a climax, and liquidates.

The casualness of the occasional compositions of a brilliant violin player and orchestra conductor made possible the gradual, undisturbed, organic development of a classical composer. In the twenties an album of dance compositions had appeared, in which pieces by Schubert, Lanner, and Strauss, Sr. lay next to each other. In Vienna especially, this commonality of great and popular music had been obvious for ages. *The Magic Flute* had combined very great and popular music for the naive public; Beethoven had written dances in the popular tone; the teacher of the young Johann Strauss, Joseph Drechsler, was a church composer and in addition the creator of the music for Ferdinand Raimund's suburban fairy tale *The Girl from the Fairy World.*

The waltz, expression of the middle-class awareness of life, had just as much right to citizenship in the realm of artistic music as the minuet before it, and even earlier the jig, allemande, saraband, and other dance forms of the suites and sonatas. The waltz appears in the works of Chopin and Glinka, in the *symphonie plastique* of Berlioz, in the works of Marschner, Schumann, Liszt, and Brahms, in Gounod's *Faust*, in Offenbach's opera, the ländler as scherzo for the Bruckner symphonies, and in the works of Gustav Mahler. The waltz is not purely Viennese, but was simply snatched up and developed in an especially joyful manner in Vienna. Over and beyond the individual piece of music, as a phenomenon, as an institution, to a certain extent as a view of the world, it was particularly important for its time, originally revolutionary, then symbol for self-assertion, as jazz was a hundred years later. Werther had already danced a waltz with Lotte; around 1800 the waltz was already well-known throughout Europe, but at first only as a rhythm, as a dance form, as expression, without regard to the compositions.

If there is a "father of the waltz" at all in artistic music, then that distinction does not belong to any Viennese, but to the North German Carl Maria von Weber, who perhaps brought his knowledge of the dance with him from Prague, where he was active as an orchestra leader from 1813 to 1816. In 1819, *Der Freischutz* appears with its waltz; in 1819 he also writes the amazing piano piece *Invitation to Dance*, and in so doing anticipates a formal development that the "classical waltz" does not attain until many decades later: an independent introduction, a series of individual waltzes, and a coda combined together to form a great musical work. When the *Invitation to Dance* appeared, the eighteen-year-old Lanner was making his debut as the first chair in a trio that was expanded to a quartet in 1820, when it was joined by the sixteen-year-old Johann Strauss. Lanner's first printed waltz appeared as opus 8, but Lanner's opus 7 was an arrangement of the *Invitation to Dance* (printed in 1827), but abbreviated, reduced to the pure dance music of the breathless "German dances" and "waltzes" of the early period. Thus Weber stands at the beginning of the "Vienna waltz."

Joseph Lanner and Strauss, Sr. reformed the waltz, gave it introductions and greater scope; Johann Strauss, the son, expanded and deepened it in his own right and gradually revised the form until it reached the level that Weber's generally well-known *Invitation to Dance* had already reached long before. Of course, Weber's piece had not been dance music, but impression, an idealistic-romantic representation of a ball—it was almost half a century before the ball realized Weber's image with the great classical waltzes of Johann Strauss, the son.

The waltz dominates the new century outside Vienna as well, but Vienna has a special affinity for it, adopts and adapts it, and gives it its own character.

Does the Vienna waltz deal directly with the joy of life? It may fill the dancer or the listener, but not the waltz music. The Vienna waltz of the classical waltz century has the entire bacchanal-dionysian trait of reeling self-assertion in conscious self-forgetfulness only once: the *Fledermaus* waltz in the finale of the second act. But otherwise the Vienna waltz is more and predominantly elegiacly nostalgic, dreamy, melancholy, in its very tempo reserved and withdrawn: the Viennese original waltz tempo, by which Johann Strauss, Jr. set especially great store, is slower than the minds of orchestra directors outside Austria imagine.

Tales from the Vienna Woods, *The Blue Danube*, *Vienna Blood*, the *Emperor's Waltz*, and even the little

Schubert waltzes do not arise from cheerfulness, from affirmation: they discover and paint the passing beauty of penumbral intermediate tones, and where they press forward into the light, the shadows always remain present as necessary complementary values.

It is much easier for two-four and four-four time than for three-four time to express and represent cheerfulness in music, the ironic, purposeful, happy, saucy gallopade, march, and cancan of Offenbach, which was alien to Johann Strauss (with the constant exception of *Die Fledermaus*), the even-numbered meter that traverses distances and clearly moves from a beginning to a goal, that can make the most of its even-numberedness or spice, "pointedly express" it with rhythmic punctuation. Actually three-quarter time is already punctuated, agitated, irregular; it is not purposeful movement, but lively persistence in the same thing, an attempt to hold on to time in the moment—the waltz revolves around its own axis, rests in itself, does not want to end, suspends time. The further the century progresses, the more decisively the waltz develops from conqueror to preserver and defender of the middle-class awareness of life, the more urgently it clings to not progressing further, not wanting to end, the more pieces of waltz music are extended, while the polka, the gallopade, and the quadrille conservatively retain their forms from the beginning and do not develop them further.

The waltz does not want to cease, and if it must cease, it flows from the peculiarity of its melodies into the general detachment of any number of meaningless, common closing phrases. In a great waltz by Johann Strauss everything is great and special, not just the conclusion, which could have been written by anyone, which dutifully and conventionally leads from infinity back into actuality. These "positive" endings should be taken no more seriously than the endings of Nestroy's plays with their engagements and shouts of hurrah! As long as the waltz lasts, time stands still, we have stolen forth from it unnoticed, glided out of it—how should we be able to find our way back without deep pain at a particular moment? A coda delays the end, perceives once more in concentrated form the "Please stay!" that is said to the moment, and can still only postpone the painful end a little bit, but not terminate the pressure to return to the even-numbered world. The ending of every waltz only demonstrates the knowledge that a waltz actually cannot end.

Joy of life? Where was the young Johann Strauss supposed to obtain it. Unlike his father, he was not even permitted to experience an intermezzo of joyful youthful pranks before he submitted himself to the trial of responsible, exposed activity. He was weighed down by his father's fame and name and burdened by his father's refusal to let his son become a musician, despite recognition of his talent. He had to bear the idea of his brilliant gift, learned to compose and play the violin (he secretly took violin lessons and earned the necessary money by giving piano lessons)—he surely wavered between serious and "light" music: as his journeyman's piece he presented his composition teacher Drechsler with a four-part gradual accompanied by wind instruments, *Tu qui regis totum orbem.*

On October 5, 1844, at the age of nineteen, he dared to do the unthinkable: as an unknown Johann Strauss he presented himself to the public with his own orchestra at Dommayer's in Hietzing, where the celebrated Johann Strauss had performed the previous May. And even though he was a success—as a violinist, orchestra director, and composer—that did not mean that the tension was resolved at all. Evening after evening he had to confirm his success anew, continue to compose, and prevail against understandable resistance in public opinion.

To advance into fame and popularity overnight at the age of nineteen demands in any case all of one's powers and nerves in a hardly conceivable manner—how much more when the breakthrough occurs under such auspices, when it is attempted against the father's will, and that father is Johann Strauss! The original situation of the crown prince tragedy is repeated; Prince Henry stole the crown while King Henry was still alive and had to defend it against his father again day after day.

We know but little about the emotional state of the young Johann Strauss in those years, but we can imagine it—he had surely inherited from his father not only his musical genius, but also his nervous temperament, and he probably also inherited from his grandfather a depressive disposition; and the crotchets and oppressions that we will find in the autumn of this life certainly have their roots in that unimaginably stormy and trying spring.

Three months after the death of his father, in the fifth year of his activity, when, at the request of the musicians, he has already taken on the direction of his father's orphaned orchestra, Johann Strauss must publish an extensive, ponderous, and humiliating text in the official *Wiener Zeitung*: "Heartfelt Thanks and Sincere Appeal to the Honored Viennese Audience," full of flattery directed toward the "noble-minded," "honored" Viennese, defensive phrases against the "often partisan judgment of the public" and the "judgment from the strict mouths of his opponents," who "exposed all of my weaknesses uncharitably enough and even invented additional ones when my own supply of youthful mistakes was not sufficient."

"At the moment when the number of my opponents increased," it then went on, "and that of my benefactors decreased," his father had died. And for the sake of his mother and siblings, "to whose only support the death of my dear father has solemnly called me," the "favor and forbearance of the honored public" is requested.

He is twenty-four when he accedes to autocratic rule. We are still in the mirror-image repetition of the already prefabricated Johann Strauss biography: a great wealth of concerts and balls; waltzes are written at the last minute, when the ball has already begun and the orchestra is meanwhile directed by the first violinist—at eleven-thirty Strauss and Fahrbach appear, lay out the parts, and the piece is premiered while being "sight-read." The announcement "Strauss in person" appears on many invitations and placards, and many a night Johann Strauss must rush from ball to ball in a cab, in order to play the violin while directing at least one or two pieces in person everywhere.

Like his father, he is favorably disposed toward the modern music of his time. On a concert program, in addition to his *Albion Polka* and his waltz *Ladybugs* he includes music from *Lohengrin*. In 1856, in honor of Liszt, he will play the *Mazeppa* in his presence, and as early as 1861 he will play music from *Tristan and Isolde* in the public garden in front of the court opera theater.

(Try to imagine Franz Lehár with his orchestra including music by Arnold Schönberg, or Paul Whiteman including music by Paul Hindemith in a program!)

The mirror-image biography also shows successful tours; the twenty-one-year-old travels through the Balkans; concert trips to Prague, Germany, and Russia soon follow.

But even the collapse as a result of excessive demands placed upon his strength is repeated. Only the extreme is not strived for and attained by sheer stubbornness—a mother is there and takes the reins in her hands: Johann must unharness himself, he must give up directing the orchestra himself.

And a third chapter of the family history begins, the most improbable among the improbabilities: the chapter about the genius against his will.

Josef Strauss, two years younger than Johann, had, of course, already played the piano as a boy; that will continue to be viewed as not peculiar. The mother, an innkeeper's daughter, had also written down the melody on one occasion when the six-year-old boy had tinkered out something in three-four time—and nobody was amazed that an ingenuous Viennese innkeeper's daughter could write notes.

But for Josef everything musical was only a sideline, a hobby. To be sure, he wrote, tried his hand at lyrical poetry and drama, and was also very talented as a sketch artist, but in spite of his multiple creative interests, he became a technician. He, too, prevailed in his choice of profession in conflict with his father, for his father wanted Josef to become a soldier, and the young man had to beseech him in a great letter:

> Just leave me where I am; let me be what I am, don't tear me away from a life that can bring me joy... Don't thrust me out into that unsettled, rough activity that destroys all feeling for what is human, to which I am not suited, to which I was not born. I do not want to learn to kill

people, do not want to be distinguished for hunting human lives...

How differently this young man writes, how much more freely, more vibrantly, with an authentic relationship to the words, when compared with his brother Johann, who wrote to his father in the same situation:

> Aware that in the difficult inner conflict in which his childish love can hardly be united with his sense of justice and his gratitude, vis-à-vis his dear father the loving son would lack the strength and firmness to choose the only thing that is truly good and noble, after mustering all the forces of my heart and mind for a step that is so important, so decisive for the future of my mother and me, I decided to use the limited talents whose development I owe to my dear mother in addition to Mother Nature, to give my meager thanks to her. Otherwise, under the current unfortunate circumstances whose improvement would depend only upon you, she would remain helpless and unprotected and completely abandoned by everyone.

Josef graduates from the secondary school that Johann has left after four years, studies at the polytechnical college, works as a construction designer, becomes an engineer, directs the construction of a dam, works in a factory, compiles a "collection of examples, formulae, problems, and tables from mathematics, mechanics, geometry, physics, etc., etc.," invents a new kind of street-sweeping machine, which—much later, to be sure—is purchased by the municipal authorities of Vienna.

According to the statement of his sister-in-law Jetty, Josef is "timid, reserved, entirely introverted," happily married to a childhood sweetheart, and is described as melancholy. Now the family presents itself against him categorically for the second time; now they do not leave him where he his, or let him be what he is; they tear him away from his life. He must take over the direction of the orchestra while Johann is recovering, and later he must share the direction with Johann.

Very hastily Josef learns music theory, he begins to educate himself as a violinist. In three years he learns to play the violin. For now he only directs; soon people see announcements with "J. Strauss" as orchestra director. The highly gifted engineer and technician makes a profession of his hobbies, raises the sideline to main endeavor. At age twenty-six, on July 23, 1853, he has his debut, and because it is also customary for dance orchestra directors to compose, he now also begins composing and plays his first waltz in August 1853.

Josef came to music only because Johann was exhausted. And he not only became a splendid director (whom Richard Wagner especially lauded on the occasion of a performance of music from *The Flying Dutchman*), he was also a gifted composer, of entirely equal rank with his father and brother. The number of compositions that he published also has three digits, the index of his works lists two hundred eighty-three, that were written in seventeen years, among them the *Village Swallows from Austria*, the *Dynamist Waltz*, which was used in *The Cavalier of the Rose*, *My Life's Career Is Love and Joy*, employed in the film *The Congress Dances* ("That must be a bit of heaven...")

He would have been capable of writing operettas; after all, he had written many poems and also a drama.

He had a legitimate relationship with the word and conceived music and words simultaneously.

A finished operetta is said to have been in his artistic estate, but the artistic estate disappeared amid mysterious accompanying phenomena and is still missing.

Josef died early, in 1870. His musical career had lasted only seventeen years. For the second time, the challenge "Strauss, see that you think of something" had called forth a rich life's work, a world wonder of inspiration and productivity—but it is the fate of every Strauss that he stands in the shadow of the other one; and thus this improbable Josef, too, is only a component of the family chronicle for his contemporaries and posterity, and not appropriately recognized as an independent phenomenon.

And nevertheless, all of them together, more world-famous than anyone else or anything in the field of music, stand in the shadows even as a combined phenomenon. The obviousness of their worth hinders a clear recognition of the individuals. For each Strauss is true, what Karl Kraus said about Nestroy: all of them are unknown to the many who know them.

There are a number of books about the Strauss family, about the father and the son (none about Josef Strauss)—to date there is no authentic, scientifically exact biography, no serious Strauss research. A fraction of what was invested in Franz Grillparzer, if dedicated to the Strauss family, would have preserved infinitely important material that is now already difficult to find. The great secular figures of the Strauss family are especially impressive examples of the fragmentary, incomplete, and misleading knowledge and self-understanding of Austria. The flight from greatness can also occur in the direction leading to the noncommittal, imprecise legend and consist of insufficient knowledge of greatness. There is no Schubert tribute without the stupid cliché "Prince of song," no Strauss tribute without "Waltz King" and "joy of life."

Because it sees itself as such and wants to be seen as such, the "City of Songs" neglects the question about the true, authentic features of its face.

In no tribute to the "Waltz King," for example, do we find the nevertheless noteworthy fact that in the church register of St. Stephen's Cathedral the marriage of Strauss, Sr.'s grandfather is recorded, who came from Budapest and received the notation "a baptized Jew." While searching for other ancestors, a genealogist accidentally found that notation while browsing and once mentioned it in the presence of National Socialists to whom he was talking. As a result, the gestapo confiscated the parish register and replaced it with a counterfeit in which the addition had been removed by means of photocopy. One day before the beginning of the siege of Vienna, in the spring of 1945, a gentleman from the gestapo appeared and returned the original to the parish office of St. Stephen's Cathedral.

In the Strauss books the birthplace of Johann Strauss, Jr. is also usually given as *Lerchenfelderstraße* 115, but it was really where the house *Lerchenfelderstraße* 15 now stands, a hundred and fifty paces from the birthplace of Joseph Lanner on *Mechitaristengasse*. The incorrect statement that *Die Fledermaus* was only performed sixteen times following the Vienna premiere, then dropped, is found inveterate in almost all the biographical works. Nor has the mystery surrounding the vanished estate of Josef Strauss ever been clearly solved.

With regard to the first decades of the life of the younger Johann Strauss, we know the titles of his works, the places where he appeared; we know some details that establish his sympathies for the revolution of 1848—that, too, reflects an extreme contrast to his conservative father who paid tribute to Field Marshal Radetzky—but his actual nature still remains in the dark. In 1859 Johann Strauss was in Russia for months. His love letters to Olga Smirnitzki have been preserved; in them, at one point an "Elise" is mentioned, to whom Johann is apparently engaged: "If my Mama has come to the conclusion that Elise cannot make me happy, she will also endeavor to remove that family in a very delicate and tender manner." A letter written by Jetty Strauss states that Johann "probably fooled many people in his life—for he was engaged thirteen times alone."

Just who was this Elise? What about the unbelievably numerous "engagements"? How and why did they collapse? We know nothing about it. We only perceive how the romantic Olga episode, with its secret rendezvous and smuggled letters, gave wings to and inspired the thirty-four-year-old man. He was never previously able to express himself as vivaciously as he did in those letters:

> There can no longer be any last kiss other than the one that I will press upon your lips before my death...—How unhappy I am—why can't you be with me?! Why can't I be like another human being?—I want to comfort myself through music—want to try it—but I cannot continue. My nerves tremble; my strength leaves me.— — —Olga, how unhappy I am! I hardly have enough strength to write these lines. I have never wept for myself—today—I confess it only to you—it happened. Oh, Olga, I feel that I will

soon die—and alone... But it is better that nobody knows what I have suffered.

Your Jean

And we almost refuse to believe that it is the same man who will later find his way back to the awkward, lifeless ponderousness of his weakness in verbal expression:

I want to give you my heartfelt thanks for the great effort and drudgery that you expended in the process of writing a biography concerning my humble self, in order to reach the goal that you had in mind, and, from what I hear, with generally satisfactory results. Unfortunately, I have not yet found the time to read your book—but since so much of it has appeared in local and out-of-town newspapers—the general opinion, which sounds as favorable as possible, is probably the same for specialists.

We know a few things about Olga, but about Elise and the other "fiancées" we know nothing. Concerning Henriette (Jetty) Treffz, whom he married in 1862, we know much, but not all. She was the life's companion of a wealthy man, the hostess of his popular salon, mother of his two daughters. She could not marry him because he had promised his father on the latter's deathbed, never to leave the Jewish religious fellowship, and because she did not want to renounce her membership in the Catholic Church. Before this union she had already given birth to one or more sons, had been lauded as a singer of Mendelssohn and Berlioz, and had been internationally successful.

When he married her, Johann Strauss grew a full beard, probably to compensate superficially for the age difference. In letters she calls him her boy: "My Jeany boy is the most well-behaved, noblest boy in the world." —"...they come is if we were going to pay them for it, and shout and cheer and idolize the boy for me."

Even though he was advised and directed and encouraged by his mother, he always had to do, handle, decide, and oversee so many things; he had not been equal to the internal and external burdens. It was not easy to be Johann Strauss; it was hardly bearable to be there in isolation and to work under the constant burden of his name and his world fame.

Schubert became Schubert because he did not know that he was Schubert. Raimund and Nestroy became Raimund and Nestroy because they considered themselves to be actors and only produced plays on the side. Grillparzer contented himself for half his life with the agonizing knowledge that he was Grillparzer and had ceased to do justice to the fact through regular creative activity. Adalbert Stifter escaped into inconspicuousness in Linz; Johann Strauss fled to the mothers, whom he married.

The great Austrian prose writer Adalbert Stifter does not begin writing prose until the middle of his life; the great Austrian dramatist Ferdinand Raimund only begins writing dramas in the middle of his life; the great Austrian prose writer Peter Altenberg only begins to publish prose in the middle of his life; the great Austrian composer Josef Strauss only turns to music in the middle of his life; in all these cases chance happenings caused the productivity.

Johann Strauss, the most successful of all operetta composers, writes his first operetta in the middle of his life. He does not want to. He is forced into the operetta, tricked, maneuvered into it. The middle of his life does not bring the breakthrough, but self-alienation, breach, and Grillparzerlike foundering in unfulfillment.

His spouse, Jetty, immediately seizes the management of the object named Johann Strauss, and the object is happy that he can finally be an object. Jetty releases him from some responsibilities and gradually makes a professional composer of him. Now he can no longer say like his father: "I did nothing to make them call me an artist, which I have never claimed to be." He has married Jenny Treffz, and in his name she does everything in that regard.

Never in his life did he have a way with words. Once, when he was already an old man, when invited to write, he himself admitted: "...here what counts is the word—a substance that has constantly been brittle and intractable for me." It seems that he only really perceived the vowels. Once he sang, so they say, from memory, accompanying himself and with no witty intention whatever, the text:

> Who runs forth admired from stone to stone
> And ends the dog's hunting slips iron from bone.

and it is a matter of the verse:

> What good is approval from all for what's done?
> The heart holds no hundred, it holds only one.

Once someone asked him which of his waltzes should be performed during a concert of the Dresden Orchestra, and in his letter of reply he named among others the waltz: *Millions, Be Greeted*. He no longer quite remembered the title (and what a title!) of the waltz *Be Embraced, Millions*, which had only been written a short time earlier.*

He was forty-two years old when music and word encountered each other again in his works for the first time since the music student's four-part gradual. For a gala of Carnival songs by the Vienna Men's Choral Society on February 15, 1876, he wrote a choral waltz, but the music was created first. The text was not added until later; it was written by the then popular lyricist Josef Weyl and is a piece of occasional poetry for Carnival that makes fun of the bad times following the lost war of 1866 while simultaneously intending to console people in Viennese fashion concerning the troubles of the times:

> Viennese, be gay!
>   Why that today?
> Just look, and you'll see!
>   What can it be?
> A shimmer of light!
>   Nothing's in sight!
> Well Carnival's here!
>   Not much, I fear!
> Thus time now defy,
>   The time, oh my!
> And your misery.
>   How bright that would be.
>
> What good is the fretting,
> Regretting?
> Thus be cheerful and free!

---

*These titles are translated literally to make the intended point.

Shrovetide law follow!
No matter how hollow
Your financing,
Let's be dancing!
Now they still perspire
Who sit by the fire
Just like the dancers all
At the ball.

The farmer scratches much,
Because hard times are such,
He takes a run with force,
Runs to the tax office and pays, of course.

His money is gone now, and how!
They won't give it back again!
But since it is Carnival now,
There's a ball going on at the inn.
There are still nice girls down there
We'll dance and we'll kick our share.
And if it's money we lack,
There's no money in anyone's sack!

A fat old landlord, he worries a lot,
He had many tenants, and now he does not.
No matter, in spite of his gall,
He's at the masquerade ball!
With six empty he'll begin
To raise the rents down the hall,
Tomorrow an artist moves in
Who'll pay nothing at all.

It's bad if he distrains,
There's nothing there to be had,

And so he wracks his brains
And dances mad.
When near the Graces the artist still
Feels good and ill
Like the fish in the rill.
Embodied he sees in the cheerful ray
The ideal he's dreamed of every day
It is he whose forehead the muse's touch meets,
Whose life becomes sweet, whom beauty greets.
Where love and great happiness blossom free,
The artist is at home, you see.

Moving, quick,
Young and slick
All the artists claim
Masterly their fame,
Thus 'tis right
When the heart
Of a lady greatly favors art.

Even political, critical men
Like to dance 'round in circles again,
Seem to fly quite boldly, yet they,
Never move away.
While they are waltzing as hard as they can,
They mentally spoil the soup in the pan.
Though they notes with exactness treat,
Here they always seem to lose the beat.

So with zest
Dance without peace or rest!
Savor the moment then,
For its joy won't come again.
Don't delay,

> Use what's yours today,
> Time will pass you by,
> And the roses of joy fade and die,
> So dance, yes, dance, yes, dance!

From the manuscript we see that this text represents the result of an adaptation. In the crossed-out original text we read among other things:

> Don't despair,
> Bravely bear...
> God helps in our greatest need.
>
> As long as the tavern still lends,
> Our life is not so hard,
> Do not lose heart and faint,
> What good is your complaint?
> Let's be brave, do what we can
> Until we are saved by heaven's plan.
>
> That Hungary of union won't hear
> Could rob us of our joy and good cheer,
> Best it is to forget it then,
> When fasting starts again.
>
> My Austria, you were e'er a blessèd land,
> A gracious hand
> Protects your strand,
> Even though clouds now deck the heavens here,
> Do not despair, Vienna dear.

It is puzzling that a piece of music with this text bears the title *By the Beautiful Blue Danube*, for the Danube is not mentioned in the text.

The line about the "beautiful blue Danube" was taken from a poem by the early nineteenth-century poet Karl Beck, who was somewhat well-known in his time. By making that author immortal, Johann Strauss, the son, paid a debt of gratitude, for Beck had once eulogized his father and Lanner:

> O Strauss and Lanner, roaming gypsy players,
> Selected by the god of dance as seers,
> Unto your violins' sweet magic prayers
> Both young and old now cling with wistful ears.
> The cheerful hall becomes a holy place;
> The heart's bell calls to dance a lovely round,
> Like choirs of men the violins resound—
> And from the stand now speaks to us the bass.

Now this same Karl Beck, the father's eulogizer, became the catalytic agent for the son's first encounter with real men's choruses in place of violins. But it did not happen in the spirit of verses from the section "Quiet Songs" in his collected poems, where there is an acquiescent eight-stanza love poem that emulates Heine: "By the Danube":

> And I saw your agony,
> And I saw you young and fine,
> Where the heart holds loyalty
> Like pure gold down in the mine
> By the Danube,
> By the beautiful blue Danube.

But she, "the restless one," goes to the colorful Orient, "on the Danube, on the beautiful blue Danube," and the singer remains alone behind...

> When I think that on the morrow,
> All too soon we now must part,
> Drives a wildly surging sorrow
> Never ending through my heart
> Like the Danube,
> Like the bottomless blue Danube.

By the light of the moon a mermaid rises "from the Danube, from the beautiful blue Danube" and inspires Lorelei reminiscences within him:

> Waters whisper tempting, mild,
> And they sing in lovely tones:
> You'd feel better, fevered child,
> Down here deep among the stones
> In the Danube,
> In the crystal-cool blue Danube.

It is difficult to explain Johann Strauss's choice of the title except in terms of what was certainly a chronic dilemma concerning titles. The audience, producers, and publishers set great store by titles, and in the indexes to the works of all waltz, polka, gallopade, and quadrille composers we find a wealth of far-fetched titles that arose out of quandaries and are not at all or only superficially related to the nature of the music: *Dashes* (waltz), *The Demons* (waltz), *The Insignificant Ones* (waltz), *Dance Recipes Waltz* (Strauss, Sr.)—*Fleeting Desire* (waltz), *Flowers of Desire* (waltz), *Nymph Gallopade*, *The Cavalry on Foot* (gallopade), *Karlsbad Mineral Water Waltz* (Lanner)—*Demon Quadrille*, *Bon Vivant Quadrille*, *Electromagnetic Polka*, *Glosses* (waltz), *Merchant Elite Quadrille*, *Telegraphic Dispatches* (waltz), *Flight of Fancy* (waltz), *Wrecker Polka* (Strauss,

Jr.). So Johann Strauss may have made a note of the phrase about the "beautiful blue Danube" for a future title, but there was no authentic congruity between the music, the title, and the text, which, from the point of view of handiwork, was adapted very casually and awkwardly to the music anyway.

The vocalized waltz, presented as the fifth of nine numbers on the program, did not fail during the premiere, as many biographies claim, but its success was not overpowering in any sense. For all that, the piece was not mentioned once in a detailed report in the *Neue Freie Presse*. Only when Johann Strauss played the waltz soon afterward in Paris and London, or when what had originally been sung had become absolute music again, did the natural phenomenon of effect take place, certainly assisted by the program that was suggested in the title.

Soon the waltz was known and loved throughout the world. As early as 1874 Eduard Hanslick called the piece a "wordless *Marseillaise* of peace" and wrote: "The Danube waltzes by Strauss have not simply achieved an unprecedented popularity, they have taken on a remarkable significance, the significance of a quotation, of a slogan... To the Austrian they are not simply waltzes, but patriotic folk songs without words. In addition to Father Haydn's anthem...in Strauss's *Beautiful Blue Danube* we have another folk hymn that celebrates our country and people... More clearly, penetratingly, and warmly than any words, this melody that has been impressed upon us all says everything flattering that can be said about the topic *Vienna*."

A consistent leitmotif in this competent tribute to a piece of music that was originally written for a song is the praise for its wordlessness. The first encounter of the absolute musician with the word was a total failure as such. A national anthem had come into being quite unintentionally, even almost against the will of its creator, otherwise he would have set store by an appropriate, generally valid text from the beginning.

Even the official Austrian Haydn hymn had bad luck with its texts, which celebrated first "Franz, the emperor," then "our emperor," and finally in the twilight of the First Republic the "wonderfully sweet earth of home." The Second Republic could not reintroduce the first Austrian hymn because its tones called forth associations with both the emperor and *Germany above All*.

And the other, unofficial Austrian hymn *O Thou, My Austria* also became popular unintentionally, in a grotesque, roundabout way, contrary to the original text. As an interlude for a dialect fairy-tale play, *The Little Mandrake* by Baron Klesheim—the author of the popular *May Breeze* song, Franz von Suppé had written a patriotic song:

> There where the snowy peaks
> Raise their heads proud and high
> Just as if they could say
> Something to the sky,
> There where the purest water
> From its sources flows,
> There where the wily hunter
> After the chamois goes
> When he upon the wall
> High on the rock cliff stands,
> Yes: That is my Austria,
> That is my fatherland.

During the premiere the female singer was booed so severely that she could hardly finish singing the song.

Many years later, the singer, comedian, and Offenbach translator Karl Treumann found the old forgotten song in the archives and employed it for a vaudeville song. Now the text was no longer political—the initial lines criticized and stood in satirical contrast to the chorus:

> There where so firm and true
> The era is fresh and new,
> Where the glow of freedom's light
> Now paints the future bright,
> Where no canals are made
> And no bad pavement's laid,
> Where in the treasury
> Not one dime's found, I fear,
> This is my Austria,
> My birth place, it is here,
> And this is my home town,
> Vienna dear!

This time the success was substantial, and from that moment on the song became the unofficial national anthem which even today gives expression to both patriotic and satirical-critical moods that in Austria, unlike other places, intersect, overlap, and get mixed up with one another... And from the text nothing but the four chorus words are popular, just as the Danube hymn, unlike hymns in other places, lives on without a text, for even the somewhat more successful new texts are foreign to the music that is intended for the violin and not to be sung.

Oh Thou, My Austria celebrates in four words the love-hate relationship to the state; *By the Beautiful Blue Danube* wordlessly sings the love of country.

But after the first failed attempt to break free of what was for him a characteristic wordlessness, Johann Strauss permitted himself to be afflicted by words again and again. What happens there in terms of tragic futility seems to be less a wrestling with words and drama than a struggle against words and drama; Johann Strauss wants to prove again and again—to whom?—that he is not a dramatic composer. He approaches the proof successfully fifteen times, but once he is blessed with failure. The hour of the operetta strikes. Johann Strauss establishes and destroys the Vienna operetta, and its existence actually last only one hour: from the beginning of *Die Fledermaus* to the middle of its second act.

He does not want to, he resists, he has had nothing to do with the theater, he has no interest in the theater, he is an Austrian, and he feels that the talent for acting, for singing on stage, and for the handiwork of the theater orchestra director is at home there, but not the talent for dramatic production. Before him Schubert ran aground on the theater; next to him Hugo Wolf will fail in the theater. The libretti are always at fault, but not the libretti alone. Schubert was certainly filled with resistance similar to that of Johann Strauss. We know of Schubert's somnambulant, entranced intensity while composing; but as Spaun reports, he wrote the music to a musical play "without great interest for the project." Schubert's music was epic and lyrical; he was just as unsuited for the dramatically pointed "expositions" as Johann Strauss was unsuited for the ensembles and the finali of the musical drama. Mozart was Austria's first and last musical dramatist; Raimund's *The King of the Alps and the Misanthrope* is Austria's only authentic dramatic play to date. Nestroy had obtained the dramatic substance from his sources, Grillparzer knew what was necessary then got stuck half way through, but Strauss was driven. When he was not willing, force was used. His wife Jetty purloined sketches and drafts from his desk. In the *Theater an der Wien* the melodies were given texts and arranged. Strauss was asked to go to the theater on a pretext. They played and sang the pieces for him. Amazed, he recognized them as his own and in that fashion was supposed to become accustomed to the idea that his music could also be sung.

What dramatic composer ever came to the musical theater at that age and in such a manner? The others promoted themselves for the theater; Johann Strauss resisted the theater. The fact that he resisted until his death did him no good; the products of his resistance are his operettas as creations of the most successful composer. Today, however, they are hardly known anymore by name for the most part, so successfully did he defend himself against the dictate—who still remembers *Woodruff*, *Blindman's Buff*, *Princess Ninetta*, *Jabuka*, or *The Goddess of Reason*?

The entire dilemma that he brought on himself and the self-destructive joy of failure are given expression in an atrocious letter:

> With respect to my work, with the best of intentions I was not able to find any inspiration for the book. It has neither a poetic nor a comical tone. It is a trite, bombastic story that actually needs no music, for the whole thing is there only to deliver the [author's] jokes, some of which are quite excellent. The action and music form the framework. The play is nothing other that the exposition of the jokes. No trace of plot, and just as little trace of a need for music.

I never had the libretto with its dialogue in front of me, only the song texts. For that reason I saw many things in a too noble light, which was detrimental to the project. In his book there is nothing that can be seen in a noble light. During the final rehearsals, where I became acquainted with the entire story, I was very shocked. No sincere feeling, no rationality in the end! Just foolishness!!! The music does not fit this crazy artless material at all. It is a mad sort of farce without music (or at most a few lively, humorous, impromptu songs). It lacks any inner feeling, any healthy reason, but also any comical situation that arises from the material. It is a tightrope act around the author's jokes! And robbers and murderers for that?!... I am happy about only one thing: that they were not able to prevent a complete revolt in Berlin. I will be even happier if the whole thing soon winds up in the nursing home. They can have it; I won't shed a tear for it."

That is not just "indolence with respect to the dramatic," as one biographer believes; that is passivity that turns into self-destructive activity.

One is reminded of Grillparzer's: "Thank God...I cut my finger." One looks disconcertedly at this self-punishment, at the artistic suicide of the composer Johann Strauss, which lasted for almost three decades.

It is also mysterious that the dramatic production begins very soon after the death of the dramatically gifted Josef Strauss. Josef dies in 1870, the first Strauss operetta premiere, *Indigo*, is in 1871. Josef's artistic estate had disappeared. Again and again suspicions have been expressed in that connection. Serious experts claim that the *Fledermaus* music or the music of *Carnival in Rome* is partially the work of Josef Strauss. Around 1912 Josef's daughter said that she suspected that Johann had used pieces by her father in *Indigo*, and Josef's family is similarly said to have recognized music by Josef Strauss in *Carnival in Rome*. The role played by Richard Genée, the librettist for five Strauss operettas and an all-around musical literary talent—author, director, arranger, and composer of operas and operettas—is also still open to question. He is said to have boasted that even *Indigo* would have been a success if he had collaborated. The melodrama at the beginning of the third act in *Die Fledermaus*, with its brilliant leitmotifs, is said to have originated with Genée. In any case, he was not only the author of song texts but also a musical advisor. In her reminiscences on the occasion of the centennial of Johann Strauss's birth a singer from the Strauss operetta period reported that Johann Strauss's musical sketches were "very meticulously sorted" in Genée's presence.

Much becomes unclear as soon as we examine the dramatic creations of the non-dramatist, but the agonizing perversity of the undertakings surrounding his operettas is quite clear; clear is the unkindness of a clique of friends and advisors under the leadership of each respective wife; very clear is the predominance of catastrophic failures that result from the synthesis of perplexity and industry.

Once Johann Strauss began composing a *Romulus*, but did not finish it. The manuscript is missing. Then he completed an operetta *The Merry Wives of Vienna*, but withdrew it because he did not agree with the casting for the female leading role. That manuscript is also missing.

It is suspected that an operetta *Don Quixote* was also composed. But nothing more is known about that either.

Indigo had its premiere on February 10, 1871. The writer of the libretto was not named in the theater program, but was replaced by the director of the *Theater an der Wien*: "Based on an older theme, adapted for this stage by Maximilian Steiner." So many hands had worked and puttered with the book that the actual situation could not be formulated in the usual manner. (*Indigo* was cooked up entirely in Vienna, and to be more precise, by so many cooks who worked with and against each other that we do not know at all who is actually responsible for the shoddy piece of work." Eduard Hanslick) In the Vienna operetta's hour of birth, one of its mortal sins has already become its godfather, one that anticipates our unfortunate film practices: the irresponsible multiplicity of collaborators and advisors. (Hanslick: "...this libretto, which has a poor plot and insultingly shallow and banal dialogue, will grievously impair the success of the operetta everywhere.")

The second operetta, *Carnival in Rome* (premiere on March 1, 1873), at least had recognizable authors, Josef Braun and Richard Genée, and a serviceable source, the play *Piccolino* by Sardou—the second mortal sin of the Vienna operetta, that it indiscriminately and unscrupulously abuses foreign material and almost never acknowledges its source. *The Count of Luxembourg* also came originally from Sardou; *The Merry Widow* (like *Die Fledermaus*) had been derived from a play by Meilhac and Halévy; *The Student Beggar* combined several unnamed sources; *Countess Mariza* was based among other things on a Hungarian piece *Teremtette*. More or less every operetta of the later period comes from the same sort of usually secret borrowings, right down to the embarrassing reminiscences of *Carmen* in *Giuditta* by Lehár.

In the *Carnival* book we are moved by the anticipation of the champagne apotheosis from *Die Fledermaus*:

> Champagne, it lets the soul take wing,
> It loosens up the tongue,
> It teaches all to sing
> Who never notes have sung.

Some texts have poetic charm, for example, the description of an evening mood by a painter:

> Colors, light,
> As they died,
> Distant scene
> Bathed in blue,
> On mats of green
> Dark shadow hue,
> The hill's bright top
> Now lined with gold,
> There I did stop,
> Let dreams unfold.

Other things, however, are irreparably and hopelessly silly and objectionable: the inversions ("Oh, could I find only of him the trail"—"I'll let myself here not be locked in") and awkward pseudolearned verses like:

> World-famed Rome of yore
> On the Tiber's shore,
> That in majesty
> Stands for centuries,
> As by night, so by day,

Nothing's like your display,
Your fame's from time gone by,
And it will not soon die.

Then comes the special case of *Die Fledermaus*, which will be treated separately.

Cagliostro in Vienna, with a text by Zell and Genée, appeared as the fourth operetta on February 27, 1875 and introduced a new mortal sin of the Vienna operetta. In a libretto like a folk play, with mostly good-natured, pleasant, naive verses, but no dramatically convincing plot, a Hungarian appears, probably because the Hungarian flavor succeeded in the czardas of *Die Fledermaus*, which preceded it. From now until the bitter Abrahamic end, a calamitous Hungarianization of the Viennese will spread and poison the real Viennese nature of the Vienna operetta. After the Orient, Rome, and the no-man's-land of *Die Fledermaus*, for the first time Johann Strauss moves the Vienna operetta to Vienna. But simultaneously its alienation from Vienna becomes imminent. In *Cagliostro* the brilliant actor Alexander Girardi appears for the first time as a collaborator in a Strauss operetta, at first providing enrichment and refinement, but later only another cause for decline. For the helpless, insecure composer later wrote many of his stage works specifically for Girardi; the interpreter came before the work, the Girardi role was compulsory, speculation about Girardi's success stood in the foreground, the popular comedian dictated the rules of the action—and once, after Strauss had played a new piece of music for him, Strauss asked Girardi: "Now, is that vulgar enough for you?"

The real and cordial friendship between the composer and his star reveals certain traits of an almost tragic attachment bordering on bondage, and Johann Strauss's loneliness, an unsated, unfulfilled need to communicate. Although they lived next door and saw each other daily, Strauss often sent letters to Girardi at night.

Prince Methuselah (January 3, 1877) is referred to as a "comic opera." The book by the Frenchmen Wilder and Delacour, who had adapted *Die Fledermaus* for Paris, was translated into German by Karl Treumann. It can be assumed that no takers had been found in Paris, otherwise the libretto would hardly have been available to Strauss. "It is a shame, however," wrote Daniel Spitzer, "that the lilting melodies of our Strauss have to carry the freight of such a boring text...the new texts are all old enough to make a person yawn, and when we see how little spirit and mood the satirical librettists applied to their task, it gives the impression that after sufficiently running down the high-ranking ladies and gentlemen of the altar, the throne, and Olympus, they even intended to make fun of a venerable theater audience."

Just like this belated, watered-down Offenbach imitation, the operetta *Blindman's Buff* (December 18, 1878, text by Rudolf Kneisel) proved unsuccessful. The second finale climaxes in the tiresomely repeated verse:

> Blinded cow!* Look at you!
> We all will lead you. Moo! Moo! Moo!

which intensifies to the apotheosis of tediousness before the curtain falls, as follows:

> Blinded cow! Look at you!
> Now at last we're through, yes through!
> Moo! Moo!

*Literal translation of the German expression for blindman's buff.

At the premiere people circulated the witticism that this time Treffz's infallibility was missing.*

Jetty had died in April of that year. Strauss left the apartment, never returned to it, and moved to a hotel. He was not present at the funeral. We will yet learn from numerous details about the condition of the man's soul who is recognized as the incarnation of the joy of life and carefree merriment. He could not bear the thought of death. Once he said: "I am afraid when I am alone."

In September, five months after Jetty's death, he marries again. Just once he attempts to be a man, takes a young, charming girl to wife, and it fails very badly, ends with adultery and divorce after four years. Johann Strauss must look for a new mother.

His next operetta, *The Queen's Lace Handkerchief* (October 1, 1880, book by Bohrmann and Genée), gives Hanslick occasion for justified criticism: "All too eager librettists, in our opinion, have impaired Strauss's talent and his successes by almost always speculating on an audience with coarse taste and a low level of education, with grotesquely outfitted caricatures, impossible situations, and forcibly wedged-in, deplorable jokes." The writer Cervantes is degraded to an operetta hero, and that prefigures the additional disaster of the operettas that will hold orgies in the desecration of Paganini, Schubert, and Goethe.

From the music to *The Queen's Lace Handkerchief* the waltz *Roses from the South* was put together. It reveals how woodenly, vapidly, desperately the words are grafted into the music of the first waltz melody, the *Truffle Song*:

---

*The original German contains a wordplay that cannot be translated.

> It always comes to mind again,
> The thing that once amused me,
> But it's betrayed by its bouquet
> So sweet, so charming, fragrant, gay...

the second waltz melody, the romance:

> Where the wild rose blossoms so fair
> It draws me there...

Freed from the text, the music takes a deep breath and can fully develop, just as it does in the Danube waltz.

Things happen in an absolutely ghastly manner in this libretto when a vaudeville song about stomach ailments is sung in the most tedious Viennese argot; and that occurs in spite of the Iberian milieu:

> No one suspects that I sit here in pain,
> As I graciously fool them all again,
> A gravy comes now, one that's sticky, plain,
> I take it, though it might well be my bane...

The Merry War (November 25, 1881, book by Zell and Genée) did not fare much better, and one critic rightfully noted that it remained "an eternal mystery, why a musician of the calibre of a Johann Strauss does not judge with more certainty in assessing what is demanded of his musical genius, his very own specialty."

Nor did *Night in Venice* (November 9, 1883, book by Zell and Genée) bring any change, but instead even caused a theater scandal during the Berlin premiere, because of the silly text. Strauss could even have obtained from Zell and Genée the significantly better script of the *Beggar Student*, but he chose the silly, formless one of *Night in Venice*. He had also rejected the libretto for *Fatinitza*, which then brought Franz von Suppé his first great success. He had no desire.

During the development of *Night in Venice*, Lili, his second wife, had still interfered. With the premiere of the operetta began the reign of the thirty-years-younger, third, and last wife, Adele, who had become a widow at the age of twenty-one and brought a daughter into the marriage. Her name was already Strauss before she married Johann Strauss. At her wedding, when she had married Anton Strauss, the son of a family friend, Johann Strauss had been a witness to the marriage. Here was a woman who was already Mrs. Strauss and did not have to be made Mrs. Strauss. She began her reign very soon after Lili's departure, even though a long time passed before they were married.

Like Raimund and Nestroy, Johann Strauss could not marry in Austria because the divorcée whom he had married too hastily was still alive. After difficult struggles he found a solution, acquired citizenship in Coburg, and married there in a Protestant ceremony in 1887.

Before that, *The Gypsy Baron* had already been written and had premiered successfully (on May 24, 1885), the product of serious, conscientious work, and yet also a further declining step in the dissociation of the Vienna operetta from Vienna, once again not Viennese, even though the third act celebrates Vienna, again with coarse Hungarian comedy that pays tribute to a life associated with raising pigs ("The ideal purpose of my life is pigs and bacon"). Above all, however, in *The Gypsy Baron* the sentimental second finale of the later operetta pattern is introduced for the first time, which draws the eternally constant pseudotragic conclusions from the class distinctions:

Barinkay: My heart I did dedicate
To the Gypsy maid—
I cannot ever dare your hand to take,
The princess I must now forsake!
Saffi *heatedly*: You don't love me!
Barinkay: Oh, if that were true,
I could without sorrow
Leave tomorrow!
Saffi: You'd leave? I cannot understand it!
It is my love for you that will demand it!

Ignatz Schnitzer, the librettist of *The Gypsy Baron*, who was a Hungarian like the Strauss librettists Braun and Dóczy (his linguistic origins are noticeable in the [German version of the] line "I cannot understand it!"), possessed the facility to intuitively provide natural texts for already existing music. It even got to the point that on one occasion, when Johann Strauss wanted the vowels A and I employed as much as possible in the lyrics to a particular piece of music, Schnitzer actually gave him the text:

How mild is the nightingale's call and song in the night:
O love, precious love, it is truly heaven's might.*

But this practice was transformed from exception to rule. A decisive weakness of the musical dramatist Johann Strauss is the fact that again and again a text must laboriously be set to the already formulated music, whereby the composer, with no sense of language, was quite indiscriminate.

*In the German original almost every word has the desired vowels.

Schnitzer reports that Strauss commended to him the cook's song from *Night in Venice* as a model:

> Tacka, tacka, tack,
> I first hack fine,
> Tacka, tacka, tack,
> This stuff of mine...
>
> Mixing, mixing, mix,
> I with my pin,
> Mixing, mixing, mix,
> Stir three eggs in...
>
> Pimperim, pimpim,
> Grind the crumbs, I do,
> Pimperim, pimpim,
> And add them too...

And when Schnitzer expressed his justified objections, Strauss said: "But look, my dear man, it sounds good!"

Strauss heard only rhythms and vowels, had little appreciation for words and actions, and apparently hated the theater so much that he could not really concentrate on his tasks as a musical dramatist at all. He only superficially considered the scripts that were to be performed, and sometimes did not even look at them. In Eduard Hanslick's obituary we read: "Strauss himself admitted to me that my suspicion was correct, and that his text writers usually had to set the words, for better or worse, to pieces of music after they were finished." And if that was not the case, the composer expressed the angry criticism that they did not have the capability "to write for existing music," as if the lack and not the exercise were a sin.

The method set a precedent. Lehár habitually had librettists add texts to his music and even had Goethe verses rewritten for the sake of the melody.

But what happened in the third wife's domain after *The Gypsy Baron* surpasses in every respect even the worst previous orgies of failure. Six more works came into being, six pitiful libretti, six failures, and all that in a nasty, hectic atmosphere of increased industry that attracted powerful journalists of the time as librettists (Max Kalbeck, Julius Bauer, Hugo Wittmann, Bernhard Buchbinder) and debased the genius of the poor, aging, fearful, helpless master to the object of commercial speculation, which furthermore had to fail because it was all too shrewdly engineered. Because *The Trumpeter of Säckingen* was a hit, an old German operetta had to be written; because *The Bartered Bride* was successful, a Slavic operetta had to be produced.

The old German operetta *Simplicius* (July 17, 1887, book: Victor Leon) lived on (and died of) the erroneous idea of having Girardi play the Parsifal figure of a sylvan. Again the composer was completely conscious of the questionable nature of his undertaking: "Simplicius and Tilly absorb all the interest. Everything else lacks characteristic representation. Armin is present, in order to have a tenor voice sing in the operetta. When he bawls out into it, it is actually nonsense, because in the plot he is the lord of uselessness."

The language also leaves much to be desired. The hero Simplicius makes his first appearance as follows:

> Sought mushrooms and roots in the woods and knelt
> In feathery moss; as though
> By accident I suddenly felt
> In my ear a terrible blow.

Then came the abortive excursion into the field of the opera *Knight Pásmán* (June 1, 1892, book: Ludwig von Dóczy), which failed both because of the prosaic philistine text and because it lacked formal dramatic power—the abortive *Princess Ninetta* (June 16, 1893, book: Bauer-Wittmann) with a wealth of textual gaffes ("...let me say what it is, that here in my heart turns, that feels where true love burns")—Strauss wrote to his brother-in-law: "I wrote this work without inspiration—it will become a piece of junk, you can depend on it"—the abortive *Jabuka* (October 12, 1894, book: Kalbeck-Davis), organized as a production to compete with *The Bartered Bride*, humorless and lacking any high linguistic standard (for the sake of a rhyme with *Stärke* the word *Marke* has to become *Märke*)—the abortive *Woodruff* (December 4, 1895, book: Davis), in which Girardi had to speak in the dialect of Saxony, intolerable because of its philistine farce humor:

> The golden tinsel flies away,
> And soon has fled the day
> Of love's sweet tender bliss!
> Now all's amiss!

And finally as the crowning low point *The Goddess of Reason* (March 13, 1897, book: Willner-Buchbinder). Johann Strauss believed in this opus so little and had been so irritated by the impertinent, almost extortionate machinations of the librettists that he did not go to the premiere.

He was an artist as long as nobody did anything to cause them "to call" him "an artist." Otherwise he was, as recorded in the obituary notice of a Vienna newspaper, "always only the milk cow for royalty-crazy bookmakers." We add: and for a wife who had married into a flourishing composition business.

(Even Ignatz Schnitzer calls Adele "enterprising" in his deliberately cautious and uncritical memoirs, which appeared while she was still alive, and speaks of her "agile piousness"; he states that she "introduced" the librettists Wittmann, Bauer, Leon, Kalbeck, Davis, Dóczy, and Willner to Johann Strauss. And Johannes Brahms, a friend of the old Strauss and guest of the family, supposedly once said that he wished the composer success in his next work, because he liked him so much, because he was so excited..."and then the woman who still gives him hell.")

An incorruptible witness speaks up for the first time as a contemporary: Karl Kraus, whose *Fackel* strikes up its dirge for Johann Strauss in its seventh issue: "One day a group of jobbers and reporters began to sway to the beat of his *Beautiful Blue Danube*; since then a ring of tarock players and theater agents has kept the creative power of the genius almost forcibly surrounded. At that time, Johann Strauss died, married, and became an honorary member of the 'concord.'"

He sentenced himself to this death; he seems to have needed it, to have fanatically affirmed it—his tender, almost humbly submissive letters to Adele prove that. He often wrote them, like the letters to Girardi, from the immediate vicinity, at night, from one room in the house to the other, because he was afraid when he was alone. With his sixteen dramatic works he invented and destroyed the Vienna operetta; from *Indigo* to *The Goddess of Reason* we can read off an entire historical development. It is situated in that area that is called "on the Vienna," because an unattractive river called the Vienna flows past there, one that could sometimes become dangerous and overflow its banks in the spring, but which has since then been regulated and tamed and rendered invisible. There, on the Vienna, *The Magic Flute* came into being and *The Vagabond* was performed, then later, when the Vienna was no longer visible, *The Princess of Czardas* and *Countess Mariza*. In the autumn of 1945 the then homeless Vienna State Opera opened in the *Theater an der Wien* with *Fidelio*. While these lines are being written, the beautiful, venerable building is being remodeled as the *Wiener Festspielhaus*.

Die Fledermaus also premiered in the *Theater an der Wien*. It stands in the middle of the disastrous development from *Indigo* to *The Goddess of Reason* simultaneously as a glowing justification, an example, and a counter-example. It is only this third of the sixteen dramatic works that makes the tragedy complete, for it shows an enormous possibility, a promise that is not realized. Its greatest charm for the connoisseurs and admirers in the auditorium is an unconscious one: People want to see *Die Fledermaus* again and again because it begins so splendidly and they continue to hope that it will go on that way to the end, but in vain: *Die Fledermaus* begins like *Così fan tutte* and ends like *Countess Mariza*.

The great hour of the operetta has struck, but word and genre have not just come into being in Paris. Even when dramatic music was gradually emancipating itself from Italian domination at the time of Mozart—and that really was not very long ago!—the term *operetta* was used for the comic opera. *The Abduction from the Seraglio*, *Così fan tutte*, and even *Don Juan* were occasionally referred to as "operettas." In 1787, Goethe wrote about operettas in his Rome notes; in 1825,

Schubert's friend Schwind wrote to Schubert's friend Schober: "If you would like to make an operetta or an opera out of *David and Abigail*, or something else, he would like to have a text, but with few words."

When Offenbach composes one-act works from 1845 on and changes to pieces that fill an evening in 1858, he does not create a form, but remains within the framework of what has long existed between the musical play and the *opera buffa—opéra comique*. The same for Franz von Suppé, born in 1819, Belgian origins, native language Italian, beginning in 1840 theater orchestra director in Vienna, creator of an infinite amount of utility music: overtures, interludes for popular farces and folk plays; the same for Karl Millöcker, born in 1842, theater orchestra director in Graz and Vienna, composer of the music for plays by Anzengruber. Suppé, like Offenbach, began with the one-act operetta (1860, *The Boarding School*), as did Millöcker (1867, *The Chaste Diana*)—both, however, arrive at the evening-filling operetta after Johann Strauss, Suppé in 1876 with *Fatinitza*, Millöcker in 1878 with *The Enchanted Castle*.

All this happened under the influence of Jacques Offenbach, who was first presented in Vienna by Nestroy, caused a sensation there, and soon appeared personally in Vienna. Offenbach's operettas, usually topical in text, were definitely operettas in the sense of Goethe, Mozart, and Schubert, cheerful comic or buffo operas, to be performed by singers, with ensembles, finali, and all the traditional formal elements of the opera—closer and more related to Nicolai, Auber, and Lortzing than to Lehár or Kálmán or even the late Johann Strauss. As operas they had the lovely, naive, but thoroughly organic matter-of-factness of the fairy-tale milieu, far from all reality, whether they played in antiquity, in satirically stylized, imaginary small countries, in the domain of the fabulous Bluebeard, or even in Paris, when the rich Brazilian, upon his arrival at the railway station, simply strews money among the people there.

In Vienna the magically intact comic-opera world of the great Parisians Offenbach, Audran, Lecocq, and Maillart was robbed of its paradisiacal unscrupulousness from the very beginning, in that it remained limited to the music, while the texts were watered down, coarsened, and "rendered idiotic." Thus a pseudo-Offenbach cliché came into being and, while abusing Offenbach, established a calamitous tradition.

Just once the miracle of the obviously paradisiacal irreality succeeded in Vienna, and it occurred thanks to a breathtaking detour.

There was a prose comedy by the Offenbach librettists Meilhac and Halévy, entitled *Réveillon*, whose basic idea had been borrowed from a comedy by the honorable German Roderich Benedix entitled *The Prison*. They did not want to play *Réveillon* as it was, either in the *Theater an der Wien* or in the *Carl Theater*, for the institution of the midnight supper, which anticipates our New Year's Eve mood on Christmas Eve, was unknown in Vienna and risky as a prerequisite for humorous entanglements. Because of a lack of confidence in the material they arrived at the solution of having the play adapted as an operetta for Johann Strauss; thus the music was a fill-in, an emergency measure, and what was to become the most Viennese of all Vienna operettas was adapted for Vienna by the East Prussian Carl Haffner and the West Prussian Richard Genée, based on a French original that was traceable to Roderich Benedix from Saxony.

It is also amazing in this case that no costumes and stylizations justify the music. We find ourselves in the present. The people acting on the stage are like those sitting in the orchestra section; until now the latter did not usually sing on the stage.

The miracle of *Die Fledermaus* is fed from many sources. What all had to happen before the libretto, against all probability and better judgment, became what it did and came into Johann Strauss's hands! And how does one explain the fact that the obscure theater artisan Haffner and the skilled old hand Genée created a mood and an atmosphere here that are radically different from everything that happened before and afterward on the operetta stage? Just as the honorable Schikaneder somnambulantly rose to the heights of the great poem about the "sacred halls," two artisans had transcended themselves for one historic moment.

The events are not localized in or near Vienna (the city is only mentioned once in the second scene of the first act, but even that is without meaning and appears to be an inadvertently remaining relic of an earlier version). We find ourselves in a "bathing resort in the vicinity of a large city," and even that is a component of the miracle, for as a result, all of the laws of actuality are sent on vacation, everyday problems can take a day off, nothing has to be as serious as it is. In the trappings of the present we encounter the spirit of the ancient comedy: the *Dottore* Dr. Blind could have his origins with Molière, Gozzi, Goldoni, or Mozart; the lady's maid Adele could be called Susanne, Smeraldina, or Despina and plays "*la serva padrona*" in their fashion.

But this *Fledermaus* also reminds us of *The Vagabond*, for it radically contradicts—and that is how the miracle becomes so wonderfully incomprehensible—the ancient, well-founded laws of the theater and of dramaturgy. An operetta in the costumes of today?—inconceivable! The title *Die Fledermaus* [The Bat]—disgusting and repellent! How does the nocturnally loathsome animal reach the point of announcing the embodiment of joyful merriment? This title (like the evil spirit called the vagabond) is only superficially tied to the action, and moreover the frame story that is marked by the title is uninteresting, indistinct, neither comical nor exciting. Even connoisseurs and admirers of *Die Fledermaus* will have difficulty repeating the actual bat story. Again (like Knieriem in *The Vagabond*) a major figure is introduced in the first act—the singing teacher Alfred—who does not appear in the second act. And the end of the second act (as in *The Vagabond*) brings no dramatic climax; the action falters and disintegrates during the general singing.

All this and more that is still to be discussed changes brilliantly to something positive under the sign of *nevertheless*.

Perhaps a specific local constellation contributed to it: As *Die Fledermaus* came into being, the ethereal awareness of life that developed fully in parties and love affairs and even remained merry in prison, was the reflection of an authentic mood. Then came "Black Friday" with the stock market crash, unrest, social insecurity, upheaval, and dissatisfaction. What was conceived as a portrait now appeared as a glorious memory. *Die Fledermaus* plays, so to speak, during the night from a Thursday to a Friday that still does not know that it is Black Friday. To be sure, its ladies and gentlemen wear the costumes of people attending a premiere, but they are really already historical figures.

Three notable works of the Austrian theater have this noteworthy tendency to pretend to be a today that no longer exists. (Just as the intact Austro-Hungarian army was still defending the monarchy in 1918, when the latter no longer existed.) At its premiere, *Die Fledermaus* showed a reflection in a mirror that was broken a year earlier. In *The Difficult Man* by Hofmannsthal, the First World War, and with it the monarchy, has ended; in spite of that the title figure is supposed to "make his debut as a speaker in the session of the upper chamber of the legislature on the day after tomorrow." The upper chamber of the legislature ceased to exist along with the monarchy, but here it is still presumed to exist; yesterday is assimilated as experience into today and "immortalized." In the cast listing of *The Difficult Man* the customary information about time and scene of the action is missing. And in Kálmán's *Countess Mariza*, which premiered in 1924, fifty years after *Die Fledermaus*, they sing: "Come along to Warasdin...there the whole world is still red-white-green." *Countess Mariza* is not a historical operetta, it plays in the contemporary world of the twenties. Red, white, and green are the Hungarian national colors, but Warasdin was ceded to Yugoslavia in the Treaty of Trianon in 1920. For political reasons, to come along to Warasdin was unthinkable for the Hungarians around Countess Mariza. In 1921 Yugoslavia had entered into the anti-Hungarian alliance of the "Little Entente" with Rumania and Czechoslovakia; all that negated the operetta, just as *Die Fledermaus* and *The Difficult Man* negated actuality. In the no-man's-land of the Austrian no-man's-time they dream of a lost paradise and assume that it still exists: just one place—the bathing resort of *Die Fledermaus*, the prewar-postwar Vienna of *The Difficult Man*, the Warasdin of *Countess Mariza* stands for the world, and there, in this one place, if one is prepared to believe in it, "the whole world still" can be read, white, and green.

Like *The Vagabond, Die Fledermaus* has no actual plot. The plot begins but is not organically continued. The action is unimportant, the mood, the attitude toward life is everything. In *The Vagabond* it is the melancholy, the deep-seated fear and anxiety, the turning toward earthly things because the comet is coming next year, the unwillingness to improve and use Lady Luck's gifts meaningfully—in *The Vagabond* the Austrian's real, authentic attitude toward life, in *Die Fledermaus* the dreamed one. Work is done here but not there. As a young married man, one is already a "pensioner," as a singing teacher one gives no lessons but sings serenades. The prison warden attends parties, the jailer gets drunk. (Zwirn: "They do nothing but work, eat, drink, and sleep—is that any kind of order?") And it is also part of this special shared disdain for action that in both *The Vagabond* and *Die Fledermaus* the plot is not rejected from the beginning and neglected in favor of pure portrayal of mood, but that in both instances it quite properly begins, gets under way, continues, and develops, only to be negated, spurned, and abandoned in favor of song at the climax. (Grillparzer: "Something possible towers above all worlds, what is real only reveals itself in space.")

"Prince Orlofsky, the wealthy lady's man is giving an intimate gala dinner this evening." Ida—"she is with the ballet, you see"—will appear there. The exclusiveness is not taken too literally, for Ida writes to her sister, the lady's maid Adele, that only one of the lady's formal dresses will be needed to make it possible to present Adele to the prince. While Adele reads the letter, the singing teacher Alfred serenades the lady. The lady has not seen him for four years—and in one sentence she brings the main key, the eternal fundamental law of the comedy world into play: "Surely he considers me unfaithful. Perhaps he believes that I love another, and all I did was get married." Adele asks for leave because she supposedly wants to visit her poor, sick aunt, but in reality she wants to attend the ball—Rosalinde will grant the leave, for she will want to be visited by Alfred. And her husband, Eisenstein, must begin a jail sentence this very day. A trio (Rosalinde-Eisenstein-the lawyer) confirms that Eisenstein has an obligation to go to jail this evening. What a concentrated comedy exposition leading to this evening from many directions! Why Eisenstein is locked up is insignificant. It is also insignificant why his friend, Dr. Falke, wants to take revenge on him, and a thousand times more insignificant that this Dr. Falke is a professional notary public. He appears to invite Eisenstein to the party where Adele will also appear. From there Eisenstein is to go to jail—and from the mutual joyful anticipation of the evening blossoms the great farewell song, the musical archetype of hypocrisy. The wife and the husband declare elegiacly: "Oh God, how this moves me"; with marital dutifulness they feign pain while both of them are filled with the most joyful extramarital expectation. Thus the sentimentality expresses itself to a certain extent in quotation marks. Then, however, the line "Oh God, how this moves me! (*moderato espressivo*) is followed by the cheerful "Oh my, oh my, how this moves me" with a jubilation that is hardly restrained any longer, the most cheerful contrasting of text and music (as in Knieriem's "The world will not stand much longer in any case"), a truly inspired musical-dramatical idea—this "Oh my, oh my" was not in the script; Johann Strauss added it while composing—and for one moment, for two vowels, he was a dramatic composer.

Eisenstein goes, Alfred comes, he drinks the wine that had been prepared for the husband's parting, he eats: "All right, I want to dream myself back into my lost paradise for a moment." Was Alfred Rosalinde's admirer, was he her lover? We experience an astonishing, a unique love scene: a love scene that omits the erotic element. In his serenade Alfred sang:

> Dove that flew away from me,
> Quench my longing, do!
> Dove that I kissed tenderly,
> Let me capture you!

Now he comes to the object of this longing. What does he do? He fills his glass, clothes himself in the husband's robe and hood, then eats and drinks, calls his beloved "dear old woman," and makes arrangements for breakfast—not a word about love, desire, tenderness, but "Let's drink (he pours) and let's sing while we do!" Music does not awaken love, does not proclaim love, but replaces it.

In all of *Die Fledermaus* we will see no ernest attempts to find the self "in love," only conventional allusions and avoidance in wine and song.

Alfred, alone with his "dove," does not want to enjoy love but the feigned memory of past love; he does not want to take pleasure in the present but in what was, and because everything is illusion anyway, it does not matter whether this past experience is authentic or imagined. He does not play the lover with Rosalinde, but the one who has loved.

As the first component of the finale he sings the drinking song, the philosophical drinking song about flight from reality. The lover informs the beloved for whom he longed and yearned a quarter of an hour earlier, that "heated love's a dream that fools us so much"—he knows that everything in life is illusion...

> Make believe gives us pleasure here,
> Though so briefly may we play,
> I believe you, never fear,
> I find joy today!

He accepts the deception and pretense, even preaches it:

> Though you were to me untrue,
> Pardon you'll receive.
> Swear again to me anew
> And I will believe!

And both unite in the tragically acquiescent knowledge:

> Happy he,
> Who'd not see
> What can never altered be!

There, in slow, three-four time (*allegretto moderato*) the synthesis of Nestroy and Grillparzer is accomplished. ("Shadows are the wealth of life, and shadows are its pleasures too, shadows, words, deep wishes, deeds...and none of it is true!") The Austrian view of the world finds no more genuine, authentic, legitimate, competent expression than this drinking song.

How did the Prussian Genée, author of the awkward song of praise to Rome ("As by night, so by day, nothing's like your display") and the silly cook stanzas ("Tacka, tacka, tack—mixing, mixing, mix—pimperim, pimpim") attain such heights?

This drinking song is the first waltz of the evening, and it is not conventional, but even more acquiescently melancholy than waltzes usually are. Up to now in this act there have been pieces in six-eight time, two-four and four-four time; only the unserious pain at parting was expressed in three-four time, but far from any thought of a Strauss waltz. In this act there will be only one more piece in three-four time, even designated "*Tempo di Valse*," when the prison warden disturbs the encounter to pick up the husband, and Rosalinde sets forth in her song, not without indirectly reproaching Alfred: the gentleman in the robe and cap who has already almost fallen asleep cannot be a lover, "can only be my husband." Here the practical application is perfectly and convincingly derived from the hymn to illusion: Rosalinde credibly offers the proof for a claim that is established as false. And now is the only moment for love because it can certainly not occur anymore: Alfred gives Rosalinde the "farewell kiss." The only tenderness between the lover and the beloved occurs under the sign of farewell. A cheerful trio concludes the grandiose prelude to a comedy. The prison warden and Rosalinde will also appear at the party in the second act; all of the prerequisites for humorous situations are present: husband and wife who each believe the other to be at home or in jail respectively—the lady's maid who is supposedly visiting her aunt and must not be recognized by her mistress here—the real Eisenstein, whom the prison warden believes is behind bars—all of them come to Prince Orlofsky's villa.

The facts that his wife also appears there and that the girl with whom Eisenstein flirts at the party is in reality his servant were successfully added by the Viennese adapters while expanding and improving the French original; even Eisenstein's repeating watch only receives its real meaning as a comic prop in the Vienna version. And everything—that, too, is an idea belonging to the operetta version—is organized because Dr. Falke wants to take revenge on Eisenstein, and because he has promised the prince that the latter will "laugh heartily." He has also, as we note in the second act, directed Adele to come here, and he forged her sister Ida's letter for that purpose.

But even in the second act, at first there is only prelude, preparation. The chorus of guests praises the event

> Everything that sets the rooms agleam
> Now seems to us like some bright dream...

and declares that they are followers of amusement. Here in this Vienna operetta an indication is given of the non-Viennese origins of the librettist:

> Chorus: The hours so quickly flee away,
> For no one is the time here long,
> There's but one slogan here today:
> *Amüs'ment! Amüs'ment! Amüs'ment! Amüs'ment!*

In *Carnival in Rome* Genée had already rhymed his "*Amüsmong*" with the "merry song."

Prince Orlofsky is introduced. As a cross between Nestroy's "disrupted man" and the Brazilian from *Paris Life*, he proclaims the principle of his life. He is a blasé "superfluous man," who is always bored and has little to say, even in the text of this self-portrayal. And now the intrigues are supposed to begin that are to make the prince laugh heartily. But here only Adele has the opportunity to give a variation of a motif from the first act: Just as Rosalinde made fiction convincingly plausible for the prison warden in a song, she, the maid, now believably proves in a song that it is impossible for her to be a maid. But now the intrigues should begin. But the husband only has a duet with his masked wife. He makes advances toward her, she takes his watch, nothing else happens.

Up to this point we have remained in the sphere of the *opéra comique*, closer to *The Marriage of Figaro* and *Così fan tutte* than to any operetta, even the previous and subsequent ones by Johann Strauss—to be more precise: on the Offenbach level. But now the momentum slackens, the book leaves Johann Strauss in the lurch, he himself no longer seems to enjoy it. The prelude was everything, the possibilities are given, but the realization mocks them. The statement "Something must happen" triumphs over the events and replaces the deed.

As an interlude, Rosalinde sings a czardas—the potential of the Vienna operetta fails under the sign of the invasion of Hungarian music. This czardas is dramatically unimportant and can easily be omitted. The dialogues drag on laboriously and increase; there is no productive misunderstanding, no recognition scene, no dramatic moment. The host has no more opportunity to laugh heartily than does the theater audience. The rest is festivity, song, dance, and champagne. To this point the second act has also gotten along without authentic waltz music, has only suggested the waltz in three-four and six-eight time, and has favored the lively, quick, two-four tempo. The first real piece of music in three-four time seals the sacrifice of drama in favor of the static element. All this is only a consequence of the Austrian self-portrayal in Alfred's drinking song, which caused the most secret string to reverberate in Johann Strauss: the turn toward illusion, the renunciation of action, the sacrifice of love in favor of marriage—joyful anticipation and memory are everything, the events are nothing, wine gives consolation through forgetfulness. Again a motif from the first act is repeated, but this time the drinking song is aimed expressly at the champagne.

Then suddenly the notary, Dr. Falke, begins to speak; nothing that we know of him up to this point, and nothing that we will learn about him in the further course of the production legitimizes him. He wanted to instigate an intrigue, he prepared it in minute detail, he wants to amuse the prince, he wants to take revenge on Eisenstein, he could still heighten the quid pro quo to its most amusing development, but no! "Stop!" he cries, then steps out of the action and looks at it. "Stop, listen to what I contrived!" He promotes the great brotherhood in a tone that from the very beginning rises above the meaningless, banal, stimulus: "...let us all a grand community of sisters and of brothers be... Take my example with glass in hand and sing to your neighbor as you here stand..."

The mood has separated itself from the track of a comedy around Rosalinde, Eisenstein, Alfred, and Adele. Something unprecedented begins, only very loosely connected to reality, a toast to human beings, a Magna Carta of brotherliness, an intoxication that no longer comes from alcohol, an embracing of the world.

> Brothers dear and sisters dear
> Let all of us be here,
> Brothers dear and sisters dear,
> Let us call each other thou...

And then a brilliant formula for the entire greatness and dubiousness of the moment:

> For all eternity just like today,
> If we later think of now!

First a kiss, but the kiss is not important; it is not a matter of that when a man and a woman have become a dear brother and a dear sister...

> First a kiss—then a "Thou"—
> Thou—Thou—always now!

The chorus joins in, and those present turn not only to each other:

> Brother dear and sister dear,
> Sing along now with us here...

With us! The whole world is addressed, eternity is evoked in the grand retardative swell of "Always now—always now—."

The great composers often set existing texts to music, but sometimes they sought for a text for the message that was to be sung and did not find an adequate one. Thus Beethoven found the totally inadequate "Ode to Joy" by Schiller; he fell into the trap of "All men everywhere are brothers" and eulogized his daughter with the soft wing and the scent of roses that one drinks from the breasts of nature. Gustav Mahler sought and did not find what he wanted and had to change from Klopstock by way of Nietzsche to the second part of *Faust* and Bethge's works in the Chinese style. Johann Strauss did not seek and found here the key word for what he wanted to say: the "kisses and grapes" and "this kiss of the entire world": all men everywhere become dear brothers and dear sisters—no more intoxication from champagne, and no drink and pledge of friendship, but a grand hymn, sublimely intensified and solemn— even more than the other Strauss creations in three-four time, the tempo of this piece can never be taken slowly enough! And the swell of the repeated "always now" is still not the conclusion, but only a transition. Johann Strauss crowns the cantus and climbs from the word, which is foreign to him, of course, up into wordlessness. Instead of *hallelujah* or *hosanna* he has them sing vowels that are more to him than words: Duidu—duidu —lala lalalala—that means nothing and everything, that means among other things (and better) "Your enchantments bind again what fashion strictly kept apart" and "He who has now in his life found a friend to share his days, he who's won a lovely wife, let him joyful anthems raise" and "Be embraced now, all you millions." Next to *The Beautiful Blue Danube*, it is a second "wordless *Marseillaise* of peace."

How can it now go on? How can we find our way back from the firmament of this supernatural, unsensual bliss to the earth, to Orlofsky's villa? Johann Strauss senses that. He lets the mood die away in wordlessness: a ballet interlude follows—"Spanish," "Scottish," "Russian," "Bohemian," "Hungarian," something vacuous, conventional, dutiful, breathless, and only after that does the first great, authentic waltz of the evening begin, and with it the only really sumptuous, jubilant, as it were "positive" waltz by Johann Strauss. The central figures, who had just become supernumeraries of the thou-ecstasies, remember their functions; the libretto provisionally remembers that we are at a party, that there has been drinking, that a quota of comical situation drama should have been filled, that the act will soon end—but it is too late. Where the world was addressed, there remains for Rosalinde and Eisenstein only a pitiful

Rosalinde:	I've a pimple on my nose,
	That is why I hide my face!
Eisenstein:	I don't think that is the case!
Adele, Ida:	That won't drive him from the place!
Eisenstein:	Now I must behold this face!

The clock strikes six. Eisenstein and Frank leave, the others remain behind and repeat their trite chorus:

> Ha, what a feast, what a night of play,
> Love and the wine so much joy inspire!
> If life were always just like today,
> Each hour we'd do just what we desire!

What kind of party was it really? A dinner, champagne, dancing. Where was the love? Where was the bliss? Expectation was everything, the rest was dance.

Joy of life was dictatorially proclaimed by the music but not realized in Orlofsky's villa. Nothing happened. For only a moment they were fraternally close to each other, and "all" were drawn into that proximity. The pleasure that the party is supposed to have aroused according to the statements of the guests, comes from the music and while avoiding the guests and the host takes hold of only the audience of the *Fledermaus* performance. Pleasure and love—yes, but only pleasure in eating, drinking, and dancing, only fraternal love. only "a kiss": the conventional kiss of the drink and pledge of friendship. And the grand "always now" does not mean the kiss, but the use of the familiar form of address. The large pause that now follows is not simply an interval between two acts. The prison act is far from the comic opera, even from its lower limit in the comical scenes of Lortzing and of the *Fra Diavolo*. It is the prototype for coming third acts of operettas that more or less summarily bring about a halfway conceivable ending. In Vienna it was customary to carry out the great premiere ceremony of the bow and the reception of wreaths and flowers right after the second act of an operetta. The second act already decided success or failure, the rest was a formality.

In the third act of *Die Fledermaus* Frosch, the jailer, appears, a speaking part, prototype of the third-act comedian, and whoever reads his role in the original book can do little with it. The role, as played everywhere today, lives on improvisations that (as in *The Vagabond*) attached themselves to the original text over time and became tradition. Frank must cover himself with a newspaper so that Frosch can say: "He sighs under the pressure of the press." Frank must ask Frosch a question so that the latter can answer: "Worthless Director" and then correct himself: "Nothing, worthy director!"* Frosch must say: "When I drink, I am a different person," then drink plum brandy and say: "The other person also wants to drink!" Instead of through the door, he must go into a closet and anxiously say: "Director, we're walled in." All this and many other corresponding things are inconceivably far below what the first two acts have promised. The difference between the first two acts and the third act of *Die Fledermaus* is like the difference between champagne and plum brandy.

*The original German offers a humorous play on words.

Now the music no longer predominates. After the introductory melodrama the act offers only two more pieces, and one of them is purely an interlude: Adele's arietta. She—solely as an occasion for music—performs for Frank so that he will promote her in the theater—although there has previously been no mention of the fact that Adele wants to get into the theater and that Frank has the appropriate connections.

The warden has come to the prison from the party with a hangover. Adele and Ida appear with him without motivation, and are removed from the scene without motivation. Eisenstein appears—he is viewed by the warden as a crony from the previous evening and not as a prisoner, and he, for his part, also sees Frank as a crony and not as the prison warden... Eisenstein learns that "Eisenstein" was already arrested the previous evening... In any musical comedy in the world, that situation would produce a piece of music with special charm; here it is disposed of in a prose dialogue.

Only when the attorney and, shortly thereafter, Rosalinde appear does the only authentic musically dramatic number of the act occur in the grand trio, a suggestion of what the first and second act promised, a legitimate comedy situation: Eisenstein disguises himself (as in Meilhac and Halévy's version) as an attorney and now learns the truth from Alfred and Rosalinde. And the situation has hardly come to a head, when it is summarily and totally put in order in prose. And then, "so that it comes to an end," as they say in Vienna, Orlofsky already appears with the entire ball group; they all hastily sing the closing song, which works with reminiscences from the already familiar music of the operetta and in so doing establishes an additional momentous tradition of the genre.

What happened? We cannot solve the double puzzle: that on only one occasion, entirely without being prepared or predestined to do so, Johann Strauss so somnambulantly rose to the comic opera, and that he suddenly lost his momentum and ended deep in the lowlands. The hour of the operetta has struck, but when the clock strikes six in Orlofsky's hall at the end of the second act, it has passed. Mozart and Offenbach were the godfathers at the birth of the child that developed its gifts, only to betray them immediately and perish miserably in plum brandy after promising beginnings. The Vienna operetta passed away when it had hardly come. The rest is Lehár.

Die Fledermaus crowned the worldwide success of the Strauss name in many dimensions. Gustav Mahler presented it in the Hamburg opera house in March 1894; the Vienna Court Opera followed in October 1894. At that time, twenty years after the premiere, the work had already been performed on about two hundred stages, also in England, Russia, North America, India, and Australia. (The co-author Haffner had died soon after the premiere, poor and forgotten.)

The world discovered its unity in the phenomenon of the worldwide success of two composers named Johann Strauss. For forty years, from *Die Fledermaus* to Sarajevo, it lived the illusion of that unity. But its herald, Johann Strauss, wrote in the autumn of 1894: *Die Fledermaus* is least suited for the opera house... If it should prove itself in the opera as a drawing card, I would refine this operetta and leave it solely to opera theaters." It did not come to that. Instead of saving his masterpiece, Johann Strauss had to set *Woodruff* and *The Goddess of Reason* to music.

The entry of *Die Fledermaus* into the Vienna Court Opera occurred within the framework of one of the grand festivities that were often bestowed upon the old Strauss in Vienna. This time it was a matter of celebrating the fifty years since his first public appearance at Dommayer's in Hietzing. On October 28, 1894 the opera director Jahn directed *Die Fledermaus*; the roles were occupied by outstanding soloists of the opera. In the great ensemble of the second act, in honor of Strauss, the greatest singers of the theater sang along (Paula Mark, Antonie Schläger, Ernst van Dyk, Hermann Winkelmann, and many others). Ten years later, in a festival performance of the New York Metropolitan Opera, Caruso, Scotti, de Reszke, and other star singers sang in the "Brother dear and sister dear" ensemble.

Nobody else would have had so much reason to be cheerful and happy, and yet we see the aging and old, the married Johann Strauss in darkening twilight. We look at his entire life and find tensions, unrest, struggles, and peculiarities. The apostle of lightheartedness, the breaker of the world's cares seems to us to be deeply unhappy and burdened, and the music of Strauss as well, especially Strauss's waltzes, frequently expresses corresponding moods. The father's waltzes had the capacity to put Hector Berlioz "in a deeply melancholy mood." Heinrich Laube said of their introductions: "...they sound tragic, like a happiness still clutched in the pains of birth." Paris journalists found a "Nordic melancholy" in them. And like nervousness and hypochondria the mood of resignation was also passed down from the father to the son and is heard specifically in his most successful and characteristic pieces. We should listen for that, at the right tempo, in *Tales from the Vienna Woods* and the *Emperor's Waltz*!

In production Strauss seeks the happiness of the man who forgets what cannot be changed anyway. But he does not succeed in forgetting. Once he wrote in a letter that could almost have been written by Grillparzer: "I...can grieve so much about something that really can no longer be undone, that in the subsequent days I really do nothing right anymore." And in this case it is only a matter of a social gathering, from which, he suspects "with horror," he will not come home "until the morning begins to dawn in front of me." And it is even unimportant things of that kind, that cannot be changed, which he cannot forget for days. Thus he is not happy.

He is afraid of nature, has a horror of going up a mountain, has probably never been in those Vienna Woods that he immortally celebrated. He does not like beautiful weather: "Just no sunshine for my work!" and "It is just now becoming beautiful in Ischl. People lose themselves, and from what I hear—it will not quit raining anymore. A magnificent prospect for me! I love it when I can work in what is for me a congenial apartment, during stormy, yes (for others) bleak weather. However, that is true bliss for me..."

He fears death, he negates it, he does not go to any funeral, not even to that of his wife Jetty, his mother.

He has a panicky aversion to railway travel: "For me, traveling by train comes right after hanging." An obituary speaks of his almost pathological disinclination toward railroad travel, and Max Kalbeck reports that Johann Strauss only traveled with the curtains down; when the train passed through a tunnel or over a bridge, Johann Strauss stretched out flat along the floor of the compartment. He always carried champagne with him, which was supposed to ease the terrors of the journey for him.

The photographs of the last years of his life show a tense, unhappy, dejected man; in the portrait by Lembach, the staring, almost panic-filled eyes reveal the mystery of his tragic spiritual condition.

After 1879—he was forty-five years old at that time—he no longer played the violin. At the age of sixty-eight, he no longer considered himself to be "in a position" to direct an operetta performance. A slow, tragic withering, from within, intensified by the activity of his efficient wife—and it does not matter whether the pains and suffering that burdened his last years were real or imagined.

What became of the revolutionary romantic who affirmed the revolution, who supported the new sound of Wagner? He never read, never went to the theater, and listened to almost no music. (Kalbeck: "Later he never attended a concert, almost never an opera.")

What Schnitzer describes in his memoirs as a "character trait of the master that was known only to those belonging to his household" reads like the story of an illness: "Sometimes the usually so jovial and gregarious man seemed suddenly changed. Sullenly, wordlessly, hardly looking up, he crept timidly around in the house for days, even weeks, or kept himself wrapped in the cocoon of his work room. Then even his wife hardly dared to speak to him, for being disturbed in this morose silence could bring him to violent agitation."

In another place Schnitzer speaks of the fact that Johann Strauss "was in a condition of almost permanent nervousness." And he tells of his last encounter, during which, before a premiere, he said in all innocence that at worst Strauss could say with Valentin: "I die as a soldier and bravely." Strauss had such an "exalted fear of the very word *die*," that Schnitzer had caused a catastrophe: "A dreadful agitation had overcome him and had not departed for hours."

From October 1898 to Pentecost 1899, Johann Strauss did not leave his house. In his letters of the last decade of his life, we read again and again of afflictions: "I have been suffering from very horrible headaches for four days."—"My right shoulder is still not doing well." —"My arthritis has not gotten any better yet."—"...that since I had the flu I must continually struggle against discomfort and neuralgia."—"Things are going just as badly with my nerves as they are with the horses. Misery everywhere!"—and even five years before his death: "...my visual capacity has significantly decreased. ...in semidarkness I already see nothing at all (including the glasses). Writing all those notes weakened my vision to a great degree... I see everything double—if I take a toothpick, I always see two in front of me. If I should have the misfortune to go blind, I will shoot myself."

A year before his death, he composed and directed his last work, and a circle closes here in a touchingly meaningful way. For the celebration of the unveiling of the Raimund monument he put together old melodies from the period of his father, Lanner, and his teacher Drechsler to form a medley: *Sounds from the Raimund Era*. When he was led through a narrow, dark corridor into the orchestra pit of the *Volkstheater* on May 31, 1898, he almost collapsed in panic. The theater still frightened him.

On Whitmonday, May 22, 1899, during the afternoon he directed the overture to *Die Fledermaus* in the Court Opera and caught a cold on the way home. A few days later, at the welfare festival in the Prater, he was still giving autographs. Eight days later, on June 3, he was dead. On June 5 the street where he spent the last years of his life had already been named *Johann-Strauß-Gasse*.

The burial was staged in the style of a royal funeral. "Could one be amazed that so few Viennese walked behind his casket? There was no place for them because so many librettists strolled along behind." (*Die Fackel*)

As Johann Strauss lay on his death bed, a twenty-thousand-dollar law suit against him regarding the American rights to the operetta *The Goddess of Reason* was tried in the Higher Regional Court.

In his memory they performed the *German Requiem*, but also *Die Fledermaus* in the court opera houses of Vienna and Berlin. Berlin had adopted the operetta into its repertoire in May 1899, under the direction of the orchestra conductor Richard Strauss. (The *Vossische Zeitung* wrote that the visibly warm affection that Richard Strauss had for the work revealed "that this artist really is an authentic and true musician, not simply an audaciously experimental composer.") During the two intermissions of the memorial performance Richard Strauss directed Strauss waltzes.

In the month of his death it was announced that the librettists Leon and Stein were in the process of putting together an operetta *Vienna Blood* from known and unknown music by Strauss. It is said that shortly before his death Johann Strauss gave his consent for the undertaking and himself shared in the decision about which pieces of music should be included in the new operetta.

"It is known, of course, that right after the death of Johann Strauss haggling and shrieking began, and while the soul of an artist entered eternity on the pinions of waltzes, in the next room they were already dallying and goggling around in the 'musical estate'... Such a silly comedy was made out of Johann Strauss's memory, and from then on his fame was exploited so disgustingly..." (*Die Fackel*, October 1899)

Since then the assistants, accomplices, arrangers, and adapters have not rested. Hugo Felix adapted *Indigo*, which led to a civil suit with the composer's widow. Later Reiterer adapted the work and gave it the title *A Thousand and One Nights*, with which, however, it did not become much better. The same adapter, together with Leon, made a new operetta *Countess Pepi* from *Simplicius* and *Blindman's Buff*. ("Since that time dispositions have been made concerning the musical estate of Johann Strauss that cannot possibly be represented as reverent execution of his last will and testament. There is tireless 'galvanizing,' tireless searching around in his drawer, tireless pasting together of 'posthumous material' to form novelties." (*Die Fackel*, 1902) Felix Salten, who was not legitimized by any special musical disposition, adapted *The Goddess of Reason* under the pseudonym Stollberg and gave the new story the title *Rich Girls*; Hagemann adapted *Night in Venice*, as did Korngold, who also concentrated and coarsened *Cagliostro in Vienna* and is responsible for a musical play with Strauss music entitled *Waltzes from Vienna*. They performed a new *Carnival in Rome* under the title *The Blue Hero*, performed "Strauss operettas" entitled *Carnival Wedding*, *Casanova* (Benatzky), *The Dancer Fanny Elssler* (Stalla and Melichar), and an additional version of *Indigo*: *Night on the Bosporus*. Authentic reverence or conscientious effort to preserve was hardly ever the primary motive. The theater business dominated, and his widow Adele permitted all this and usually encouraged it. Karl Kraus protested alone against the "impudent manipulations of the works of a man who was no less defenseless after his death than he was while still alive," against a practice in which "perfect business sense and a feeling for three-four time participate."

In 1929, before the end of the copyright period, Max Reinhardt, together with Rössler, Schiffer, and Korngold, organized a mammoth production of *Die Fledermaus*. ("Wherever that most tasteful destroyer of the German stage walked, nothing but grass grew on it." *Die Fackel*, 1929)

Here, before Alfred appears in the first act, Adele helps her mistress undress and put on her negligee, while Rosalinde sings among other things:

> Here no rest, head to toe!
> Say, why won't it come free?
> Are the whalebones sticking me?
> Do my own shoes, too small today, scratch me there?
> Or does it even catch beneath my underwear?
> Would I were free of these things of mine!
> They pinch me like an Eisenstein.

In the Orlofsky song it says:

> Til now the lovely ladies were
> My one and sole complex...

And Adele, who wants to get into the theater, must sing in her arietta:

> However I did please them best
> At my demonic sexiest,
> When then my gaze eroticized,
> The strongest man then hypnotized...

In 1932, Nestroy's farce *He Wants to Do It for Laughs* was misused in creating an operetta that plays in the 1890s, *Enjoy Life*, with music by Johann and Josef Strauss. In 1946, *The Strauss Boys* (Text: Hubert Marischka and Rudolf Weys, with music by Johann and Josef Strauss, "employing previously unpublished posthumous music") was performed in Vienna, as a counterpart to *The House of Three Girls* a no less loathsome, but fortunately less successful "house of three boys."

Mrs. Strauss	*goes to Johann and tries to calm him down, then says:* Be smart, Schani, believe me, it was better that way—and don't think badly of the girl.
Johann	*says:* You're right, Mother.
	sings: What once was, won't come back someday, At last all songs must fade away, Bliss flees again, Will not remain.
Mrs. Strauss	*almost spoken:* 'Tis what is apt, You must adapt!
Johann:	Come, Mother.

And then he goes into the house and composes an immortal waltz amid the pain of farewell.

Eduard, the youngest "Strauss boy," born ten years after Johann, originally destined for consular service, a fruitful, but not very original composer, and a brilliant arranger and conductor, had directed since 1862, had taken over sole responsibility for conducting the Strauss orchestra in 1870, after Josef's death, had played successful concerts in Vienna and abroad, and had not gotten along especially well with his two brothers. He was distrustful, suspicious, misanthropic, and paranoid. As an old man, he published his memoirs, which, however, are suspect as a source and above all anxious to move his own, less important figure into the proper light.

Johann once thought that Eduard was "a somewhat difficult gentleman" and wrote him, when he was already almost seventy and Edward was almost sixty years old: "You always see black—always think that I want to do something to you. Just stop these derogatory remarks—just how old do you have to become before you see at last that you don't have to see an enemy in your brother?"

When Eduard Strauss was sixty-two years old, through foolish manipulations of his wife and his two sons, he lost almost his entire fortune and had to earn wealth a second time with intensive tour activity in Germany, Holland, England, and America. In 1901 he dissolved the orchestra after his right shoulder was injured in a railroad accident in America and he was hampered in directing as a result of it.

When Eduard Strauss was seventy-two years old, he had a carload of waste paper burned in a Viennese stove factory. On the basis of an agreement that had supposedly been made with his brother Josef, the surviving brother was supposedly obliged to destroy all the Strauss orchestra's sheet music. In that manner many original manuscripts and unprinted works by the entire family, which had not been copied, perished—invaluable material and historical works, and this only because, according to Eduard Strauss, there was a danger that with the "orchestra arrangements that were very valuable for any concert undertaking...if strangers had somehow gotten hold of them, the authors of these orchestra arrangements would probably not have been named in the programs for public performances"!

On October 22, 1907, the stove manufacturer reports, "first a load of many heavy packets of sheet music came in a police car and were unloaded. Before two o'clock in the afternoon, Eduard Strauss appeared in my office with his personal servant. I encouraged him to rescind the order. Strauss stared into space for a while; then he cried: 'I cannot!' So we went into the factory where there were two large furnaces for firing tile stoves and earthenware. The one had been prepared to receive the sheet-music archive. Eduard Strauss sat down in an armchair in front of the furnace; my workers opened the packets and threw the sheets of music into the rising flames of the man-high firebox before the eyes of the court-ball music director. With certain packets of music that contained special family memories, Strauss was visibly moved. He stood up, looked away, or went back into the office for a short time. But he did not leave the factory until the last sheet of music was burned. One can perhaps get an idea of the size of the archive, when I say that the burning of the music lasted from two o'clock in the afternoon until seven o'clock in the evening. That had been, by the way, only a part of Johann Strauss's archive. Strauss had two additional carloads of music burned in a factory on *Porzellangasse*. There, too, he witnessed the burning in each case."

When Eduard Strauss was eighty-one, he died—he had disinherited his wife and sons and had established the children of his older son Johann as his heirs.

The preserved memorabilia were in the possession of Adele's daughter and Johann's stepdaughter Alice when, in June 1939, the *Stürmer* unleashed a campaign because Strauss relics were "in the hands of Jews." In the owner's absence SA agents appeared in her apartment and confiscated many things that were auctioned off in Vienna and thus lost during the war. The rest was "given" to the state and was purchased by the city of Vienna; the two violins belonging to Johann Strauss, father and son, were "stored" and lost at the end of the war. Shortly before that, Alice, née Strauss, died in Vienna. In the course of a restoration process, a large portion of the manuscripts, documents, and other relics that still existed were later acquired a second time by the city of Vienna. The effort was made to classify the entire collection as historical monuments and to preserve it for Austria, but this attempt failed because of a protest by the heirs and their assignees. Thus, among other things, the original manuscript of *Die Fledermaus* left the country.

What the city of Vienna finally retained is packed away in the Vienna city hall. It is not yet "catalogued," and is thus temporarily inaccessible to researchers.

The city of Vienna erected a Johann Strauss monument in the Vienna city park. It had already been projected in 1899, was completed in 1906, and was solemnly unveiled on June 26, 1921 in the presence of the widow Adele and her daughter Alice. The veil fell while the Vienna Philharmonic Orchestra under the direction of Arthur Nikisch played *By the Beautiful Blue Danube*.

Every year, when the Vienna Festival opens at the end of May, the Danube waltz rings out in front of the Vienna city hall, and after the introduction, to the rhythm of the number one waltz, the city hall lighting is turned on.

The Vienna Philharmonic Orchestra has the custom of ringing out the old year on New Year's Eve with

Strauss music and beginning the new year with Strauss music on the morning of New Year's Day.

At midnight on New Year's Eve, when the twelve chimes have faded away, Radio Austria plays the waltz *By the Beautiful Blue Danube*. The Austrian Ministry of Education has established a Johann Strauss Prize "to honor especially outstanding Austrian creators of cheerful music."

And the Austrian Air Lines named one of its airplanes the *Johann Strauss*.

Vienna is also the seat of a Johann Strauss Society that was established in 1936 and reemerged in 1948 after an interruption caused by the times. In 1948 it announced that it would "promote and reinforce" Vienna's musical culture through a series of events; in 1950 it announced that it would organize an annual festival week of Vienna music. In 1955 it made the decision to publish a "historically revised complete edition of the works of Johann Strauss, the son." These announcements were not realized. Until further notice, the main activity of the Johann Strauss Society will consist in recording Johann Strauss music on records in collaboration with a recording company; in this work the president of the Johann Strauss Society is frequently active as the conductor.

In 1887 the great edition of the works of Johann Strauss, Sr. appeared with an introduction by his son. Just as foreign countries (Germany and England) had taken on the publication of Joseph Haydn's works, the obligation of honor with respect to this great Austrian had been seized not in Vienna, but in Leipzig.

The son's famous and beloved standard works understandably existed and exist in numerous editions. The less common ones, even though musically very precious, were and are missing for the most part, and only present here and there, scattered in archives. It was not possible to interest any major publishing house in a task that was fascinating and promising in every respect, that of looking after the Vienna classical composer as a publisher. In 1952, an inquiry in the Austrian Ministry of Education made a decision that favored a complete edition in principle, but it had no practical consequences. It was left to a small music and publishing house in the fifteenth district of Vienna to publish an index of the works of Strauss, the son. Since 1950, new individual editions of the works of Johann Strauss, father and son, and Josef Strauss have continuously appeared there, remaining as true to the originals as possible, for orchestra, chorus with orchestra or piano accompaniment, singing, and solo instruments. Not only the "classical," but also forgotten pieces are requested in this edition in great numbers by music stores, orchestras, and radio stations all over the world.

To date, no solid scholarly Strauss biography has appeared; a cultural-historical musical reference work *Das Jahrhundert des Walzers* [The Century of the Waltz], which was projected for several volumes, was not continued after the appearance of the first volume (Johann Strauss, the father). Nor have Johann Strauss's letters been collected. Only a much too sparse, insufficiently annotated selection has appeared, which was published by Adele Strauss in 1926. Adele, about thirty years younger than Johann Strauss, lived about thirty years longer than he did and thoroughly justified her nickname: "Cosima in three-four time." She was enterprising and efficient and "actively pious" to the end. When the thirty-year term of copyright ended, and with it her income from the works of Johann Strauss, she exhibited intensive activity, sought intervention by the

Austrian Ministry of Education and the Ministry of Justice, among others, requesting that the state extend the term of copyright, thus her income, through a special edict. But the planned *Johann Strauss Law* did not come into being; only with the ordinance of December 15, 1933 was the copyright term in Austria lengthened to fifty years. On January 1, 1930 the music of Johann Strauss became public domain and was no longer subject to royalties. Ten weeks later Adele Strauss was dead.

Vienna, Spring 1958—Spring 1960

AUTHOR'S AFTERWORD

In order to avoid any suspicion of scholarship from the very beginning, I intend to do without footnotes as well as a detailed bibliography. This does not mean at all, however, that the text itself has not employed sources. Their meagerness and their fragmentary nature, their history and their "Austrian fates," occasionally already mentioned in the text, fit harmoniously into the Austrian panorama of the six chapters.

When we conjure up Franz Schubert and his image in the minds of posterity, we must remember the great Viennese scholar Otto Erich Deutsch with admiration. He devoted the work of a lifetime to the life and works of Franz Schubert, and from his first Schubert anthology (Berlin, 1905) to the great index of his works, he created the bases for Schubert research. The history of this life's work is rich in tragic and tragicomic episodes and had to hold its own arduously against world history: Of the work *Franz Schubert, die Dokumente seines Lebens und Schaffens* [Franz Schubert, the Documents of his Life and Creative Work], which was originally planned for four volumes, volume three, *Sein Leben in Bildern* [His Life in Pictures], and the first half of volume two, *Die Dokumente seines Lebens* [The Documents of His Life], had appeared in Munich in 1913 and 1914 respectively, without annotation and index. The final, annotated edition with index still exists only in English (London, 1946; New York, 1947)—with the dedication: "To Vienna's Past and Future." The Schubert bibliography, planned as volume one, appeared in 1938 in Regensburg, edited by Willi Kahl. The reminiscences about Schubert, planned as the second part of volume two, appeared in 1957 in Leipzig, in 1958 in London and New York. The chronological-thematical work index still exists only in English and appeared in 1951 in London and New York. As a place of publication, Vienna is represented only in the important expanded and revised edition of the *Briefe und Schriften* [Letters and Writings] (1954).

Otto Erich Deutsch is not only a Schubert researcher, but a music scholar of great breadth, an art historian, an iconographer, and a literary scholar, a rare example of the polyhistorian. When, on the occasion of his seventy-fifth birthday in 1958, he was asked what he was working on, he said: "On a bibliography of the books that I would still like to write." Fortunately for us and for the Schubert image of the future, the books that were to be written about Franz Schubert did not have to be included in that bibliography.

Of the numerous Schubert biographies, the one by Walter Dahms (14th to 17th edition, Berlin, 1922) and especially Alfred Einstein's *Schubert, ein musikalisches Porträt* [Schubert, A Musical Portrait] (Zurich, 1952) are unquestionably the most preferable.

The quoted sentences by Hermann Hesse about genius come from *Dank an Goethe* [Thanks to Goethe] (Zurich, 1946).

Like his image in novels, operettas, and biographies, Franz Schubert's outward appearance is usually adulterated. Only nine authentic pictures of Schubert exist, among them an insignificant caricature and three pictures that portray Schubert within a group. The aquarelle by W. A. Rieder, from the year 1825 (Vienna City Museum), can be viewed as the most important portrait.

Schubert research began all too late; the Schubert biographers usually do not do justice to their material and do not perceive that he was one of the great ones whom one cannot "pat benevolently on the shoulder... and whom his early perfection only makes all the greater" (Alfred Einstein).

The Schubert literature is accordingly all too extensive.

In comparison, the literature about Ferdinand Raimund is dismayingly meager, and Raimund research is hardly appropriately developed. Above all, infinitely important and valuable letters by the author fell victim to a lack of prompt care.

The great historical-critical complete edition of his works had been planned by a Munich publisher in 1914 and began to appear in Vienna in 1923. After the sixth (*Die Gesänge der Märchendramen in den ursprünglichen Vertonungen* [The Songs of the Fairy-Tale Plays in Their Original Settings]), fifth, and fourth volumes came out in 1924, the project was interrupted; the second and third volumes could not be published until 1933—with respect to the volumes that were to contain the dramas in their revised texts with critical apparatus, there were differences between the editors and the publisher, because the latter objected to the all-too-large size; the edition was not published in its completeness with a reduced apparatus of different readings until 1934. It is also a curiosity in that the first volume contains addenda to the fourth and sixth volumes.

Outside this edition only two portrayals of Ferdinand Raimund exist, both of them valuable and informative, but marked by the time of their genesis and publication: Heinz Kindermann's *Ferdinand Raimund, Schicksal und Wirkungsraum eines Deutschen Volksdramatikers* [Ferdinand Raimund, Story and Sphere of Activity of a German Folk Dramatist] (Vienna, 1943) and Walter Erdmann's *Ferdinand Raimund, dichterische Entwicklung, Persönlichkeit und Lebensschicksal* [Ferdinand Raimund, Poetic Development, Personality, and Life Story] (Würzburg, 1943). Thus the great Austrian Raimund biography remains to be written.

A beautiful Raimund essay by Felix Braun, *"Ferdinand Raimund und die Komödie"* [Ferdinand Raimund and the Comedy], is included in the volume *Das musische Land, Versuche über Österreichs Landschaft und Dichtung* [The Land of the Fine Arts, Essays About Austria's Landscape and Literature] (Innsbruck, 1952); Heinz Politzer's essay on *The King of the Alps* appeared in *Die Neue Rundschau* (January 1955); the quoted Raimund essay by Egon Friedell appeared on January 25, 1931 in *Das Neue Wiener Journal.*

The invaluable contemporary source is formed by the diary pages of the imperial and royal court actor and director Carl Ludwig Costenoble *Aus dem Burgtheater* [From the *Burgtheater*] (Vienna, 1889)

Hofmannsthal's essay on Raimund is the introduction to *Ferdinand Raimunds Lebensdokumente* [Documents of Ferdinand Raimund's Life] (Vienna, 1920).

Like Franz Schubert, Johann Nestroy also owes the preservation of his image and the late scholarly establishment of textual and biographical authenticity to the life's work of a great, admirable and honorable Viennese scholar: Otto Rommel. In the monographic contributions to the two editions that he edited (Large edition, volume 15—small edition, volume 1), as in his fundamental work *Die Alt-Wiener Volkskomödie vom barocken Welt-Theater bis zum Tode Nestroys* [The Old Viennese Folk Comedy from the Baroque Theater of the World to the

Death of Nestroy] (Vienna, 1952), Otto Rommel—also meritorious as Ludwig Anzengruber's editor—performed an undying, invaluable work and prepared and made possible the Nestroy renaissance of our day.

Next to Rommel, Karl Kraus is to be praised as a promoter of the Nestroy renaissance: *"Nestroy und die Nachwelt"* [Nestroy and Posterity] (*Die Fackel*, May 1912) and a wealth of appreciative articles, references, and polemics in all annual volumes of *Die Fackel*, among others: *"Der Zerrissene (Causa Herzl contra Nestroy)"* [The Disrupted Man (The Case of Herzl versus Nestroy)], *"Girardi und Kainz"* [Girardi and Kainz] (May 1908), *"Nestroy-Feier"* [Nestroy Celebration] (June 1912), *"Die Wortgestalt"* [The Word Form] (June 1921), *"Nestroy und die Literaten"* [Nestroy and the Men of Letters], *"Zur Nestroy-Feier"* [On the Nestroy Celebration] (July 1922), *"Nestroy-Zyklus"* [Nestroy Cycle] (April 1923), *"Notizen"* [Notes] (June 1923), *"Ein zeitgenössischer Kritiker Nestroys"* [A Contemporary Nestroy Critic] (August 1924), *"Um Nestroy"* [About Nestroy] (December 1924), *"Nestroy und das Burgtheater"* [Nestroy and the *Burgtheater*] (January 1925), *"Tischlerlied"* [Carpenter's Song] (March 1925).

An informative, valuable book that reflects appreciation of Nestroy, Otto Forst de Battaglia's *Johann Nestroy: Abschätzer der Menschen, Magier des Wortes* [Johann Nestroy: Assessor of People, Magician of the Word] (Leipzig, 1932), does not satisfy the longing for a great, classical Nestroy biography in any way. A very substantial long essay *"Johann Nestroy und seine Kunst"* [Johann Nestroy and His Art] by Franz H. Mautner forms an introduction to the one-volume *Ausgewählte*

Werke [Selected Works] (Vienna, 1937); additional Nestroy essays: Ludwig Speidel in *Persönlichkeiten* [Personalities] (Berlin, 1910), Otto Stoessl in *Geist und Gestalt* [Spirit and Form] (Vienna, 1935), Egon Friedell (*Neue Freie Presse*, June 19, 1929), Richard Schaukal (*Wiener Zeitung*, September 10, 1929), Leopold Liegler (*Die Freyung*, March 1930; *Die Waage*, March 1925; *Plan*, October 1945), a reference by Ernst Křenek in the essay "*Von der Aufgabe, ein Österreicher zu sein*" [On the Task of Being an Austrian] (*Die Freyung*, April 1931), many references by Alfred Polgar in *Ja und Nein* [Yes and No] (Hamburg, 1956). Johann Nestroy's *Gesammelte Briefe und Revolutionsdokumente* [Collected Letters and Documents of the Revolution] appeared in Vienna in 1938.

In addition to numerous short essays and two oral presentations about Nestroy, since 1935 I have written supplemental Nestroy verses for performances in Austria, Germany, and Switzerland, assisted with Nestroy adaptations, and prepared four Nestroy plays for Vienna's *Burgtheater* and the Salzburg Festival. On the occasion of the sesquicentennial of his birth, a longer essay, "*Johann Nestroy oder Die Kunst und ihr Gegenstand*" [Johann Nestroy, or: Art and Its Object] appeared in *Monat* in December 1951.

The editions of Grillparzer's works and the Grillparzer literature are indeterminable and suggest, to compensate for their boundlessness, special moderation with regard to the references:

Berndt von Heiseler's Grillparzer essay in *Ahnung und Aussage* [Idea and Expression] (Gütersloh, 1952), Rudolf Kassner's Grillparzer essay in *Geistige Welten* [Worlds of the Spirit] (Berlin, 1958)—Hofmannsthal's introduction to *The Waves of the Sea and of Love* in the Pantheon edition (Berlin, 1903), *"Grillparzers politisches Vermächtnis"* [Grillparzer's Political Legacy] as the foreword to volume one of *Die Österreichische Bibliothek* [The Austrian Library] (Leipzig, 1915), Hofmannsthal's Grillparzer speech in *Die Neue Freie Presse* of July 23 and 25, 1922—Ferdinand Kürnberger's obituary *"Grillparzers Lebensmaske"* [Grillparzer's Life Mask] in *Literarische Herzenssachen* [Literary Things of the Heart] (Munich, 1911), Karl Kraus on Grillparzer, especially in *Die Fackel*, May 1922 (*"Grillparzer-Feier"* [Grillparzer Celebration]) and March 1925 (*"Notizen"* [Notes]), Egon Friedell on Grillparzer in *Das Neue Wiener Journal*, June 25, 1931—Carlyle on Grillparzer, quoted by Emil Kuh in *Zwei Dichter Österreichs* [Two Austrian Poets] (Pest, 1872), an essay *"Heimatmundart und Dichtersprache"* [Local Dialect and Poetic Language] by Edwin Rollett in *Grillparzer-Studien* [Grillparzer Studies] (Vienna, 1924), a reference by Richard Schaukal in *Einsame Gedankengänge* [Lonely Thought Processes] (Munich, 1947). The anecdote about Raimund and Grillparzer in the menagerie in *Ferdinand Raimunds Lebensdokumente* [Documents of Ferdinand Raimund's Life] (Vienna, 1920).

In contrast to the Grillparzer literature, the literature about Adalbert Stifter is, on the other hand, comparatively meager, so that one is almost inclined to believe in an Austrian law of the inverse proportionality of greatness and journalistic-historical expression.

The works of Stifter have kindly become available again through the editions of the Insel, Winkler, and Kraft publishing houses; more recent Stifter research has its focus in the Adalbert Stifter Institute in Linz, which was able to celebrate the tenth anniversary of its beneficial work a short time ago and is in the process of making amends for the omissions of many decades through scholarly and publicistic activity.

Aside from the classical biography of A. R. Hein (Vienna, 1952) that was mentioned in the text, few other and no truly exemplary Stifter biographies based on new knowledge exist, but on the other hand there are several collections of letters, documents, and quotations, a collection of the cultural-political essays (Zurich, 1948), a basic portrayal of the phenomenon *Adalbert Stifter als Maler* [Adalbert Stifter as a Painter] (Vienna, 1941) by Fritz Novotny, who is also to be thanked for the essay *Klassizismus und Klassizität im Werk Adalbert Stifters* [Classicism and Exemplariness in the Works of Adalbert Stifter] (Vienna, 1959). The cited essay by Franz Glück about *Two Sisters* is in the Vienna *Adalbert-Stifter-Almanach für 1947* [Adalbert Stifter Almanac for 1947]. Besides other valuable publications about the writer, Otto Jungmair wrote the especially important *Adalbert Stifters Linzer Jahre* [Adalbert Stifter's Linz Years] (Graz, 1958) in which he also treated the problem of the supposed suicide, to which a medical study, *"Adalbert Stifter, seine Krankheit und sein Tod"* [Adalbert Stifter, His Illness and His Death] in the *Wiener Klinische Wochenschrift* of January 30, 1959 is also dedicated.

Further: a Stifter Essay by Felix Braun in *Das musische Land* [The Land of the Fine Arts] (Innsbruck, 1952) and two essays by the same author, *"Adalbert Stifters Welt"* [Adalbert Stifter's World] and *"Meine Begegnungen mit Adalbert Stifter"* [My Encounters with Adalbert Stifter], in *Die Eisblume* [Frostwork] (Salzburg, 1955), a Stifter essay by Oskar Loerke in *Dichtung von Dichtern gesehen* [Literature as Seen by Writers] (Frankfurt, 1954), a *Witiko* essay by Berndt von Heiseler in *Ahnung und Aussage* [Idea and Expression] (Gütersloh, 1952), references and quotes in *Die Fackel* (April and May 1916)—on the other hand, Hofmannsthal's essay about *Indian Summer* as an afterword to the Epikon edition (Leipzig, 1925), unfavorably discussed in *Die Fackel* (April 1926), and the article by Martha Karlweis about Stifter's death in *Die Wiener Zeitung* of January 20 and 27, 1935.

All this does not relieve the contemporaries of the duty to publish a usable, accessible, unified new historical-critical complete edition and causes the wish for a major, basic Stifter biography and bibliography to seem very urgent.

At this point I must personally make a confession and make amends for a wrong. When I attended secondary school in Vienna, Dr. Gustav Wilhelm was my principal there and also my German teacher for a short time. Not only for me, but for all the pupils he was the subject of jokes and childish-roguish aggressions. He only won our respect in 1924, when, after a student suicide affair, he was suspended and bore it with a philosophical demeanor. I had no special connection to him and participated vigorously in the actions that made life difficult for him. When I visited him once again in the winter of 1945-1946 (and made him happy with my visit), this gesture arose less from respect, gratitude, or regret, than from the longing to see the figures of the past again.

The true reunion, however, did not occur until I found Gustav Wilhelm's tracks again in everything concerning Adalbert Stifter. For his entire life—even while we tormented and imitated him and did not take him seriously—Gustav Wilhelm had been unwearyingly and productively active in service to Adalbert Stifter and had promoted the publication of the complete edition of his works, research, and the erection of the Vienna monument in invaluable selfless devotion. His collected essays, *Begegnungen mit Stifter* [Encounters with Stifter], appeared in Munich in 1943. Otto Jungmair lauded him in a brief study *Gustav Wilhelm, ein Lebensbild* [Gustav Wilhelm, a Life Portrait] (*Schriftenreihe des Adalbert-Stifter-Instituts* [Publications of the Adalbert Stifter Institute], 1956). Other important prominent figures of Stifter literature and Stifter cultivation whom I admire, Franz Glück, Fritz Novotny, and Max Stefl have bowed gratefully before him in obituaries, and faced with an honestly felt debt, nothing remains for me here but to acknowledge it.

The literature about Johann Strauss, Sr. and Joseph Lanner is meager; the first and presumably irrevocably final volume of the series *Das Jahrhundert des Walzers* [The Century of the Waltz] (Vienna, 1954) by Max Schönherr und Karl Reinöhl, a work index with characterizations of the works, examples of scores, cultural-historical portrayals, and a wealth of pictorial material about Johann Strauss, Sr., must be acknowledged as the only exception. Similarly valuable is the Johann Strauss calendar by M. E. Engel (Vienna, 1901), which has completely disappeared.

Max Schönherr is working on a manuscript about Johann Strauss, the son, and on a Johann Strauss bibliography, but the care and cataloging of the Strauss legacy takes place primarily outside the authorities and institutions that are given responsibility for it, in a patriarchal manner and on a voluntary basis, the way people otherwise pursue only unusual hobbies. Max Schönherr knows where orchestra material or other sheet music for which works can be found, counsels interested people who inquire of him, all over the world, and cares for the new editions of the Ludwig Krenn publishing house in Vienna's fifteenth district.

In 1956 a new bibliographical *Verzeichnis sämtlicher Werke von Johann Strauss, Vater und Sohn* [Index of the Complete Works of Johann Strauss, Father and Son] also appeared there, produced by another venerable member of the voluntary and selfless Johann Strauss community: Alexander Weimann.

Several biographies of the younger Johann Strauss are available, but they are more or less imprecise, incorrect, uncritical, and contradictory. It was my endeavor to avoid the traditional errors (which have recurred inveterately to some degree since the first biography by Eisenberg, Leipzig, 1894) as conscientiously as possible. I hope that I was at least able to reduce them.

The Strauss biographies by Siegfried Löwy (Vienna, 1924) and Ernst Decsey (new edition, Vienna, 1948) are already characterized by the respective subtitles *Der Spielmann von der blauen Donau* [The Musician of the Blue Danube] and *Ein Wiener Buch* [A Vienna Book]. They come from the domain of the later librettists of Strauss operettas and repeatedly attain epitomes of misunderstanding and stylistic false notes. "The musician of the blue Danube loved both people and his creative fiddle, across which he could glide so refreshingly with enchanting sincerity and warmth of feeling, that you would almost think he was holding a lover in his arms, whom he tenderly fondled in the intoxication of romance." (Löwy)—"Strauss ruled uncrowned and perpetually, the musical seducer melted down all hate. His music poured honey into the Austrian powder keg." (Decsey)

The omissions in the purely biographical sphere may at least be explained by the established statement of one of the two authors, who said: "I shall never again write the biography of a musician whose widow is still alive!"

Somewhat more tolerable: the Strauss biographies by Karl Kobald (Vienna, 1925) and especially Werner Jaspert (Berlin, 1939); the biography by Erich Schenk (Potsdam, 1940) neglects the biographical element in favor of commendable thorough musical form analyses, but it, too, is not free of errors.

The portrayal of the two Johann Strauss's by Heinrich Eduard Jacob (*Johann Strauss und das neunzehnte Jahrhundert* [Johann Strauss and the Nineteenth Century], Amsterdam, 1937—new edition *Johann Strauss, Vater und Sohn, die Geschichte einer musikalischen Weltherrschaft* [Johann Strauss, Father and Son, the Story of a Musical World Supremacy], Hamburg, 1953) suffers similarly from many inaccuracies and subjective statements, but it is nevertheless the most competent, readable, and informative publication to date.

Not absolutely reliable and occasionally inclining to superficiality: the work *Die Operette* [The Operetta] by Otto Keller (Vienna, 1926), which was dedicated to Adele Strauss; more precise and useful because of new material is *Die Wiener Operette* [The Vienna Operetta] by Hadamowsky-Otte (Vienna, 1947).

Further, the fragmentary, superficially edited collection *Johann Strauss schreibt Briefe...Mitgeteilt von Adele Strauss* [Johann Strauss Writes Letters...Imparted by Adele Strauss] (Berlin, 1926), which was mentioned in the text, and the loquacious, philistine, not entirely believable, but occasionally informative reminiscences of Ignatz Schnitzer, *Meister Johann* [Master Johann] (Vienna, 1920). The oppressively informative letter by

Johann Strauss that is imparted on pages 288-289 (Jacob states that it had been written after the premiere of *Night in Venice*; Jaspert states that it had been written after the premiere of *Princess Ninetta*) is in Paul Lindau's memoirs *Nur Erinnerungen* [Only Memories] (Stuttgart, 1919) with the addition: "I have suppressed the date, the name of the author, and that of the operetta out of consideration for the still living text writer." Since Zell and Genée, the librettists of *Night in Venice*, were no longer alive in 1919, it can be assumed that it concerned a later operetta from the Adele era.

The statement repeated in all biographies, that in 1874 *Die Fledermaus* was dropped by the *Theater an der Wien* after sixteen performances, is refuted by A. Bauer in the October 1942 issue of the journal *Die Musik*.

The statement repeated in some biographies, that Johann Strauss, the son, was born in the house at *Lerchenfelderstraße* 115, is refuted by a memorial plaque on the house at *Lerchenfelderstraße* 15.

My thanks to Otto Erich Deutsch and Otto Rommel; I have already given my thanks to Gustav Wilhelm. I still have the pleasant duty to thank Otto Jungmair of the Adalbert Stifter Institute for very substantial and valuable instruction, the Johann Strauss expert Max Schönherr for similarly valuable and substantial advice, the archivists of the Vienna Society of Music Lovers, the Vienna Men's Choral Society, and Johann Strauss, the grandson of Eduard Strauss, who were helpful to me on my path to Johann Strauss, as well as the ladies and gentlemen of the music collection in the Austrian National Library.

In addition, I would like to mention with special gratitude my many friends in Vienna's secondhand bookshops, who brought to light in overwhelming abundance the extremely rare material that I sought, but very especially the dream of a lifetime among libraries, the Eldorado of all who seek material: the Vienna City Library.

TRANSLATOR'S AFTERWORD

In his essay on Franz Grillparzer, Hans Weigel argues that the Austrian writer "at least partially portrayed himself" in his novella *The Poor Musician*, where he created an almost archetypal representation of the artist who is out of tune with a society that neither understands nor appreciates him. Because of the disharmony between the protagonist and the traditional world of family and practical expectation, and because of the human foibles that are a part of his nature, weaknesses that contribute to his inviability in the middle-class environment of business and social involvement, the title figure is condemned to a tragic life where he must labor at tasks for which he does not feel suited and which bring him no fulfillment. He fails miserably in his relationships with his father, women, and others, allows himself to be exploited as a result of his naivete, orients his life according to standards that do not match those of the people around him, and ultimately dies, leaving behind a legacy of contribution to life, a contribution whose true essence is grasped by only a few.

Weigel's writings on selected Austrian cultural figures suggest that each of the artists suffered a fate similar in many respects to that of Grillparzer's Jakob; and these critical portrayals of their lives and careers almost seem like variations based on a pattern established in the earlier author's narrative prose. Even the central theme of the essays, the idea that there is something peculiarly Austrian in the fact that these men "fled" from greatness, failed to measure up to their true potential, or at the very least achieved greatness unconsciously or unwillingly, corresponds to what is revealed about the poor Viennese musician in the sacrificial acts that complete his life in a revelation of the true greatness of his spirit.

An important focus of the essay on Franz Schubert is the "wretched insignificance" of a life that was "so small and inconspicuously anonymous." Like Grillparzer's musician, Schubert lived in isolation within a society from which he was alienated by a lack of talent for social intercourse. For both figures an inability to communicate effectively is a key factor in the failure to enter into or maintain important relationships with the people encountered in the course of everyday life. When Jakob's Barbara visits him for the last time before leaving to marry the butcher, Jakob is unable to say more than her name. In portraying an encounter between Schubert and August Heinrich Hoffmann von Fallersleben, Weigel quotes the German poet as saying: "Schubert stands before me confused, doesn't quite know what to say, and after a few words, he says good-bye and—I never see him again." Based on this meeting, Fallersleben concluded that Schubert was "a common, indifferent, or even impolite person" who was "in no way different from any other Viennese."

As if to underscore the similarities between Schubert and the central character of the novella, Weigel also describes a scene in which the "lonely and unrecognized" master meets a real-life poor musician and reveals much about his perception of himself during the encounter. The portrayal of Schubert asking the organ grinder, "the strange old man whose plate always remains empty, whom nobody wants to hear, whom nobody looks at," if he should join him, if the beggar wants to play his (Schubert's) songs, identifies the composer concretely with Grillparzer's symbolic figure.

In the novella, the great tragedy of the poor musician's life is the miscarriage of his relationship with the grocer's daughter Barbara. The potential for marriage and subsequent happiness in family life is destroyed by Jakob's mistakes in situations where he is required to deal effectively with the practical aspects of existence.

Weigel's portrayals of Ferdinand Raimund, Johann Nestroy, and Franz Grillparzer place special emphasis on the failure or lack of traditional marital ties as a common element in their inability to find lasting fulfillment in love. For Raimund and Nestroy, the involvement with "eternal fiancées" was the result of mistakes and a specifically Austrian circumstance. Both of them entered into early, hasty, unhappy marriages that were soon terminated. Because Austrian law did not permit them to marry again as long as their divorced wives were alive, their subsequent alliances with women could not lead to wedded bliss. In Grillparzer's case, however, the situation was different. He, too, had an "eternal fiancée" whom he never married, but for him marriage was prevented only by the fact that he was "not capable of love," as he eventually acknowledged.

An additional characteristic of these "Austrian fates" that is shared by Grillparzer's artist figure is the involuntary participation in activity that does not bring complete fulfillment, or to which the individual is or feels unsuited. Jakob must earn a meager living as a musician, even though he plays very poorly, and his only reward is the opportunity to give violin lessons to Barbara's son who symbolizes the personal fulfillment that he has lost. The parallel in Raimund's life lies in the fact that he botched a serious acting role and became a comedian by accident, when in his own mind he had the makings of a tragedian. Nestroy, who began as an actor with a remarkable singing voice, was compelled by circumstances to move away from the opera into the realm of utility theater. Grillparzer wrote plays only because he needed the money and was, in Weigel's estimation, remarkably ungifted in the use of language. Adalbert Stifter felt that he was destined to make his artistic mark as a painter, earned a living for much of his life as a school official, and only found time to write his significant prose narratives on the side, as a hobby. In each case the conflict between inclination and necessity, between vision and reality resulted in accomplishment with lasting value, while leaving the artist himself unfulfilled.

In a sense, the essay on Johann Strauss, which is really an essay on the Strauss family, may be interpreted as something of a grand finale, a summary statement on the "Austrian fate" that relates the history of an entire musical dynasty to characteristics found in the title figure of Grillparzer's *Poor Musician*. An especially important contributing factor in Jakob's tragedy, for example, is the conflict between father and son. Weigel makes much of the fact that the lives of Johann Strauss, father and son, were deeply impacted by paternal rejection that played an important role in what they eventually became.

The problem of failed marriages is also significant for the lives of both men. Like Raimund and Nestroy, Johann Strauss, the father, ended what he saw as an undesirable union and spent the rest of his life with a female companion. Johann Strauss, the son, married three different women, none of whom brought him real happiness.

There is an almost ironic relationship between the life that Strauss, the younger, lived with his respective wives and the "what-might-have-been" that Grillparzer projected for Jakob and Barbara. Prior to the events that lead to their separation, Barbara is prepared to assume responsibility for the management of Jakob's practical life in a benevolent manner because she recognizes his inability to cope with the necessary tasks of everyday reality. The mistake that results in the loss of his inheritance, however, frustrates the realization of that possibility. Johann Strauss, Jr., on the other hand, married women who assumed substantial control over the business aspects of his life, but in a self-serving rather than benevolent manner. In some respects the result for him was something akin to indentured servitude in which he devoted his time to composing music for operettas, a task that he detested.

In spite of the similarities between the life stories of these Austrian cultural figures and that of Grillparzer's poor musician, there are also obvious differences. Like the people described in Weigel's essays, the misunderstood artist Jakob *does* have timeless impact on posterity, but it is the literary impact of a *created* character and not the spiritual effect generated by a *creative* individual. And perhaps it is only the latter who has the capacity to "flee" not from but into greatness.

Lowell A. Bangerter

A BRIEF BIOGRAPHY OF HANS FRONIUS

Hans Fronius, famous Austrian painter and graphic artist, was born in 1903 in Sarajevo and died in 1988 in Vienna. From 1922 to 1928 he studied at the Academy of Fine Arts in Vienna. Beginning in 1945 he had more than seventy personal exhibitions in Austria and abroad, among others at the Albertina Graphics Collection in 1952 and 1972, the Gutenberg Museum in Mainz in 1968, the Austrian Gallery in the Upper Belvedere in Vienna in 1973, the Bamberg Royal Residence in 1975, and the East German Gallery in Regensburg in 1975. Among the foreign exhibitions were those in the State Museum in Mexico City (1957) and in the national libraries in Madrid (1965) and Brussels (1976).

Fronius received numerous prizes and honors, among others the Great Austrian State Prize in 1966 and the Austrian Cross of Honor for Art and Science, First Class, in 1974.

Numerous monographs have been written about him, among others: Otto Benesch and Werner Hofmann, *Hans Fronius* (Graz, 1953); Walter Koschatzky, *Hans Fronius. Bilder und Gestalten. Mit einem Oeuvrekatalog der Druckgraphik von Leopold Rethi.* [Hans Fronius, Pictures and Figures, with a Catalogue of the Graphic Prints by Leopold Rethi] (Vienna, 1972).

His works in illustrated books and folio volumes consist of more than eighty publications.

ARIADNE PRESS
Autobiography, Biography, Memoirs Series

Quietude and Quest
Protagonists and Antagonists in the
Theater, on and off Stage
As Seen Through the Eyes of
Leon Askin
By Leon Askin and C. Melvin Davidson

On the Wrong Track
By
Milo Dor
Translation and Afterword
By Jerry Glenn

Unsentimental Journey
By
Albert Drach
Translation by Harvey I. Dunkle
Afterword by Ernestine Schlant

Reunion in Vienna
By Edith Foster
Afterword by
Heinrich von Weizsäcker

I Want to Speak
The Tragedy and Banality of Survival
in Terezin and Auschwitz
By Margareta Glas-Larsson
Commented by Gerhard Botz
Translated by Lowell A. Bangerter

Remembering Gardens
By
Kurt Klinger
Translated by Harvey I Dunkle
Preface by Ernst Schönwiese
Afterword by Joseph P. Strelka

Night over Vienna
By
Lili Körber
Translation by Viktoria Hertling and
Kay M. Stone
Commentary by Viktoria Hertling

Thomas Bernhard and His Grandfather
Johannes Freumbichler
"Our Grandfathers Are Our Teachers"
By
Caroline Markolin
Translated by Petra Hartweg
Afterword by Erich Wolfgang Skwara

When Allah Reigns Supreme
By
Susi Schalit
Translation and Afterword
by Sabine D. Jordan

View from a Distance
By
Lore Lizbeth Waller

ARIADNE PRESS
New Titles

Walk about the Villages
By Peter Handke
Translated by Michael Roloff

The Giant File on Zwetschkenbaum
By Albert Drach
Translated by Harvey I. Dunkle

Woman's Face of Resistance
By Marie-Thérèse Kerschbaumer
Translated by Lowell A. Bangerter

Ice on the Bridge
By Erich Wolfgang Skwara
Translated by Michael Roloff

"It's Up to Us!"
Collected Works of Jura Soyfer
Selected, Edited and Translated
By Horst Jarka

The House of the Linsky Sisters
By Florian Kalbeck
Translated by Michael Mitchell

Springtime on the Via Condotti
By Gustav Ernst
Translated by Todd C. Hanlin

Against the Grain
New Anthology of Contemporary
Austrian Prose
Selected by Adolf Opel

The Final Plays
By Arthur Schnitzler
Translated by G.J. Weinberger

New Anthology of Contemporary Austrian Folk Plays
Edited by Richard H. Lawson

Shooting Rats, Other Plays and Poems
By Peter Turrini
Translatedy by Richard Dixon

Rilke's Duino Elegies
Edited by Roger Paulin
and Peter Hutchinson

Phantom Empires
The Novels of Alexander Lernet-Holenia and the Question of Postimperial Austrian Identity
By Robert Dassanowsky

Waking the Dead
Correspondences between Walter Benjamin's Concept of Remembrance and Ingeborg Bachmann's Ways of Dying
By Karen Remmler

Dirt
By Robert Schneider
Translated by Paul F. Dvorak

ARIADNE PRESS
Translation Series

Lerida
By Alexander Giese
Translated by Lowell A. Bangerter

Three Flute Notes
By Jeannie Ebner
Translated by Lowell A. Bangerter

Siberia and Other Plays
By Felix Mitterer

The Sphere of Glass
By Marianne Gruber
Translation and Afterword
by Alexandra Strelka

The Convent School
By Barbara Frischmuth
Translated by
G. Chapple and J.B. Lawson

The Green Face
By Gustav Meyrink
Translated by Michael Mitchell

The Ariadne Book of Austrian Fantasy: The Meyrink Years 1890-1930
Ed. & trans. by Michael Mitchell

Walpurgisnacht
By Gustav Meyrink
Translated by Michael Mitchell

The Cassowary
By Matthias Mander
Translated by Michael Mitchell

Plague in Siena
By Erich Wolfgang Skwara
Foreword by Joseph P. Strelka
Translation by Michael Roloff

Memories with Trees
By Ilse Tielsch
Translated by David Scrase

Aphorisms
By Marie von Ebner-Eschenbach
Translated by David Scrase and Wolfgang Mieder

Conversations with Peter Rosei
By Wilhelm Schwarz
Translated by Christine and Thomas Tessier

Anthology of Contemporary Austrian Folk Plays
By V. Canetti, Preses/Becher, Mitterer, Szyszkowitz, Turrini
Translation and Afterword
by Richard Dixon

Try Your Luck!
By Peter Rosei
Translated by Kathleen Thorpe